MANAGING PROJECTS

WITH MICROSOFT®

PROJECT FOR WINDOWS™

VNR PROJECT MANAGEMENT SERIES

MANAGING PROJECTS
WITH MICROSOFT®
PROJECT FOR WINDOWS™

Gwen Lowery

VNR VAN NOSTRAND REINHOLD
New York

Library of Congress Catalog Card Number 90-12592
ISBN 0-442-00411-7

Printed in the United States of America

Van Nostrand Reinhold
115 Fifth Avenue
New York, New York 10003

Chapman & Hall
2-6 Boundary Row
London SE1 8HN, England

Thomas Nelson Australia
102 Dodds Street
South Melbourne, Victoria 3205, Australia

Nelson Canada
1120 Birchmount Road
Scarborough, Ontario M1K 5G4, Canada

16 15 14 13 12 11 10 9 8 7 6 5 4

Library of Congress Cataloging in Publication Data

Lowery, Gwen, 1950–
    Managing Projects with Microsoft Project for Windows /
Gwen Lowery.
        p. cm.
    Includes index.
    ISBN 0-442-00411-7 (pbk.)
    1. Microsoft Project for Windows (Computer program).   2. Industrial
project management—Data processing.   I. Title.
HD69.P75L69 1991
658.4'04'0285543—dc20   90–12592
                                                            CIP

To
Lucie and Pete
who told me I could do anything

Contents

Preface

In these incredibly fast-paced times, how successfully you manage the multitude of projects for which you are responsible is one of the keys to how well you do in business. The project management software available today is truly amazing; it does much of what was tedious about project management and does it very fast, giving you almost instant results so you can make educated decisions for the remainder of the project.

But as powerful as the software is, even more important to your success is a thorough understanding of the steps you, as project manager, must follow to make a project happen. You are in control of the planning, tracking, and managing of the project to get from where you are today to the goal—on time and on budget. This book is about managing projects—not just about using Microsoft® Project for Windows™ but about how you get from here to there—successfully.

Part 1 briefly describes project management and Microsoft Project for Windows. In Parts 2, 3, and 4, each chapter covers one step in the project management process. Each chapter in these three parts contains two types of information: information about project management and information about Microsoft Project for Windows.

The general project management information is at the beginning of each chapter. Read this information, up to the "Using Microsoft Project for Windows" section, if you want to know about the project management theory behind the step covered in the chapter. If you just want information about using Microsoft Project, skip the introductory sections.

Because Microsoft Project is so flexible and allows you to do things in several ways, the "Using Microsoft Project for Windows" sections often include more than one method to accomplish a step so that you can pick the method that is best suited to your work style. For example, more

than one method is presented for entering tasks and for entering resources.

Part 5 includes information specific to Microsoft Project. It covers
topics that will make your life easier but are not strictly part of the
project management process, such as how to work with multiple
projects, how to share information with other software packages, and
procedures for using Microsoft Project tools.

A companion disk to this book is available from Editorial Services. The
disk contains all the custom views, tables, filters, and reports discussed in
this book. By opening the file on the disk in Microsoft Project, you'll
have at your fingertips the library of reports, views, tables, and filters
used in this book, ready to use with your project data. If you want to
purchase the disk, use the order form included at the end of the book.

Acknowledgments

Thanks to the following people: Lois Oien, Jim McKendry, and Jim Dunnigan for their patience in reviewing the book and for offering so many valuable suggestions; the development team of Brian MacDonald, Jeff Lill, John Clifford, Cory Reina, and Glenn Slayden for creating such great software; Bob Argentieri and Gene Dallaire of VNR for making sure the book happened; and Dennis Stovall, Linny Stovall, Judy Binder, and Chris Silva at Blue Heron Publishing, Inc. for editing, design, and typesetting services.

MANAGING PROJECTS
WITH MICROSOFT®
PROJECT FOR WINDOWS™

PART 1

PROJECT MANAGEMENT AND MICROSOFT® PROJECT FOR WINDOWS™

How well you manage a project has a direct effect on the outcome of the project. There are several parts in the project management equation, two of which are the project management steps and the tools you have to support these steps. Part 1 introduces both the project management process and one tool to help you track and manage your project, Microsoft Project for Windows.

Chapter 1 discusses the benefits of project planning and of using a computer. You'll also learn about Microsoft Project for Windows and how it schedules your project.

Use Chapter 2 as a reference to Microsoft Project for Windows. The chapter includes:

- How Microsoft Project sees a project
- Description of Microsoft Project tables, filters, and views and how these three tools are used to give you the information you want about your project
- Basics of working with Microsoft Project for Windows, including how to use menus, commands, and dialog boxes
- Table showing what you can change in Microsoft Project to match the way you work so that it gives you exactly the information you want, the way you want it, as efficiently as possible

About Project Management

A *project* is a one-time set of activities that ends with a specific accomplishment. It originates when something out of the ordinary has to be accomplished. A project has the following characteristics:

- A set of nonroutine tasks performed in a certain sequence leading to a goal
- A distinct start and finish date
- A limited set of resources which may be used on more than one project

A project is not an ongoing process, such as preparing weekly payroll, or manufacturing a product on an assembly line. These processes have no real completion date, which is a requirement of a project, nor are they in any way unique. Rather, they are part of the everyday business.

Project management is the defining, planning, scheduling, and controlling of the tasks that must be completed to reach your goal and the allocation of the resources to perform those tasks. Defining and planning are necessary so you know what you will do. Scheduling is important so you know when you will do it. And controlling is important because things never work out exactly as planned. To meet your goal, it's important that you be on top of changes. This means constantly tracking and rescheduling as the project progresses.

As a project manager, you are successful when you satisfy the requirements of your client or management, and meet your project goals on schedule and within your budget. Project management software simplifies and speeds up this process. It gives you easy access to important information so you can make decisions while there is still time to take corrective action. The software lets you model your project so you can plan your resource requirements and avoid conflicts.

Why Plan?

One of the most tedious and possibly time-consuming steps for the project manager is creating the initial plan before the project is even under way. But, it is also the most important step. A plan simulates the project and lists what you will do. It is a model of your project used to predict the future.

Creating your schedule involves three basic steps. First, you specify *what* you are going to do by defining the tasks that must be completed to reach your goals. Then you specify *when* by scheduling the tasks. Actually, the computer does the scheduling for you; you just give it information about the sequence of the tasks, how they are related to one another, and if any tasks must start or finish at a specific time. Then you specify *how* by assigning people, equipment, and costs to complete the tasks. The computer program creates the schedule based on the information you provide.

Of course, the steps are not independent. After seeing the first schedule, you will probably reevaluate your task and resource lists to ensure you are creating the best schedule to fit the situation. And you can't do this alone. You will have a better schedule and more support for the project if you involve the project team in the planning process.

You can use a project plan and its schedule for many things. For example, it can help you:

- Communicate to others in your organization what you are going to do
- Get support from project team members
- Gain approval for the project or justify the need to management
- Show a customer how you will deliver a product or service
- Prove the need for additional staff and manage resource work loads
- Determine cash flow needs
- Keep a record of what happened on the project, to be compared to the original plan

You can also use a project schedule as the baseline against which you check the progress of your project.

So, you plan to know what is to be done, when it will be done, who will do it, and how much it will cost. Having a plan helps everyone to see who needs to do what and when they need to do it. It helps communication, makes everyone aware of deadlines, and reduces uncertainty. And by tracking the actual progress of the project and comparing it to your original schedule, you can see deviations from the plan, anticipate any problems, and correct any delays before they become severe. With a plan, there is a better chance of completing the project successfully!

How a Computer Helps you Plan and Manage a Project

When you use project management software, the most tedious job, calculation of the schedule, is performed by the computer program. It is up to you to define the project goals, plan the tasks and resources, and implement and manage the project. But, the computer can help you immeasurably. It provides up-to-date information, and it gives you the ability to test ideas and see the results in the schedule and costs.

First, a computer-based project management system calculates the schedule for you. Imagine how time-consuming it would be to manually calculate the schedule dates for all the tasks. And imagine trying to create the optimal schedule; you could spend a long time just doing calculations. The truth is, you wouldn't have time to do this.

When you use a computer and project management software, any change you make to a task is automatically incorporated as the computer recalculates the schedule for you, leaving you with more time to spend on planning and tracking your projects. The more complex the project, the more important it is to have the computer system.

There are several other benefits of using project management software:

- The schedule is created and revised quickly; you can easily analyze the schedule, resources, and costs to evaluate alternative schedules, and to find the best solution to scheduling problems

- Because you have one scheduling tool, it helps centralize planning throughout an organization

- Output is in a standard format, quick and easy to produce, accurate and consistent for all projects

- Since the same information can be presented in detail or summarized, as appropriate, for each level of management, everyone has timely and valid information for making decisions

- You have the information you need to track progress and control your schedule, resources, and costs

When you are using a computer to schedule your project, you must input:

- All the tasks that must be done to complete the project
- The sequence in which the tasks must occur, and their dependencies on other tasks and dates
- The resources used to perform the tasks and the cost of using each
- Calendar information, such as working days and times

Project management software calculates the schedule, completion date, total work, and cost to complete the project. You save this information as a baseline schedule so you can compare progress to this plan.

In the comparison or tracking stage, you input progress on tasks, including:

- Actual start and finish dates
- Percent complete of tasks in progress
- Actual work
- Actual costs

The Critical Path Method

The critical path method (CPM) is the scheduling method used in virtually all project management software today, including Microsoft Project for Windows. CPM was developed by DuPont and Remington Rand in the 1950s to improve project scheduling techniques. It is a modeling process that defines all the project's critical tasks—those tasks that must be completed on time if the entire project is to be completed on time—and calculates the start and finish dates of tasks in the project.

With CPM, calculations of the schedule are based on the durations of the tasks and the relationships between the tasks. The schedule is calculated twice—first from the earliest start date forward, and then from the latest finish date backwards. The difference between the pairs of start and finish dates for each task is float or slack time for the task. Slack time is the amount of time that a task can be delayed without delaying the project completion date. The critical path is that sequence of tasks which represent the longest total time required to complete the project. A delay in any task on the critical path causes a delay in the completion of the project. Noncritical tasks—tasks not on the critical path—have slack time.

One advantage of this method is that you can experiment with accelerating the project by shortening various critical tasks, and then check the time, costs, and resources to see how they are affected by the change. By experimenting in this way, you can determine the optimal schedule for a project.

Once you have entered this "actual" information, you can use the software to do the following:

- Compare the actual dates with the baseline schedule to spot delays
- Check resource availability and reschedule as necessary
- Compare work and costs with the baseline schedule to see if you are within budget
- Look at alternatives to decide how best to keep the schedule on track

Another advantage to tracking your project is that you create an accurate record of the project and the time it took to perform each task. This historical data can help you make estimates for future projects.

Remember that project management software is just a tool. It cannot help you determine the tasks and their relationships, but it can help you optimize the schedule and reduce time and costs. The software does all the schedule calculations quickly so you can experiment with options. By simulating the project, you can do "what-if" analyses to find the optimal balance of costs, resources, and time.

WHY USE MICROSOFT PROJECT FOR WINDOWS?

Microsoft Project for Windows is a powerful tool that will help you control your projects and complete them successfully. It gives you flexible viewing of project information, a powerful scheduling tool, resource management capability, and quality reports.

When selecting project management software, there are certain features important to the project manager. The following list describes some of the features of Microsoft Project that will make your life easier. This list gives you only a glimpse of the power of Microsoft Project for Windows:

- Save the original schedule so you have something to compare to progress; Microsoft Project saves your original schedule separately from the current schedule so you can compare the two.
- Track progress on tasks by entering actual start and finish dates, actual durations, remaining durations, actual cost, and actual work.
- Allocate resource usage so resources are available when needed for tasks, but are not assigned to too many tasks simultaneously.
- Create calendars for each project and modify the calendar for each resource; Microsoft Project uses the calendars to schedule the tasks.

- Change the presentation of information, from spreadsheet-like tables, to charts and graphs, showing task information or resource information according to your needs.
- Change the type of information presented about each task or resource so you get just the information you need at a given time. For example, you can look at a list of tasks and their start and finish dates, then change the information to see the tasks and their resources and predecessors.
- Filter the information shown to display only those tasks or resources that include certain information. For example, you can list only those tasks that use a certain resource.
- Change the order of the information, such as alphabetizing the list of resources.

Besides these, Microsoft Project includes other features designed to make the application's power more accessible and useful:

- Drop-down menus that list all the commands
- Windows so you can change from one view of your data, such as a Gantt Chart or PERT Chart, to another view, such as a spreadsheet presentation
- Built-in tutorial and Help system
- Quick-to-use reporting system to generate reports showing exactly the information you want, in the format you want
- Special mouse capabilities so you can graphically change the schedule of a task

Because Microsoft Project uses the graphic environment of Microsoft Windows, you can easily share information with other Windows products, such as Microsoft Excel and Microsoft Word for Windows.

CHAPTER 2

About Microsoft Project for Windows

Microsoft Project for Windows is easy to use, yet has the power and flexibility to do exactly what you need. For example, you can create a simple schedule quickly by entering all your tasks and then using one command to make each task start after the task before it finishes. Or you can create a detailed schedule, entering all the project information you have gathered—including tasks, resources, costs, and detailed work information for each resource—and use this schedule to track the progress of the project. Either way, Microsoft Project can give you exactly what you need.

As with every software product, understanding a few basics will make it easy for you to take advantage of the features in Microsoft Project. If you are a Microsoft Windows user or have used another Microsoft Windows product such as Microsoft Excel or Microsoft Word for Windows, you'll find that you already know the basics: the window has the same basic features, the commands are listed in the menus at the top of the window, you choose commands in the same way, and use dialog boxes in the same way. If you are unfamiliar with these concepts, they are covered briefly at the end of this chapter. But, for more information, see your Microsoft Windows documentation and the "Menus, Commands, and Dialog Boxes" topic in the *Microsoft Project Reference*.

CONVENTIONS USED IN THIS BOOK

Throughout the book, the following conventions are used when referring to Microsoft Project commands, key combinations, and the mouse:

- Commands are listed with the menu name first and then the command name. For example, to choose the Edit Copy command, you select the Edit menu, and then choose the Copy command.

- Key combinations indicate you need to press more than one key. They are presented in two ways depending on how you press the keys.

Key Combination	Description
Plus between two keys—for example, Alt+Down Arrow	Press and hold down the first key, press the second key, and then release both keys—for example, hold down Alt while you press the Down Arrow key.
Comma between two keys—for example, Alt, Spacebar	Press one key after the other—for example, press and release Alt, and then press and release Spacebar.

- Terms used for mouse actions are described in the following table.

Mouse Term	Description
Point	Position the mouse pointer so it is over the item of interest.
Click	Point to an item and click the left mouse button.
Drag	Point to the starting position with the mouse pointer, press and hold down the left mouse button, move the pointer to the new location, and then release the mouse button.

- Select means to highlight the tasks or resources you want a command to act on. For example, if you want to copy a group of tasks, you first select them and then choose the Edit Copy command.

To Select	Keys	Mouse
One task or resource	Use direction keys to move to the item	Click the item
Adjacent tasks or resources	Shift+direction keys	Drag over the items
Nonadjacent tasks or resources—called a multiple selection	Press F8 and select the first group; press Shift+F8 and move to the next group; repeat the steps until all groups are selected	Select the first group, and then hold down Ctrl to select the next group

How Microsoft Project Keeps Track of Project Information

Whether or not you use a computer, a project has two lists—a list of all your tasks and a list of all your resources. The two lists are connected by assigning the resources to the tasks.

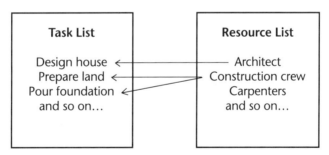

When you enter a task into Microsoft Project for Windows, over 60 fields are created to describe the task. Picture it as a big spreadsheet that includes the task ID, task name, duration, start date, finish date, cost information, and much other information.

ID	Name	Duration	Start	Finish	Milestone	Fixed	Cost	Work	and so on...
7	Build walls	1 week	1/11/91	1/15/91	No	No	$1000	80h	

The values in these fields are either entered by you or calculated by Microsoft Project. Some are used for scheduling the task, some for keeping track of progress on the task, some for keeping a record of the original schedule, and so on. There may not be values in all fields. For example, if you choose not to keep track of the progress on a project, you won't enter values in the fields for progress information.

When you enter a list of resources—called a resource pool—Microsoft Project creates over 20 fields for each resource, including resource ID, resource name, rate of pay, and so on. Again, some fields are entered by you and some are calculated; there may not be values in every field.

You link the two lists together by assigning the resources to the tasks. Again, there are fields, called resource assignment fields, which contain this information. For example, there is a field for the amount of work a resource has to do on each task to which the resource is assigned.

Microsoft Project has three basic tools to look at the tasks, resources, and resource assignments.

- *Tables* specify which fields you see.
- *Filters* control which tasks or resources are displayed—all, or a subset of your choosing.
- *Views* display your project information in a variety of perspectives, such as in a spreadsheet-like presentation, a chart presentation, or in a form. Some views show task information, some show resource information, and some show either task or resource information plus resource assignment information.

You change the table, filter, and view to see the fields you want, the tasks or resources you want, displayed in the format you want.

MICROSOFT PROJECT TABLES

Obviously, you are not going to use all 60 task fields simultaneously—probably only a handful at any time, depending on what you want to accomplish. For example, if you are entering new tasks, you'll want one set of fields, such as task ID, task name, task duration, and resources assigned to the task; if you are entering progress information about a task, perhaps you'll want, besides the task ID and name, a field for the date when the task actually started and another showing the percentage of the work finished on the task.

Tables are just a way to control which fields are displayed for the tasks or resources; you change the fields by applying a different table.

Microsoft Project for Windows comes with 17 tables. Each includes the appropriate fields to show a certain type of information. For example, initially, the Entry table is applied to two of the views that show task information. You use this table to enter basic task information; it includes fields you'll most likely use when entering new tasks, including the ID field, Name field, Duration field, Scheduled Start and Scheduled Finish date fields, Predecessors field (where you list the tasks that this task depends on), and the Resource Names fields (where you list the resources you want to use on the task). If, instead, you want to see cost information for the task, you would apply the Cost table; to enter progress information for the tasks, you would apply the Tracking table.

If you have a different combination of fields that you want to use when entering tasks or tracking tasks—or for reporting information about tasks, you can create your own table showing just those fields you want.

You use the Table menu to apply the tables and to change the fields in a table. Most of the tables that come with Microsoft Project are listed on the Table menu. The Table menu has a different list depending on the active view: one list for task views and one list for resource views. Not all views use tables. If a view does not use a table, no tables are listed on the Table menu. The tables that come with Microsoft Project are listed below.

Task Tables	Resource Tables
Constraint Dates	Cost
Cost	Entry
Earned Value	Export
Entry	Summary
Export	Usage
Plan	Work
Schedule	
Summary	
Tracking	
Variance	
Work	

TO APPLY A TABLE

    1. Select the Table menu.

    2. Choose the table you want to apply.

To apply those tables not listed on the Table menu, choose Table Define Tables, select the name of the table in the Tables box, and then press Enter or click the Set button.

You also use the Table Define Tables command to change or create tables. When you change or create a table, you specify the fields in the table, the width of the columns, and the column titles. You can use any of the fields in Microsoft Project in a table. Microsoft Project also includes several "custom" fields; use a custom field when Microsoft Project doesn't include a field you need, changing its title so you know what the field contains. For example, if you want to include an accounting code, you can use a custom field for this code. For more information about creating tables, see Chapter 16, "Using Microsoft Project Tools."

Because you can add new tables or remove tables from the Table menu, you can customize the menu to contain only those tables you use most often.

Microsoft Project Filters

Filters are just a way to control the tasks or resources displayed in a view. When you apply a filter, Microsoft Project displays only those tasks that fit the "criteria"—the requirements named in the filter. For example, you can apply a filter that shows only those tasks that are critical, or are in progress, or are over budget. A filter can contain a combination of requirements such that, for example, all critical tasks in progress are displayed.

Microsoft Project comes with 18 filters. Each includes certain requirements that the task or resource must meet to be displayed. When you apply a filter, Microsoft Project compares the value in a field with the value you specify. For example, the Critical filter checks the Critical field to see if it contains a "Yes" or "No." If a task is critical, it will contain "Yes" in the Critical field and will be displayed when you apply the filter. If the task is noncritical, it will not be displayed when you apply the filter.

Some filters compare the values in two fields. For example, the Slipping filter compares the original finish date (the value in the Planned Finish field) with the date a task is now scheduled to finish (the date in the Scheduled Finish field). Such filters are called calculated filters.

When you apply some filters, you must specify the value or values against which the filter is to compare. For example, if you apply the Date Range filter to display all tasks scheduled to start between two dates, Microsoft Project prompts you to specify the two dates each time you apply the filter. You don't have to recreate the filter each time you want to check for tasks expected to start during the next week or month. Such filters are called interactive filters.

If you want to look for a different set of tasks or resources, you can create your own filter. A filter can look for information in any of the task or resource fields. You can also create your own calculated filters and interactive filters.

You use the Filter menu to apply, change, or create filters. The Filter menu has a different list depending on the active view: one list for task views and one list for resource views. The filters that come with Microsoft Project are listed below.

Task Filters	Resource Filters
All Tasks	All Resources
Completed	Cost Overbudget
Constrained	Group
Critical	Overallocated
Date Range	Resource Range
In Progress	Work Overbudget
Milestones	
Overbudget	
Should Start	
Slipping	
Task Range	
Using Resource	

TO APPLY A FILTER

> 1. Select the Filter menu.
> 2. Choose the filter you want to apply.

You use the Filter Define Filters command to change or create filters and to apply filters not on the menu. When you change or create a filter, you change the criteria in the filter so Microsoft Project looks for a different set of tasks or resources. Because you can add new filters or remove filters from the Filter menu, you can customize the menu to contain only those filters you use most often. To apply a filter not listed on the Filter menu, choose Filter Define Filters, select the name of the filter in the Filters box, and then press Enter or click the Set button. For more information about creating filters, see Chapter 16, "Using Microsoft Project Tools."

MICROSOFT PROJECT VIEWS

In Microsoft Project for Windows, you look at different aspects of your project information by using the different views. Some views show you tasks, some show resources; some are in a spreadsheet-like format, others show information as a chart. Each view gives you a different perspective. For example, you can look at a view showing the project tasks and how they relate to one another; or you can use a view to see when the resources are scheduled and whether any are overallocated. Each view shows you a subset of the task, resource, and resource allocation fields.

Microsoft Project comes with the following views:

Task Views	Resource Views
Gantt Chart	Resource Form
Task Entry	Resource Histogram
Task Form	Resource Sheet
Task Sheet	Resource Usage
PERT Chart	
Task PERT Chart	
Tracking Gantt	

TO DISPLAY A VIEW

1. Select the View menu.

2. Choose the view you want to display.

The Tracking Gantt Chart is not on the View menu; to display this view, or any view not on the View menu, choose View Define Views, select Tracking Gantt or the name of the view you want to display, and then press Enter or click the Set button.

You also use the View Define Views command to change or create views. When you change or create a view, you pick the basic style you want, and then pick a table and filter, if the view can use either. This allows you to create custom views that you can use, for example, to generate status reports in the same format, week after week. Once created, a custom view is always available; the next time you want to present information in that format, just display and print the view. For more about creating views, see Chapter 16, "Using Microsoft Project Tools."

Because you can add new views or remove views from the View menu, you can customize it to contain only those views you use most often.

The next several pages contain information about each view included in Microsoft Project. Use this information as a reference when you need help with using the view or changing the appearance of the view.

Gantt Chart

The Gantt Chart shows a list of your tasks on the left side of the screen, and a bar chart on the right side of the screen. The bar chart shows graphically the duration and schedule information for each task. At the top of the bar chart is a timescale which can be changed to show the time periods you want (from minutes to years).

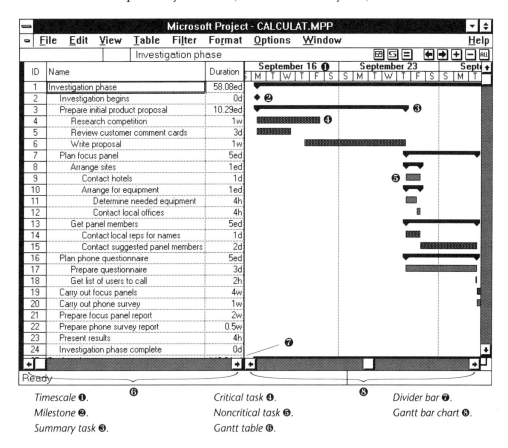

Timescale ❶.
Milestone ❷.
Summary task ❸.

Critical task ❹.
Noncritical task ❺.
Gantt table ❻.

Divider bar ❼.
Gantt bar chart ❽.

The pattern and color of the bars indicate the type of bar. For example, in the above illustration, the critical tasks (those tasks that must be completed on time for the project to be completed on time) are a darker pattern (▬▬) than the noncritical tasks (▬▬). On a color monitor or printer, critical tasks are red and noncritical tasks are blue. Summary tasks are used in outlines and span all tasks that they summarize. You can change the bars using the Format Palette command.

The Gantt table has more columns than you can see at one time. Use the direction keys or the scroll bar to scroll the table, or move the divider bar between the bar chart and the table.

The Tracking Gantt is a custom Gantt Chart, showing each task as it was originally scheduled, as it is currently scheduled based on the latest information you have entered about progress on tasks, and the percent complete for each task. You format and move on the Tracking Gantt just as you do on any Gantt Chart.

Gantt Chart History

During World War I, Henry L. Gantt used a bar chart to show tasks that needed to be done, plotted on a timescale to show start and finish dates. This bar chart was later called a Gantt Chart in honor of the inventor.

Uses

Use the Gantt Chart when you are first entering tasks, to create an outline, and to see your schedule graphically as the tasks are displayed over time. Use the Tracking Gantt to compare your current schedule to the original schedule after the project is under way.

Formatting

Command	What It Does
Format Sort	Sorts the list of tasks in the order you specify
Format Text	Changes the font, size, and color of the text on the Gantt Chart
Format Gridlines	Changes the pattern and color of the lines on the Gantt Chart
Format Outline	Controls outlining features, such as indentation of subordinate tasks and numbering
Format Timescale	Changes the amount of time and the scale of the time displayed on the bar chart
Format Palette	Controls the color and pattern of Gantt bars, the shape, type, and color of symbols, which bars appear, and text on the bar chart
Table commands	Changes the fields in the Gantt table
Filter commands	Changes the tasks that are displayed

Moving

To Move	Keys	Mouse
Up and down through the list of tasks	Up Arrow Down Arrow PgUp PgDn	Click the task Use the vertical scroll bar
Left and right through the fields in the table	Left Arrow Right Arrow Ctrl+PgUp Ctrl+PgDn	Use the horizontal scroll bar below the table
Through time on the bar chart	Alt+Left Arrow Alt+Right Arrow Alt+PgUp Alt+PgDn Alt+Home Alt+End	Use the horizontal scroll bar below the bar chart
Divider bar	Shift+F6, Left or Right Arrow, Enter	Drag divider bar (pointer changes to ⇔)

When you drag the vertical scroll box with the mouse, Microsoft Project shows the task ID that will be at the top of the window if you release the mouse button. When you drag the horizontal scroll bar below the bar chart, Microsoft Project shows the date that will be on the bar chart if you release the mouse button.

Task Form

The Task Form (next page) shows information about one task at a time. At the bottom are fields you can change to see different information related to the task. Initially, the Task Form shows the resources fields (resources assigned to the task) and the predecessors fields (tasks on which this task depends). These fields show information about the resource assignments that can't be viewed elsewhere. To change the fields, use the Format commands described in the "Formatting" section.

Use the entry bar at the top of the window to enter information in the form. The boxes and buttons in the form work just like a dialog box.

When you enter information in the Task Form, the Prev. (previous) and Next buttons change to OK and Cancel. When you finish entering information about the task, press Enter or click OK with the mouse. If you want to cancel all information you have entered, press Esc (Escape) or click Cancel. After you press Enter or Esc, or click OK or Cancel, the buttons change back to Prev. and Next so you can go to another task.

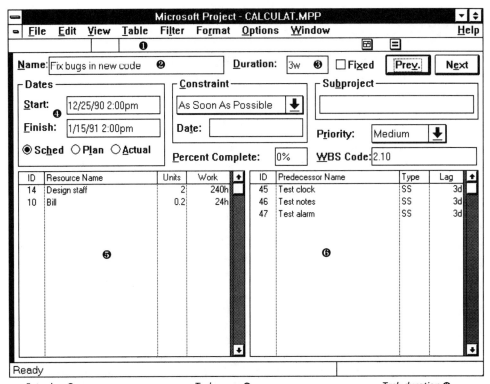

Entry bar ❶.   *Task name* ❷.   *Task duration* ❸.

Start and finish dates for the task ❹.   *The resources fields* ❺ *show the resources assigned to the task.*

The predecessors fields ❻ *shows the tasks on which this task depends, i.e., those that must come before this task.*

The Edit Form dialog box for tasks is similar to the top of the Task Form, and works the same way. Use it when you want to change several tasks at once or when the Task Form is not displayed.

Uses

Use the Task Form for entering new tasks or assigning resources to a task. You also use the Task Form to review information about a task. For example, you can see the resources scheduled to work on the task and the start and finish date for each resource. Or, you can see cost or work information for each resource on the task.

Formatting

Command	What It Does
Format Sort	Sorts the list of tasks in the order you specify; when you step through the tasks, you do so in the sort order rather than ID order
Format Resources & Predecessors	Places the resources and predecessors fields at the bottom of the form so you can enter and review resources and predecessors for this task
Format Resources & Successors	Places the resources and successors fields at the bottom of the form so you can enter and review resources and successors (tasks that depend on another task) for this task
Format Predecessors & Successors	Places the predecessors and successors fields at the bottom of the form so you can enter and review predecessors and successors for this task
Format Resource Schedule	Places the resource schedule fields at the bottom of the form so you can review the schedule for each resource assigned to this task
Format Resource Work	Places the resource work fields at the bottom of the form so you can review the amount of work for each resource assigned to this task
Format Resource Cost	Places the resource cost fields at the bottom of the form so you can review costs for each resource assigned to this task
Format Notes	Places the Notes box at the bottom of the form so you can enter a note about this task
Filter commands	Changes the tasks that are displayed; when you step through the tasks, you see only the filtered tasks

Moving

To Move	Keys	Mouse
To the next option	Tab	Click the option
To previous option	Shift+Tab	Click the option
To any option	Alt+underlined letter in the option name	Click the option
Into the fields at the bottom of the form	Alt+1	Click the field
From field to field	Direction keys	Click the field
To the next resource	Enter (to cchoose the Next button)	Click Next
To the previous resource	Shift+Enter (to choose Prev. button)	Click Prev.

Task Sheet

	Microsoft Project - CALCULAT.MPP					
File **Edit** **View** **Table** **Filter** **Format** **Options** **Window**						**Help**

Investigation phase ❶

ID	Name	Duration	Scheduled Start	Scheduled Finish	Predecess	Resource Nar
1	Investigation phase	58.08ed	9/17/90 8:00am	11/14/90 10:00am		
2	Investigation begins	0d	9/17/90 8:00am	9/17/90 8:00am		
3	Prepare initial product proposal	10.29ed	9/17/90 8:00am	9/27/90 3:00pm		
4	Research competition	1w	❷ 9/17/90 8:00am	9/21/90 5:00pm	2	Marcia,Market
5	Review customer comment cards	3d	9/17/90 8:00am	9/19/90 5:00pm		Marketing staf
6	Write proposal	1w	9/20/90 3:00pm	9/27/90 3:00pm	4FS-25%,5	Marcia,Janet
7	Plan focus panel	5ed	9/27/90 3:00pm	10/2/90 3:00pm		
8	Arrange sites	1ed	9/27/90 3:00pm	9/28/90 3:00pm		
9	Contact hotels	1d	9/27/90 3:00pm	9/28/90 3:00pm	6	Cheryl
10	Arrange for equipment	1ed	9/27/90 3:00pm	9/28/90 3:00pm		
11	Determine needed equipment	4h	9/27/90 3:00pm	9/28/90 10:00am	6	Marketing staf
12	Contact local offices	4h	9/28/90 10:00am	9/28/90 3:00pm	11	
13	Get panel members	5ed	9/27/90 3:00pm	10/2/90 3:00pm		
14	Contact local reps for names	1d	9/27/90 3:00pm	9/28/90 3:00pm	6	Marketing staf
15	Contact suggested panel members	2d	9/28/90 3:00pm	10/2/90 3:00pm	14	
16	Plan phone questionnaire	5ed	9/27/90 3:00pm	10/2/90 3:00pm		
17	Prepare questionnaire	3d	9/27/90 3:00pm	10/2/90 3:00pm	6	Roberto
18	Get list of users to call	2h	10/2/90 1:00pm	10/2/90 3:00pm	17FF	
19	Carry out focus panels	4w	10/2/90 3:00pm	10/30/90 3:00pm	15	Marcia,Market
20	Carry out phone survey	1w	10/2/90 3:00pm	10/9/90 3:00pm	18	Research Inc.

Entry bar ❶.

The table applied controls the field names ❷ listed at the top of each column and the type of information shown about each task.

The Task Sheet lists task information in a spreadsheet-like format, with the information organized in rows and columns. The table applied to the Task Sheet controls the fields displayed.

Uses

Use the Task Sheet to enter new tasks or as a convenient way to review the entire list of tasks. You also can use this view to brainstorm a list of new tasks or to create a project outline. Use it when creating reports to show only the fields you want by changing the table applied, or use it when exchanging data with another program, such as Microsoft Excel.

Formatting

Command	What It Does
Format Sort	Sorts the list of tasks in the order you specify
Format Text	Changes the font, size, and color of the text on the Task Sheet
Format Gridlines	Changes the pattern and color of the lines on the Task Sheet
Format Outline	Controls outlining features, such as indentation of subordinate tasks and numbering
Table commands	Changes the fields on the Task Sheet
Filter commands	Changes the tasks that are displayed

Moving

To Move	Keys	Mouse
Up and down through the list of tasks	Up Arrow Down Arrow PgUp PgDn	Click the task Use the vertical scroll bar
Left and right through the fields	Left Arrow Right Arrow Ctrl+PgUp Ctrl+PgDn	Use the horizontal scroll bar

When you drag the vertical scroll box with the mouse, Microsoft Project shows the task ID that will be at the top of the window if you release the mouse button.

PERT Chart

The PERT Chart shows each task as a box or node, with lines between the nodes indicating a relationship exists between the tasks. Each node initially contains the task name, ID number, duration, and the scheduled start and finish dates; these fields can be changed to contain any five fields you want.

The borders on the nodes show the type of task. For example, in the following illustration, the bold borders indicate critical tasks; the double border on "Investigation begins" indicates a milestone. The thin border is a noncritical task. On a color monitor or printer, the critical tasks and milestones are red; the noncritical tasks and milestones are black. You change the colors and patterns using the Format Borders command.

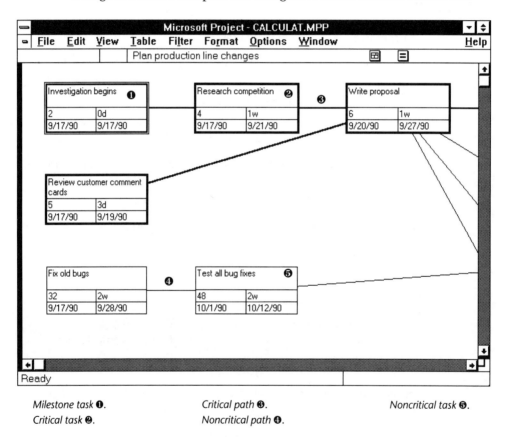

Milestone task ❶.   Critical path ❸.   Noncritical task ❺.
Critical task ❷.   Noncritical path ❹.

On the PERT Chart, there are some extra things you can do with the mouse. For example, you can create new nodes with or without a relationship to another task, and you can move single nodes, groups of nodes, or a node and all its successors.

Uses

Use the PERT Chart to see which tasks depend on other tasks. You also can enter new tasks on the PERT Chart, and you can create relationships between tasks by dragging the mouse between the tasks.

FormattingFormat command

Format Command	What It Does
Text	Changes the font, size, and color of text on the PERT Chart
Borders	Changes the pattern and color of the node borders
Palette	Changes the fields shown in each task node
Zoom	Shows a "big picture" view with the ID number only
Layout Now	Arranges the nodes in the view

Moving

To Move	Keys	Mouse
From node to node	Direction keys	Click the node
To first or last task	Home or End	Use the scroll bars
From field to field within a node	Tab	Click the field
A node	Ctrl+direction key	Point to the node border and drag the node to the new position
A group of nodes		Click the border of each node and drag to the new position
A node and successors		Hold down Shift and drag a node

Task PERT Chart

The Task PERT Chart shows one task at a time, with its immediate predecessors (tasks that it depends on) and successors (tasks that depend on it). Each task is in a box or node, with predecessors to the left, and successors to the right. The type of relationship between each pair of tasks is shown on the line between the tasks.

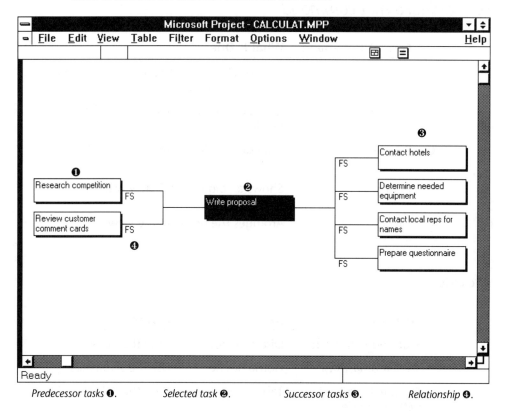

Predecessor tasks ❶.   *Selected task* ❷.   *Successor tasks* ❸.   *Relationship* ❹.

Uses

Use the Task PERT Chart to quickly identify the immediate predecessors and successors to a task. This view is best used at the bottom of a combination view—two views in one window—to see the predecessors and successors of the task selected in the top view.

Formatting

Command	What It Does
Format Sort	Sorts the list of tasks in the order you specify; when you step through the tasks, you do so in the sort order rather than ID order
Filter commands	Change the tasks that are displayed; when you step through the tasks, the selected task is a filtered task

Moving

To Move	Keys	Mouse
To first or last task	Home or End	Use the scroll bars
To previous or next task	Left Arrow Right Arrow Shift+Left Arrow Shift+Right Arrow	Click the task Use the horizontal scroll bar
Up or down through the predecessors or successors if not all visible	Up Arrow Down Arrow PgUp PgDn	Click the task Use the vertical scroll bar

Resource Form

The Resource Form (next page) shows information about one resource at a time. At the bottom of the Resource Form are fields you can change to see different types of resource assignment information for the resource. Initially, the Resource Form shows the schedule fields.

Use the entry bar at the top of the window to enter information in the form. The boxes and buttons in the form work just like a dialog box.

The fields at the bottom of the form show information about the resource assignments that can't be viewed elsewhere. To change the fields, use the Format commands, described in the "Formatting" section.

When you enter information in the Resource Form, the Prev. and Next buttons change to OK and Cancel. When you have finished entering information about the resource, press Enter or click OK with the mouse. If you want to cancel all you have entered, press Esc or click Cancel. After you press Enter or Esc, or click OK or Cancel, the buttons change back to Prev. and Next so you can go to another resource.

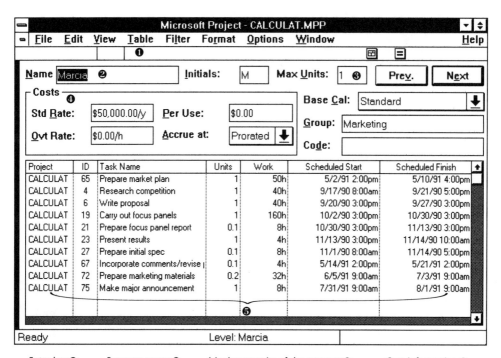

Entry bar ❶.   *Resource name* ❷.   *Maximum units of the resource* ❸.   *Cost information* ❹.
Schedule fields ❺ *show the tasks the resource is assigned to and the scheduled start and finish date for the resource on each task. You can change these fields to show other information such as work or cost for the resource on each task.*

The Edit Form dialog box for resources looks like the top half of the Resource Form and works the same way. You use it when you want to change a detail about a resource—or several resources at once—when the Resource Form is not displayed.

Uses

Use the Resource Form for entering new resources. You also use the Resource Form for reviewing resource assignment information. For example, you can see the list of tasks that the resource is scheduled to work on and the start and finish date for the resource on each task. Or you can see cost or work information for the resource on each task.

Formatting

Command	What It Does
Format Sort	Sorts the list of resources in the order you specify; when you step through the resources, you do so in the sort order rather than ID order
Format Schedule	Places the schedule fields at the bottom of the form so you can review the schedule for this resource on each task to which it is assigned
Format Cost	Places the cost fields at the bottom of the form so you can review the cost for this resource on each task to which it is assigned
Format Work	Places the work fields at the bottom of the form so you can review the amount of work for this resource on each task to which it is assigned
Format Notes	Places the Notes box at the bottom of the form so you can enter a note about this resource
Filter commands	Changes the resources that are displayed; when you step through the resources, you see only the filtered resources

Moving

To Move	Keys	Mouse
To next option	Tab	Click the option
To previous option	Shift+Tab	Click the option
To any option	Alt+underlined letter in the option name	Click the option
Into the fields at the bottom of the form	Alt+1	Click the field
From field to field	Direction keys	Click the field
To the next resource	Enter (to choose the Next button)	Click Next
To the previous resource	Shift+Enter (to choose Prev. button)	Click Prev.

Resource Histogram

The Resource Histogram shows the peak demand for one resource, period by period. It is a graphic representation of a resource's work load over time. On the histogram is a line showing the capacity of the resource—the maximum number of units available for the project. The graph shows the peak number of units of this resource allocated during the period on the timescale. For example, if the timescale shows weeks, and an allocation of five, it does not necessarily mean that five units are allocated on each day, but on at least one day.

In the following histogram, the capacity line is at three units, showing that you have a maximum of three marketing staff. The bars show that during three days, the resource is overallocated, which means you have more than three units assigned to tasks; during six days, the resource is working below capacity, which means you have assigned fewer than three units to work on tasks.

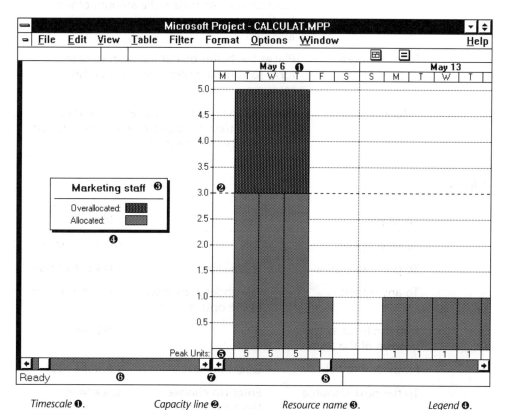

Timescale ❶.   Capacity line ❷.   Resource name ❸.   Legend ❹.
Peak units allocated during each period ❺.   Use this scroll bar to scroll through the resources ❻.
Divider bar ❼.   Use this scroll bar to scroll through time ❽.

The legend to the left shows the resource name and the color or pattern for the bars. You can change the colors or patterns using the Format Palette command.

You can move the divider bar to show more or less of the histogram timescale.

Uses

Use this view to check for overallocated or underallocated resources so you can determine how to shift tasks and resources to optimize resource use.

Formatting

Command	What It Does
Format Sort	Sorts the list of resources in the order you specify; when you step through the resources, you do so in the sort order rather than ID order
Format Text	Changes the font, size, and color of the text on the Resource Histogram
Format Gridlines	Changes the pattern and color of the lines on the Resource Histogram
Format Timescale	Changes the time period displayed on the histogram timescale
Format Palette	Controls the color and pattern of the histogram bars
Filter commands	Changes the resources that are displayed; when you step through the resources, you see only the filtered resources

Moving

To Move	Keys	Mouse
Through the resources	Left Arrow Right Arrow Home Down	Use the horizontal scroll bar below the
Through time on the histogram	Alt+Left Arrow Alt +Right Arrow Alt+PgUp Alt+PgDn Alt+Home Alt+End	Use the horizontal scroll bar below the histogram
Divider bar	Shift+F6, Left or Right Arrow, Enter	Drag divider bar (pointer changes to ◀▶)

When you drag the horizontal scroll bar below the histogram, Microsoft Project shows the date that will be on the histogram if you release the mouse button.

Resource Sheet

The Resource Sheet lists resource information in a spreadsheet-like format, with the information organized in rows and columns. The table applied to the Resource Sheet controls the fields displayed.

Resources that are overallocated, such as Marketing staff, are shown in bold (or red on a color monitor or printer). You can change this using the Format Text command.

Uses

Use the Resource Sheet to enter new resources or as a convenient way to review the complete list of resources. Use it when creating reports to show just the fields you want by changing the table applied and use it when exchanging data with another program, such as Microsoft Excel.

ID	Name	Initials	Group	Max. Units	Std. Rate	Ovt. Rate	Cost/Use	Accrue At	Code
1	**Marcia**	M	**Marketi**	1	**$50,000.00/y**	**$0.00/h**	**$0.00**	**Prorated**	
2	**Marketing staff ❸**	M	**Marketi**	3	**$32,000.00/y**	**$0.00/h**	**$0.00**	**Prorated**	
3	Jim	J	Marketin	1	$32,500.00/y	$0.00/h	$0.00	Prorated	
4	Janet	J	Marketin	1	❷$47,500.00/y	$0.00/h	$0.00	Prorated	
5	Roberto	R	Marketin	1	$30,000.00/y	$0.00/h	$0.00	Prorated	
6	Carmen	C	Marketin	1	$60,000.00/y	$0.00/h	$0.00	Prorated	
7	Dave	D	Design	1	$30,000.00/y	$0.00/h	$0.00	Prorated	
8	Cheryl	C	Marketin	1	$16,000.00/y	$11.50/h	$0.00	Prorated	
9	Shop crew	S	Producti	1	$15.00/h	$22.50/h	$0.00	Prorated	
10	Bill	B	Design	1	$25,000.00/y	$0.00/h	$0.00	Prorated	
11	Computer time	C	MIS	1	$60.00/h	$0.00/h	$50.00	End	
12	**Research Inc.**	R	**Vendor**	1	**$500.00/d**	**$0.00/h**	**$0.00**	**Start**	
13	Terri	T	Design	1	$6.50/h	$9.75/h	$0.00	Prorated	
14	**Design staff**	D	**Design**	3	**$25,000.00/y**	**$0.00/h**	**$0.00**	**Prorated**	
15	Documentation dept	D	Docume	1	$20.00/h	$0.00/h	$0.00	Prorated	
16	Testing staff	T	Testing	3	$25,000.00/y	$0.00/h	$0.00	Prorated	
17	Marilynn	M	Testing	1	$32,500.00/y	$0.00/h	$0.00	Prorated	
18	Nancy	N	Producti	1	$32,500.00/y	$0.00/h	$0.00	Prorated	
19	Production team	P	Producti	3	$25,000.00/y	$0.00/h	$0.00	Prorated	
20	Jeff	J	Sales	1	$29,000.00/y	$0.00/h	$0.00	Prorated	
21	Karen	K	Sales	1	$35,000.00/y	$0.00/h	$0.00	Prorated	
22	Sales engineers	S	Sales	3	$32,000.00/y	$0.00/h	$0.00	Prorated	
23	Rick	R	Sales	1	$10.00/h	$15.00/h	$0.00	Prorated	
24	Bob	B	Producti	1	$8.00/h	$12.00/h	$0.00	Prorated	
25	Mary	M	Sales	1	$20,000.00/y	$0.00/h	$0.00	Prorated	

Entry bar ❶.

The table applied controls the field names listed at the top of each column and the type of information shown about each resource ❷.

Bold text indicates a resource is assigned work beyond its capacity ❸.

Formatting

Command	What It Does
Format Sort	Sorts the list of resources in the order you specify
Format Text	Changes the font, size, and color of the text on the Resource Sheet
Format Gridlines	Changes the pattern and color of the lines on the Resource Sheet
Table commands	Changes the fields on the Resource Sheet
Filter commands	Changes the resources that are displayed

Moving

To Move	Keys	Mouse
Up and down through the list of resources	Up Arrow Down Arrow PgUp PgDn	Click the resource Use the vertical scroll bar
Left and right through the fields	Left Arrow Right Arrow Ctrl+PgUp Ctrl+PgDn	Use the horizontal scroll bar

When you drag the vertical scroll box with the mouse, Microsoft Project shows the resource ID that will be at the top of the window if you release the mouse button.

Resource Usage View

Entry bar **❶**.　　Timescale **❷**.

Bold shows that this resource is assigned work beyond its capacity sometime during the project **❸**.

Work assigned to this resource during the timescale period, in this case, the week of October 7 **❹**.

Resource list **❺**.　　Divider bar **❻**.　　Resource allocation information **❼**.

The Resource Usage view shows a list of resources and information about resource use over time. The period covered by the boxes on the right can be changed so you can look at resource allocation for any time period, from minutes to years. You can see the time each resource is scheduled to work for each period, the amount of time resources are overallocated during each period, what percentage each resource is allocated, or the cost of each resource for the period.

Overallocated resources, such as Marketing staff in the previous illustration, are shown in bold (or red on a color monitor or printer). You can change this using the Format Text command.

To show more or less of the table and chart, move the divider bar.

Uses

Use the Resource Usage view to check the allocation of resources during each period. You also can enter resources on this view. If you have several projects that share resources, this view can show you resource use for all the projects.

Formatting

Command	What It Does
Format Sort	Sorts the list of resources in the order you specify
Format Text	Changes the font, size, and color of the text on the Resource Usage view
Format Gridlines	Changes the pattern and color of the lines on the Resource Usage view
Format Timescale	Changes the time period displayed on the timescale
Format Allocation	Shows the amount of work each resource has been assigned during the period on the timescale
Format Overallocation	Shows the amount of work beyond the resource's capacity, if overallocated for the period on the timescale
Format Percent Allocation	Shows what percentage of a resource's total capacity has been allocated during the period on the timescale
Format Cost	Shows the scheduled cost for each resource during the period on the timescale
Table commands	Changes the fields on the Resource Usage view
Filter commands	Changes the resources that are displayed

Moving

To Move	Keys	Mouse
Up and down through the list of resources	Up Arrow Down Arrow PgUp PgDn	Click the recource Use the vertical scroll bar
Left and right through the fields	Left Arrow Right Arrow Ctrl+PgUp Ctrl+PgDn	Use the horizontal scroll bar below the table
Through time on the chart	Alt+Left Arrow Alt+Right Arrow Alt+PgUp Alt+PgDn Alt+Home Alt+End	Use the horizontal scroll bar below the boxes
Divider bar	Shift+F6, Left or Right Arrow, Enter	Drag the divider bar (pointer changes to ✥)

When you drag the vertical scroll box with the mouse, Microsoft Project shows the resource ID that will be at the top of the window if you release the mouse button. When you drag the horizontal scroll bar below the boxes, Microsoft Project shows the date that will be on the chart if you release the mouse button.

Combination Views

Microsoft Project also comes with one combination view, the Task Entry view. A combination view consists of two views in the same window, one on top and one on the bottom. The bottom view shows information about the task or resource selected in the top view. You can combine any two views that are not already combination views to create your own combination views.

When you start Microsoft Project for the first time, you see the Task Entry view, a combination view with the Gantt Chart on top and the Task Form on the bottom.

In a combination view, such as the Task Entry view, commands or typing affect the active view. The active view bar along the left side of the view shows which view is active.

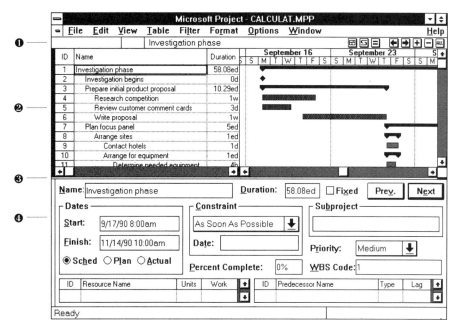

The Task Entry view has the Gantt Chart on top ❶, showing tasks and durations, and their Gantt bars.
Active view bar ❷ shows the Gantt Chart is the active view.
Split bar ❸; the split box is at the left end of the bar.
The Task Form is on the bottom ❹, showing the details about the task selected on the Gantt Chart.

To	Do This
Switch between the top and bottom views	Press F6 or click the view
Change a view in a combination view	Select the view you want to replace, and choose another view
Change a single pane view to combination view	Display the view you want on top; hold down Shift and choose the view you want on the bottom
Replace combination view with a single-pane view	Hold down Shift and choose the view from the View menu
Split a single-pane view	Press Shift+F6, press the direction keys to move the split bar, and press Enter; with the mouse, drag the split box halfway up the window
Close a pane in a combination view	Press Shift+F6, press the Up Arrow or Down Arrow key to close the top or bottom view, and press Enter; with the mouse, drag the split bar up or down

MICROSOFT PROJECT BASICS

This section will help you if you are unfamiliar with Microsoft Windows. It explains briefly the parts of a window, menus, commands, and how to use dialog boxes. It also explains how to use the entry bar, where you enter information into Microsoft Project.

The following illustration shows the parts of the window.

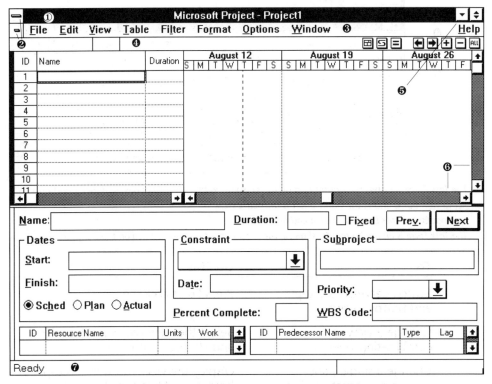

Title bar shows the application and project name ❶.

Control menus for the application and project, used to move, size, and close the windows ❷.

Menu bar lists the menus ❸.

Entry bar is used to enter information ❹.

Maximize and minimize boxes shrink or enlarge the window when clicked with the mouse ❺.

Scroll bars are used with the mouse to scroll through information ❻.

Status bar tells you about commands or what Microsoft Project is doing ❼.

Choosing a Command

The menu bar at the top of the screen contains the menus on which you'll find all the commands in Microsoft Project for Windows.

To choose a command, first select the appropriate menu, and then choose the command from the menu. You can choose a command with the keys or the mouse.

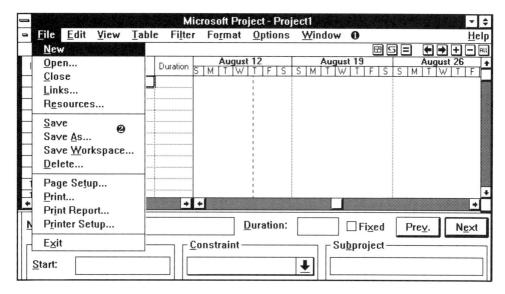

Menu bar ❶.
Commands on the File menu ❷.

TO CHOOSE COMMANDS WITH THE KEYS

1. Press Alt to select the menu bar.
2. Press the letter underlined in the menu name.
   For example, to select the File menu, press Alt followed by F.
3. Press the letter underlined in the command name.
   For example, to choose the Save command, press S.

TO CHOOSE COMMANDS WITH THE MOUSE

1. Click the menu name.
   For example, to select the File menu, click File.
2. Click the command name.
   For example, to choose the Save command, click Save.

Using a Dialog Box

When you choose certain commands—those followed by an ellipsis (...)—Microsoft Project displays a dialog box in which you set other options for the command. In a dialog box, you either type or select information. If you can select information, there is either a box containing a list of items, or there is an arrow at the right end of the option.

To move from option to option in a dialog box, press Tab. To move to a specific option, hold down Alt and press the underlined letter in the option name. To move around a dialog box using the mouse, click the option.

The following illustrations show what you do for each type of option.

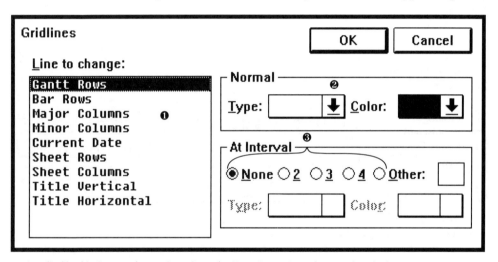

In a list like this ❶, you select an item. Press the Up or Down Arrow key to select the item you want, or click it with the mouse.

An arrow means there is a list of items from which you can select ❷. Select the option and press Alt+Down Arrow, or click the arrow to see the list. Press the Up or Down Arrow key to select the item you want, or click it with the mouse.

These are called option buttons ❸. You can select only one in a group. Press Alt+the underlined character or click the button with the mouse to select it.

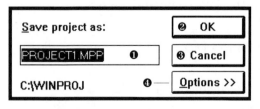

In a text box, type the text you want ❶.

Press Enter or click the OK button when the settings are as you want them and you want to carry out the command ❷.

Press Esc or click the Cancel button to cancel the command ❸. In some dialog boxes, this button changes to Close after you have done things that cannot be canceled, such as created a new table.

Choose a button like this to see another dialog box with more options ❹. To choose the button, press Alt+ the underlined letter in the option name.

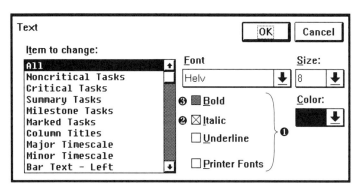

These are check boxes ❶. *You can turn on more than one check box in a group of check boxes.*

To turn on or off a check box, press Alt+the under-lined letter (such as Alt+B for Bold) or click the box with the mouse. An X in the box ❷ *indicates it is on; if the box is grayed* ❸, *it means the selected information has a mixture of settings, for example, bold and not bold text.*

Using the Entry Bar

The entry bar is used to enter information into Microsoft Project. Often, there is a list of choices from which you can select. You know if there is a list because the entry bar arrow appears when you select the field. Then you can choose from the list instead of typing. For example, you can choose a resource from the list in the entry bar.

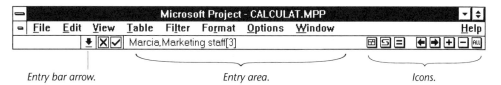

Entry bar arrow.   Entry area.   Icons.

1. *Select the field or box where you want to enter information.*

2. *Type the information or select it from the entry bar list.*

   If you can select information, the entry bar arrow (⬦) appears on the entry bar.

   To see the list, press Alt+Down Arrow, or click the arrow with the mouse. Then press the Up or Down Arrow key to select the item you want, or click the item with the mouse.

3. *To indicate that you have finished with your entry, press Enter, or click the Enter box (☑).*

   To cancel what you have done so far in the entry bar, press Esc, or click the Cancel box (☒).

At the right end of the entry bar are icons—shortcuts to use if you have a mouse. The last five icons are used for outlining, and appear only if you are using the Gantt Chart or Task Sheet, the two views on which you can outline. The table on the following page shows the meanings of the various icons.

Icon Meaning

Icon	Meaning
⊞	Edit form icon—Same as choosing the Edit Form command. Shows the Edit Form dialog box for tasks if a task is selected; shows the Edit Form dialog box for resources if a resource is selected.
⑤	Link icon—Same as choosing the Edit Link command. Links the selected tasks with finish-to-start relationships.
⊟	Calculate icon—Same as choosing the Options Calculate Now command. Calculates the project schedule if you have selected manual calculations in the Options Calculation dialog box.
←	Promote icon—Promotes a task so it becomes a summary task.
→	Demote icon—Demotes a task so it becomes a subordinate task.
⊞	Expand icon—Expands the selected summary tasks so their subordinate tasks are shown.
⊟	Collapse icon—Collapses the selected summary tasks so their subordinate tasks are hidden.
⊞	Expand All icon—Expands the outline so all tasks show.

Customizing Microsoft Project

There are several things about Microsoft Project you can change. The following table shows what you can customize and how you do it in Microsoft Project. For information and examples for creating all the elements, see Chapter 16, "Using Microsoft Project Tools."

What You Can Customize	How To Do It
Create new views, change existing views, change the View menu	View Define Views command
Create new tables, change existing tables, change the Table menu	Table Define Tables command
Create new filters, change existing filters, change the Filter menu	Filter Define Filters command
Create new reports or change existing reports	File Print Report command
Create new calendars or change existing calendars	Options Base Calendars and Options Resource Calendar

There are also a number of preferences you can set. For example, you can change the color of dialog boxes, or how Microsoft Project displays the time. The following table shows items you can change and the setting you change in the Options Preferences dialog box.

You Can Change	Change This in the Options Preferences Dialog Box
Initial view displayed when you start Microsoft Project	Default View
Color in dialog boxes and forms	Dialog Color and Form Color
Whether you want the duration tracking fields to determine the resource work and cost tracking fields, or if you prefer to enter work values yourself	Auto Track Resources
Whether you want to see the status bar, entry bar, and scroll bars	Show Status Bar, Show Entry Bar, Show Scroll Bars
Number of hours worked each day	Default Hours/Day
Number of hours worked each week	Default Hours/Week
Amount of slack time that makes a task critical	Show As Critical If Slack <=
Whether you want to be asked if you want to add a new resource to the pool, or if you want Microsoft Project to add it automatically	Auto Add Resources
Messages which warn you about scheduling inconsistencies	Schedule Messages
Units used (minutes, hours, days, or weeks) when you don't type a unit	Default Duration Units and Default Work Units
Format of date and time	Date Order, Date Format, Time Format, Date Separator, Time Separator
Text that follows the time to indicate morning or afternoon	0:00 to 11:59 Text and 12:00 to 23:59 Text
Standard and overtime rates for resources when you don't specify one	Default Standard Rate and Default Overtime Rate
Appearance of currency	Currency Symbol, Symbol Position, Currency Digits, Thousands Separator, and Decimal Separator
Whether Gantt bars are rounded to days (or to the minor timescale unit if it is smaller) or not rounded	Gantt Bar Rounding

PLANNING YOUR PROJECT AND CREATING THE SCHEDULE

In Part 2, you learn the basic steps for gathering project information and entering that information into Microsoft Project for Windows. These steps include:

- Setting your project goals
- Listing the tasks
- Estimating how long each task will take
- Deciding the sequence of the tasks and the relationships between tasks
- Assigning people, equipment, and costs for the tasks

In following these steps, you and your planning team spend the majority of your time gathering and analyzing information. Then you just enter the information into Microsoft Project for Windows. Once all this information is entered, you'll see the power of Microsoft Project as it helps you analyze your project model.

Each chapter in Part 2 describes a discrete step. In reality, each step depends on the others. You may find it easier to do all your planning at once, and then enter all the information into the computer. Or you may want to do one step at a time as you go through each chapter.

CHAPTER 3

Setting Project Goals

When planning a new project, setting the goals is the first and the most important step. This means deciding what you want to accomplish, when it has to be finished, and what your budget is. Setting goals ensures that everyone understands and agrees with the purpose of the project. Without goals, you have no way of measuring when the project is complete, and you have no way of knowing if others support your goals.

When you list your goals, be sure to include the scope of the project and the assumptions on which your goals and scope are based. Scope defines the area covered by the project and the limits of the project. Assumptions are what you expect will be true. For example:

Goal: Install New Phone System

Scope	Do:	Replace trunk lines
		Add lines
	Do not:	Rewire existing lines
		Replace existing phones
Assumptions	Existing wiring is OK	
	Existing phones will work with new system	

If you later discover that some of the wiring has been eaten by squirrels, obviously your first assumption is no longer valid, and the scope of the project has now changed.

As the project manager, you must drive the goal setting and make sure the scope and assumptions are included. Depending on your organization, you'll probably want to work with project team leaders to further analyze and define the project, and to ensure your assumptions are valid and the goals and scope realistic. By including others in the planning, you increase their commitment to make the project successful, and end up with a more solid plan.

Once you have determined project goals, scope, and assumptions, you can enter some general information about the project into Microsoft Project for Windows. For example, you can record the project title, company name, project manager, project start date, and notes about the project, including the goals, scope, and assumptions.

This is also a good time to set up your calendar. The calendar tells Microsoft Project the working hours and days for the project, and is also the place you specify holidays and other days off that affect all the workers on the project.

SETTING CLEAR PROJECT GOALS, SCOPE, AND ASSUMPTIONS

When you set goals, make sure they state clearly what you are trying to accomplish or what the project is. There are a several ways you can analyze your goals as you develop them. For example, try the following approaches.

- Think about what you want to achieve or where you want to be at the end of the project—what is the end product?
- State the goal in user or customer terms—what does this person want?
- Decide how you will know when you are finished.
- Look at where you are now and then contrast it with where you want to be.
- Analyze alternatives to your goals to decide if there is a more appropriate goal.
- Think of other ways to state the goal to be sure you are pinpointing exactly what the project is.

Once you have determined your goals, test the goals by answering the following questions.

- Are the goals measurable and specific in terms of time, cost, quality, quantity, and the end result?
- Are the goals realistic and achievable?
- Are the goals stated clearly so they are understandable and unambiguous to everyone working on the project?

If the answer to any of these questions is "no," restate the goals so the goals pass the tests.

Scope

By defining scope, you define the work that needs to be done and that will not be done. Explicitly stating the scope helps others understand what the project is and what it isn't, and helps you and others as you complete the necessary steps to plan the project. Stating the scope also helps you as the project progresses because any changes in scope will be easy to identify and justify. Even if you are not sure of the scope, getting your best guess down on paper gives you a starting point, helping you identify when the scope has changed.

One way to define scope is to state what is and what is not part of the project. For example, you could decide that a new product will be manufactured by an outside contractor; that the scope of the project is to complete the design and final specifications only. If it is later decided to manufacture the product in house, it will be obvious that the scope has changed, and that the original budget, time, and schedule no longer match the scope.

Defining scope is especially important when working with outside contractors. If you do not accurately define scope, the work they do may be either inadequate or overdone, and can adversely affect your schedule and budget. If you just assumed a contractor understood the scope, you may be charged for work you considered part of the project, but the contractor considered extra. You can't expect others to do what you want unless you tell them clearly what it is.

Assumptions

When you plan anything, you always make assumptions. Explicitly stating your assumptions now helps you later identify when things have changed, and helps you know how to get the project back on track. It is important to state assumptions clearly and concisely so everyone knows the premises on which your goals and the schedule are based.

Many of your assumptions may turn out to be inaccurate. What is more important than the eventual accuracy or inaccuracy of the assumptions is that you are conscious of the assumptions you make. By stating them clearly, you will better be able to tune into changes when they occur.

Suppose, for example, that you are assuming an outside contractor will be available to manufacture your new product. You state this up front, so that everyone understands that your goals and scope hinge on this assumption being true. If the contractor is not available, your assumption becomes false, and your scope changes, requiring a change in the plan.

If incorrect assumptions could dramatically affect the schedule, be sure to put together a contingency plan and be ready to go with it. For example, if your outside contractor is not available to manufacture the new product, what will you do instead? If you plan for this contingency now, you'll know exactly what to do if it occurs, and you'll lose the least amount of time in the schedule.

It is crucial that all project team leaders review the assumptions and agree that your assumptions are sound. Assumptions let others understand how and why you came up with your schedule and budget.

How do you decide what assumptions you are making? Think about the following questions to help you get started listing your assumptions.

- What are you assuming will have been done before you start?

- What external factors, out of your control, are you expecting to go a certain way? The weather? Or materials that must come from an outside vendor? That inflation won't go through the roof, driving your costs over budget?

- What are you expecting to happen at the end? Do you consider, for example, that the project will be finished when you hand the manufacturing plans to the outside contractor to begin production? Or do you assume you will monitor the outside contractor?

When you have prepared your goals, scope, and assumptions, share them with others. You may end up repeating the goal-setting process several times until you have the agreement and support of both your management and the rest of the project team.

USING MICROSOFT PROJECT FOR WINDOWS

In this first step, you enter general project information into Microsoft Project for Windows, such as the project name and description, the company, manager, and project start date. You can also set the calendar so Microsoft Project will schedule tasks only when you want them scheduled.

Entering General Project Information

You enter general project information in the Options Project Info dialog box. This dialog box includes an area for notes, where you can state your project goal, scope, and assumptions.

Choose Options Project Info.

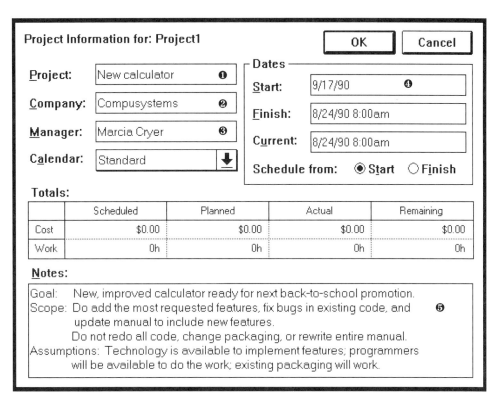

Type the name of the project here ❶.

You can also type a company name ❷ *and manager* ❸.

Type the project start date here ❹.

In the Notes box ❺, *type your goal, scope, and assumptions. At the end of each line, press Enter. After you finish typing in the Notes box, press Tab and then press Enter, or click OK.*

When you enter a project start date, Microsoft Project for Windows schedules your project forward from this date, scheduling each task to begin as soon as possible. If you enter a target project finish date in the Finish box, Microsoft Project schedules backwards from this finish date, with each task finishing as late as possible to make the finish date. Type a finish date only when you want Microsoft Project to calculate the latest possible date that you can start and still make the schedule. This does not create the ideal schedule, however, because if any task is late, the project end date will slip. It does give you useful information, though, if you want to know the latest possible start date.

Setting the Calendar

In Microsoft Project for Windows, calendars define the working and nonworking days and hours for the project. You set the calendars so Microsoft Project will schedule tasks and resources at the times you want them scheduled. Tasks are scheduled only on the working days and hours in the calendars.

Calendars in Microsoft Project look like a wall calendar with each month appearing alone. Microsoft Project has two kinds of calendars—base calendars and resource calendars. In the base calendar, you indicate the hours and days that are most standard for your company or for this project. It is your way to tell Microsoft Project the normal working hours for the project. For example, if you normally work Monday through Friday, 8 a.m. to 5 p.m., with an hour for lunch, you put this information in the base calendar. You also show holidays and other time away from work that apply to the project or the group of workers.

Resource calendars establish hours for individual resources. Each resource has a calendar; the information in each resource calendar, such as holidays, working days, and working hours, comes from the base calendar. You change the information in the resource calendar only if the resource does not work the same hours as those in the base calendar and to schedule vacation or other time away from work that is different from other resources. For more information about resource calendars, see Chapter 7, "Assigning People, Equipment, and Costs to Tasks."

When scheduling tasks that have resources assigned, Microsoft Project uses the working days and hours in the resource calendars for the resources assigned to the tasks. For those tasks that do not have resources assigned, or for tasks that do not depend on the number of resources for their duration, the base calendar is used.

You may find it convenient to create more than one base calendar. For example, if you have groups of resources working similar hours and days—such as three shifts—you can create three base calendars, one for each shift. Each calendar would contain the most general information, such as working days and hours plus holidays, for one shift. By choosing the appropriate base calendar for each resource, the working days and hours in the resource calendar are correct and all you have to do is add vacation hours, or other changes specific to each resource. For more information about creating multiple base calendars, see Chapter 16, "Using Microsoft Project Tools."

You don't have to create any calendars. If you don't, Microsoft Project uses its default calendar, which has the following settings:

- Workdays: Monday–Friday
- Work hours: 8 a.m.–12 noon and 1 p.m.–5 p.m.
- No holidays

Use the default calendar as it is, or change it to fit your project. The default calendar is called Standard.

Changing Working Days and Hours

To change the Standard calendar, choose Options Base Calendars, and then choose the Edit button. The Calendar dialog box shows the current working days and hours. To change working days, select in the calendar the day or days you want to change and select Working or Nonworking.

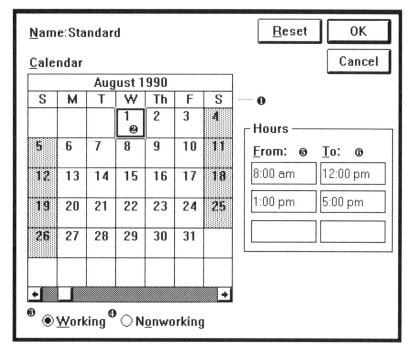

Select a day title at the top of the calendar to change that day in all weeks ❶.

Select one or more days to change only those days ❷.

To make the selected days workdays, select Working ❸.

To make the days nonworking days, select Nonworking ❹.

To change working hours for the days selected in the calendar, type the starting time for each work period in the From boxes ❺.

Type the finishing time for each work period in the To boxes ❻.

To change working hours for the selected days, type the hours in the Hours box.

Using Multiple Base Calendars

In a project, you may have one base calendar, or you may have several. You can create as many base calendars as you need. For example, you can take a single base calendar and make variations of it to suit the schedules of different groups within the company. If you have three shifts working on a project, you can create three base calendars, one for each shift, and name each one appropriately, such as Day, Swing, and Graveyard. Or if one group of resources takes every other Friday off, create a base calendar just for that group. You specify the base calendar to use when you enter your resources.

If you need to use multiple base calendars, first create one base calendar that is the most general—it should include the holidays and working days and hours that apply to most of the tasks and resources. (You can create this calendar by editing the Standard calendar, or by starting with a new calendar.) Then copy this calendar, and change those parts that are different. For example, if you have three shifts, make the Day calendar first, and then copy the Day calendar, name it Swing, and change the working hours. The holidays and working days are carried over from the Day calendar.

You can edit any calendar, create a new calendar, or copy an existing calendar and change it. When you want to:

- Change an existing calendar permanently (for example, your staff always works Monday through Thursday, 7 a.m. to 12 noon and 1 p.m. to 6 p.m. so you want the Standard calendar to have these working days and hours): Choose Options Base Calendars, select the calendar you want to change, and then choose the Edit button. The Calendar dialog box will show the current setting for the selected calendar. Once you change these settings, the original settings will no longer exist.

- Create a new calendar: Choose Options Base Calendars and choose the New button. The Calendar dialog box will show the settings from the original Standard calendar. Type a name for the calendar, and set the working days and hours as appropriate.

- Create a calendar that uses the settings of an existing calendar, but doesn't wipe out the existing calendar: Choose Options Base Calendars, select the calendar you want to copy, and then choose the Copy button. The Calendar dialog box will show the current settings for the selected calendar. Change the settings as required, and change the name of the calendar. The calendar you copied and the new calendar will both exist.

For more information about creating calendars, see Chapter 16, "Using Microsoft Project Tools."

Saving Your Calendars

When you exit Microsoft Project for Windows, your base calendars are automatically saved in a file called CALENDAR.MPC. You can also save base calendars yourself and change the name of the file containing the calendars.

To Save Base Calendars in Another File
1. Choose Options Base Calendars
2. Choose the Save button
3. Type a name for the file
4. Choose OK

By saving base calendars in different files, you can have several sets of calendars, one for each project, if appropriate. You can also pass calendar files to others in your organization. If one group, such as personnel, has all the information on the working days and hours for your organization, it can create the calendar file containing base calendars for each group. Everyone in the organization can use this file to ensure consistency within the organization.

Now that you know your goals for this project, the next step is to break the goals into the separate tasks needed to reach the goals.

CHAPTER 4

Breaking Your Project into Tasks and Milestones

OK. So, you have decided on your project goals. You stated the scope and assumptions. The next step is to break your project into the tasks that must be accomplished to meet these goals and to list the milestones that will help you track the project. Creating this list of tasks is a fundamental step in your plan because any task missing from the list won't be scheduled, making the plan invalid.

How do you determine what these tasks and milestones are? The best way is to have those who will do the work or manage the work take part in creating the list of tasks and milestones. Listing and organizing tasks and milestones requires the knowledge, skill, and experience of those responsible for and experienced in doing the work. Once you have your task list, you enter it into Microsoft Project for Windows.

But, just what is a task? And what is a milestone? And why do you need them in your project?

WHAT ARE TASKS AND MILESTONES?

Tasks are activities that must be finished to achieve the end result of the project. Milestones are checkpoints used to track your project. They represent the completion of a certain set of tasks or a certain portion of the project. For example, if your goal is to prepare a marketing plan, the tasks could include "Research competition" and "Perform cost analysis." A milestone might be "Research phase complete."

Since tasks and milestones provide the basis for the rest of your plan and for tracking the progress of your project, it is important that the task list be detailed and clear. You want tasks and milestones to be clearly worded and unambiguous so those using the plan know exactly what is expected as the result of each task.

Tasks

A task has an identifiable start and end; it usually requires people or equipment to complete it; and it is specific enough to permit both intermittent progress and the final result to be measured. For example, the task "Research competition" calls for one or more people to do the research. Progress on the task can be measured by comparing the number of competitors you plan to study with the number you have finished studying; you know when you are finished because you have studied all the competition.

Precise and Detailed. Identify tasks as precisely as possible and in as much detail as necessary. Tasks should be detailed enough that the time to complete each one is short compared to the overall project. For example, if you plan to study six competitors in depth, you may want to break the "Research competition" task into six tasks, one for each competitor. This helps you make a more reliable estimate of the task duration (the time to complete the task) and the people and equipment needed to complete the task.

Significant. Tasks must also be significant enough to be included in the plan. Insignificant or non-schedule related tasks only clutter your project task list. For example, in the "Research competition" task, the fact that you may go to the library to get financial information on competitors may be important in completing the task, but it is not significant enough to include as a separate task and does not affect how the tasks are scheduled.

Appropriate Level of Detail. The level of detail in your list of tasks should be appropriate to the amount of planning and control you want. For example, if you are hiring an outside consultant to do a study, you are interested in when the consultant starts and when the study will be in your hands, but you aren't interested in the detailed tasks performed by the consultant. In your list of tasks, you would include one task for the study, showing the start and finish date for the whole, rather than many tasks indicating each step in the study.

But, if you are doing the study yourself, the separate steps in completing the study are crucial to you. Your list of tasks would include every task necessary to do the study.

Task Scope and Assumption. Just as you set your project goals, when you list your tasks and milestones you must be aware of the scope of the tasks and the assumptions on which the tasks and milestones are based. This helps you identify changes and measure progress.

Complete. Be complete. Remember to include reports, reviews, and coordination activities in your list of tasks. And remember, also, to include tasks for anticipated rework or modifications after a task has been completed, such as revising a manual or reworking and retesting a new product.

Naming Tasks. Name a task using a verb and noun, such as "Build walls," "Install second floor phone outlets," or "Distribute design for review." Make the names as explicit as possible, and the style of the names consistent throughout. This consistency will help others understand each item in your schedule.

Milestones

A milestone is a task with a duration and cost of zero. Milestones help you measure the progress of your project and can increase motivation and productivity of those working on the tasks by giving them interim goals. By placing your milestones appropriately, you keep track of the project schedule throughout its life, instead of being surprised when the project isn't on schedule at the end. Milestones help you catch scheduling problems early, enabling you to act to bring the project back on schedule.

Placement. Usually you'll want to put a milestone at the start and end of a series of tasks so it stresses the importance of completing the tasks by a certain time. For example, at the beginning of the research phase, you could include the milestone "Research phase begins" and at the end, "Research phase complete."

Appropriate Level of Detail. Since milestones serve as checkpoints to help you track the schedule throughout the project, include milestones only down to the level of detail you want to monitor. If it is not important to you when the Research phase starts, don't include the milestone.

Related to Tasks. Be sure that milestones are related to tasks so you know when the milestone is achieved. For example, the milestone "Research phase complete" is directly related to the completion of the tasks preceding it. It will be obvious when you reach the milestone because the tasks in the Research phase will be complete. On the other hand, if you are writing the documentation for a new software product, the milestone "First testing release finished" won't tell you anything about the state of the documentation because it is not related to the writing tasks.

Events Outside Your Control. Include milestones that represent events outside your control if they influence your schedule. For example, include a milestone showing when you must have a bank loan to be able to proceed with a building project. As you approach the milestone, you can check on the loan to assure it will be in your hands when it is needed. Or, include the milestone "First testing release finished" because, while it is not directly related to your writing tasks, you know that your milestone "First draft of manual finished" must follow the testing release by one month.

Identifying Milestones. Milestones should be identified by the managers and workers who use them and must meet them. For example, if milestones are to help top management know how a project is progressing, these managers should take part in identifying milestones.

Naming Milestones. Name a milestone in a way that it is clear when the milestone is reached. Use a noun and a verb, such as "Walls complete," "Funding request due," "Loans approved," or "Manuscript reviewed." Make the names as clear as possible. The style of the names should be consistent throughout. This consistency will help others understand each item in your schedule.

LISTING TASKS AND MILESTONES

To determine your list of tasks and milestones, there are two basic methods you can use:

- Top-down method—start with major project phases, and then complete the details for each phase
- Bottom-up method—list all possible tasks, and then group the tasks into phases

Use the method that best suits what you know about the project. For example, if you are planning for a project that is new to you, such as creating a product using a new technology, you may not be able to use a bottom-up approach because you are not yet familiar with all the necessary tasks. Or you may use a combination of the two—a top-down approach to create the basic structure of the project, and then bottom-up to fill in that structure.

Whether you start with the major phases, or with the details, there are several ways you can generate your task list. For example, you can use brainstorming—a method in which members of a group spontaneously propose ideas and solutions—to identify major phases or detailed tasks. You can begin with the last milestone—the goal or purpose of the project—and work backwards to the start of the project; or start with the present and work forward to the goal.

Whatever your approach, it is especially important that those involved in doing the work also participate in creating the task list. The schedule will be more accurate and the chances are increased that the project will be completed successfully and punctually. The team members understand the necessary tasks better than any single person can, and support for the project will be stronger because the team will have confidence in the list of tasks and the plan.

When you list your tasks, answer the following questions for each one:

- Does it have an identifiable start and finish?
- Is the scope of the task clear?
- Is it clear who or what organization is responsible for getting it done?
- Is it significant, is the level of detail appropriate, and does it clearly play a role in the schedule?

If the answer to any of these questions is "no," either break the task into more detailed tasks, or change the scope of the task. Or, if it is unimportant, do not include it.

Top-down Method

Using the top-down method, you identify the major phases first, and then identify the milestones and tasks within each phase. You continue breaking tasks into smaller and smaller units until you reach the level of detail you want.

One advantage of this approach is that you have a version of the plan, although not very detailed, as soon as you decide the major phases. Once you determine this top-level schedule you can distribute the major phases to the appropriate managers and have them work with their teams to create the detailed schedules.

For example, suppose your project is to add a new calculator to your product line. The major phases might be Investigation, Design, Testing, Manufacturing, and Sales. The manager in charge of each phase can then work with the appropriate team members to create the individual task lists for each phase.

Bottom-up Method

Using the bottom-up method, you list all the tasks and milestones, and then organize them into logical groupings or by work flow. For example, you could identify all tasks that would be performed by each department, such as all marketing department tasks to market a new product, all manufacturing tasks to manufacture a new product, and all procurement tasks to procure materials for a new product.

Since it may not be easy to know how the tasks from different departments are interrelated, this method works best to create the initial list of tasks for smaller projects that involve one department.

ORGANIZING TASKS AND MILESTONES

Organizing your tasks helps you make sure the task list is complete and helps you ensure that the flow of the tasks makes sense. There are a couple of tools you can use to organize the tasks. One is outlining; the other is a work breakdown structure.

Outlining

Using an outline makes the organization of the project obvious, and helps you spot missing tasks or flaws in the logical flow of the tasks. It's an easy way to organize your tasks and makes it easy to share the appropriate level of information with others.

You can create an outline using either the top-down or bottom-up method. Either way, the main outline headings are the main phases in your project. For example:

        I   Investigation Phase
        II   Design Phase
        III Testing Phase
        IV   Manufacturing Phase
        V   Sales Phase

Under each main heading are the tasks that you must do to complete the phase. For example:

        I   Investigation Phase
             A) Prepare initial product proposal
             B) Set up focus panel
             C) Plan phone questionnaire
             D) Carry out focus panel
             E) and so on
        II   Design Phase
             A) Meet with marketing staff for report
             B) and so on
        III Testing Phase

Under each task, you list the more detailed tasks that must be done to complete the task. For example:

I Investigation Phase
   A) Prepare initial product proposal
      1) Research competition
      2) Review customer comment cards
      3) and so on
   B) Set up focus panel

You continue filling in and indenting the more detailed tasks until you get to the level of detail you want.

When you want to share information about the project, you can share just the main phases or as much detail as required by the recipient of the information by showing as much of the outline as appropriate. For example, to top management, you might share the five main phases; to the marketing manager, you might share the five main phases, plus all the tasks in those phases in which the marketing staff is involved, such as the Investigation phase and the Sales phase.

Work Breakdown Structure

A work breakdown structure, or WBS, is a tree-type of structure that includes every task and every result. It looks like an organizational chart for your company but is task oriented instead of people oriented. Each level of the WBS depicts the project at a different level of detail; the higher the level on the WBS, the less detailed are the tasks. Usually, there are three to five levels, depending on the project.

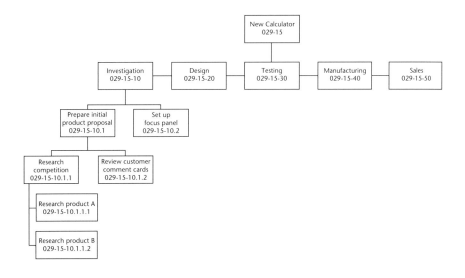

At the bottom or lowest level of a WBS is a "work package;" this is where the actual work is done and the resources are assigned. The characteristics of a work package are similar to those of a task. In the previous illustration, "Research product A" and "Research product B" are examples of work packages.

Each task is given a code number. This number shows the level of the task and where the task fits in the hierarchy. You can use these codes for sorting and filtering information to look at a limited part of the project information. For example, if a department code is part of the WBS code, you could filter the task list such that only those tasks that include a certain department code are displayed.

When you create a WBS, you start with the project goals, and then divide and redivide tasks until you get to the desired level of detail. This assures that all required tasks are logically identified and grouped. In the previous illustration, the first divisions are by project phases, but they could also be by work units (engineers, programmers, production line, etc.), financial cost codes, departments (marketing, lab, accounting, etc.), or major units of the product (if you are building a car, for example, the major units might be engine, transmission, body, suspension, and so on), depending on the organization of your project and company.

USING MICROSOFT PROJECT FOR WINDOWS

Now that you have your list of tasks and milestones, you are ready to enter them into Microsoft Project for Windows. Of course, you can also brainstorm a list of tasks at the computer, entering them as they come to mind. If you do this, just be sure that you share this list with the rest of the team to get their input and to ensure the list is complete.

This section includes steps for entering tasks and milestones, organizing the tasks and milestones in either an outline or work breakdown structure, and then printing the list so you can check your work and share it with others.

Entering Tasks and Milestones

Entering tasks and milestones into Microsoft Project is easy. When you start Microsoft Project, you see the Task Entry view with a blank Gantt Chart on top and a Task Form on the bottom. The first field is selected on the Gantt Chart, ready for you to type your first task.

You don't have to type a task number. Each task is numbered sequentially by Microsoft Project.

Entering a Task

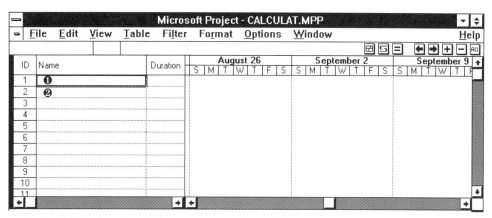

The first field is selected, ready for you to type a task name ❶.

Type the task name.

To go to the next row so you can type the next task, press the Down Arrow key or click the row ❷.

Initially, all tasks are scheduled to occur simultaneously and have a duration of one day (1d).

Entering a Milestone

Entering a milestone is similar to entering a task, except you need to specify that it is a milestone by typing "0" (zero) in the Duration field.

	Microsoft Project - CALCULAT.MPP																												
File	**Edit**	**View**	**Table**	**Filter**	**Format**	**Options**	**Window**																				**Help**		

Type the milestone ❶.

In the Duration field, type "0" ❷.

After you press Enter or click the Enter box (☑), the Gantt bar changes to a diamond ❸ to indicate it is a milestone.

You enter tasks and milestones on the Task Sheet in the same way.

Entering a Task on the PERT Chart

You can also enter tasks and milestones on the PERT Chart. Hold down Shift and choose View PERT Chart. (By holding down Shift, you get a full screen PERT Chart.)

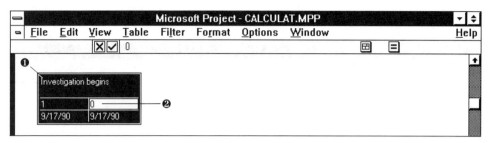

To create a task node, press Ins, or drag the mouse.
Type the task or milestone name here ❶.
If this is a milestone, type "0" here ❷.

To enter another task, repeat the steps. To move tasks around so you can see all the tasks, either press Ctrl+direction key or drag the node with the mouse.

Changing Several Tasks to Milestones Simultaneously. If you want to change several tasks to milestones, you can select all the tasks to be changed, and then choose the Edit Form command or click the form icon (▣). Type "0" in the Duration box. Choose OK.

Changing a Task with a Duration to a Milestone. Although milestones usually have zero duration, in Microsoft Project you can make any task a milestone, even one with a duration other than zero. To do this, select all the tasks that will be milestones, and then choose the Edit Form command or click the form icon (▣). Turn on the Milestone check box. Choose OK.

Importing an Existing List of Tasks. If you already have a list of tasks created in a spreadsheet or database program, such as Microsoft Excel, you can import this list into Microsoft Project for Windows. Microsoft Project can read files created in dBase II, III, and III Plus, Lotus 1–2–3, and ASCII or other text file formats. For more information, see Chapter 15, "Sharing Information."

Changing the Default View. The Task Entry view is the default view displayed when you start Microsoft Project for Windows or open a project. If you prefer to use another view most of the time, such as the PERT Chart, you can change the default view. Choose Options Preferences, select the Default View option, and then select from the list the view you want as the default view. Choose OK.

Changing Your Position When You Press Enter. You can add a line to the WINPROJ.INI file so that when you press Enter on the Gantt Chart or the Task Sheet, the next row down becomes the active row. To do this, open the WINPROJ.INI file in any word processing program, and then add the line "entermove=1" to the file. For more information about changing the WINPROJ.INI file, see the Preferences topic in the *Microsoft Project Reference*.

Moving Tasks. After you enter a list of tasks, you may need to move them around to organize them. Select the tasks, choose Edit Cut, move to the new location, choose Edit Paste. You can also use Microsoft Project's outlining feature to group the tasks and reorganize them.

Adding Cost Account Numbers. If you have cost account numbers that you use for your tasks, you can add a column to the Task Sheet to enter these numbers. You use a custom field such as Text1. Microsoft Project for Windows includes six custom text fields. Choose Table Define Tables, add the custom field to the table, and change the title to reflect the contents. You can then sort and filter on this field to show exactly the information you need. For more information about adding a column to a table, see Chapter 16, "Using Microsoft Project Tools."

Subprojects. A subproject is a group of tasks which has its own project file, but is represented as a single task in another project. Use subprojects to keep the most detailed tasks in a project separate from the master project, or when you have similar sets of tasks that you perform in many projects. For more information, see Chapter 14, "Managing Multiple Projects."

Using a Project Template. Use a project template when many of your projects have basically the same steps—such as construction jobs or similar types of publications done repeatedly. To use a template, open the template file, and choose the File Save As command to rename it. Change the start date or personnel as appropriate. For more information, see Chapter 14, "Managing Multiple Projects."

Organizing Tasks and Milestones

In Microsoft Project for Windows, you can organize your tasks using an outline or a work breakdown structure. When you create an outline, Microsoft Project for Windows also creates a WBS for you.

Outlining

Outlining is a powerful feature of Microsoft Project for Windows. You use outlining to:

- Enter and organize your tasks and milestones
- Reorganize your task list by moving summary tasks (all their subordinate tasks are moved with them)
- Collapse and expand your task list to see different levels of detail
- Present summary level information, including cost, work, and duration for the tasks

In an outline in Microsoft Project, tasks fall into two categories: summary tasks and subordinate tasks. A subordinate task is any indented or "demoted" task. A summary task:

- Has tasks indented beneath it
- Summarizes cost, work, and duration of the indented tasks
- Cannot have resources assigned to it

In Microsoft Project, an outline looks like this:

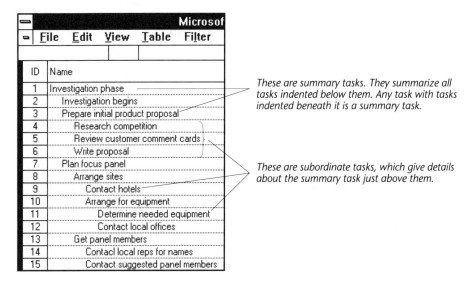

These are summary tasks. They summarize all tasks indented below them. Any task with tasks indented beneath it is a summary task.

These are subordinate tasks, which give details about the summary task just above them.

In the preceding illustration, tasks 2 through 15 are subordinate to task 1, "Investigation phase." Several tasks—3, 7, 8, 10, and 13—are also summary tasks because they have tasks indented beneath them. In Microsoft Project, you can create up to five levels; a summary task can be at any level except five.

You can create an outline using either the top-down method, in which you list the major phases first and then insert the more detailed tasks for each phase, or the bottom-up method, listing all the tasks first, then grouping them into like categories until you work your way to the major phases.

To create an outline, you just assign tasks or milestones to an outline level using the outlining key combinations, or the outline icons in the entry bar if you are using a mouse. Microsoft Project indents, or "demotes," the task or milestone to show its outline level.

Select the tasks and then:

To	Press	Click
Demote a task or add one level of indentation	Alt+Shift+Right Arrow	⮕
Promote a task or remove one level of indentation	Alt+Shift+Left Arrow	⬅

In Microsoft Project, you can outline on the Gantt Chart or Task Sheet.

Creating an Outline Using the Top-down Method. The following illustrations show how to create an outline using the top-down method, listing major phases first, and then adding the details.

Type all the major phases in your project. These will all be summary tasks ❶.

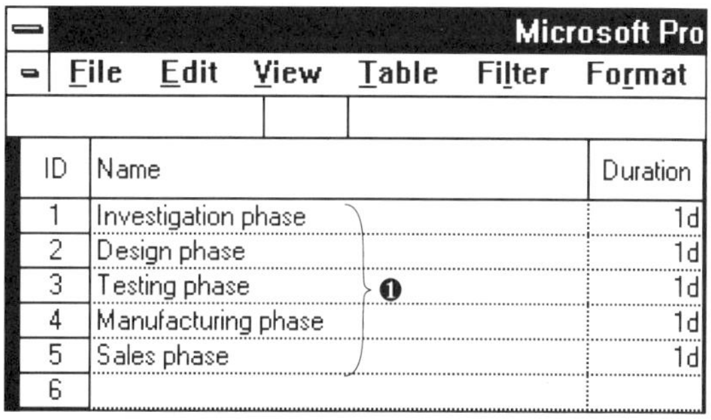

ID	Name	Duration
1	Investigation phase	1d
2	Design phase	1d
3	Testing phase	1d
4	Manufacturing phase	1d
5	Sales phase	1d
6		

To insert tasks under a phase name, select the number of rows you want to insert, starting with the row below where you want to insert.

To add space for the tasks under "Investigation phase," select the same number of rows as tasks that you want to insert. For example, to add eight tasks below "Investigation phase," select the eight rows below it ❶.

Press Ins.

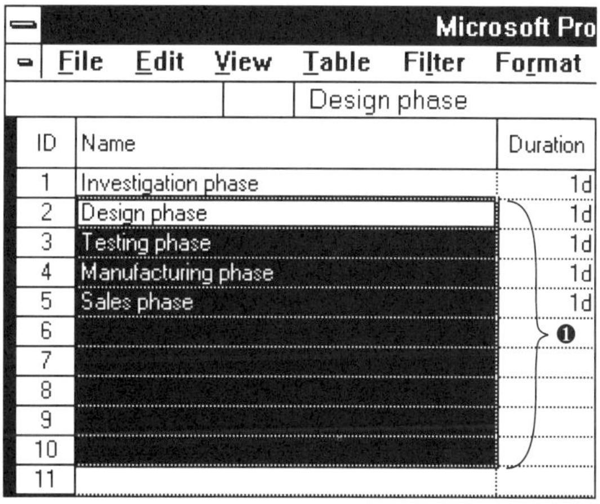

ID	Name	Duration
1	Investigation phase	1d
2	Design phase	1d
3	Testing phase	1d
4	Manufacturing phase	1d
5	Sales phase	1d
6		
7		
8		
9		
10		
11		

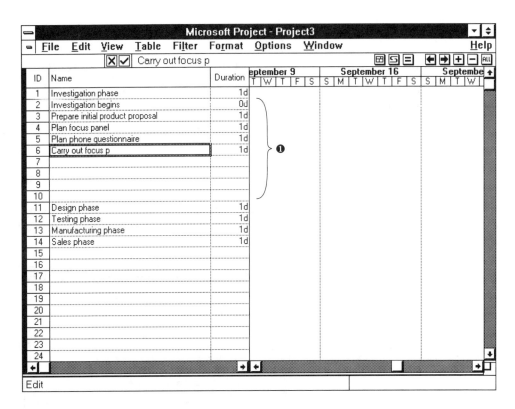

Type the tasks in the blank rows you inserted ❶.

If you need more room, insert more rows.

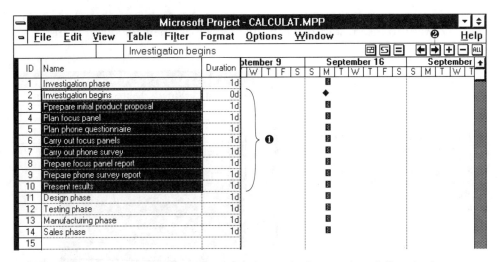

Select all the tasks you just typed so you can indent them under the summary task "Investigation phase" ❶.

To indent the tasks, press Alt+Shift+Right Arrow or click the demote icon ❷.

```
┌──────────────────────────────────────────────┐
│ ▭                          Microsoft Project   │
│ ▫ │ File  Edit  View  Table  Filter  Format    │
│   ┌──────────┬─────────────┐                   │
│   │          │             │                   │
│ ┌───┬────────────────────────────┬──────────┐  │
│ │ID │ Name                       │ Duration │  │
│ ├───┼────────────────────────────┼──────────┤  │
│ │ 1 │ Investigation phase        │  0.38ed  │  │
│ │ 2 │    Investigation begins    │     0d   │  │
│ │ 3 │    Pprepare initial product proposal │ 1d │ │
│ │ 4 │    Plan focus panel        │     1d   │  │
│ │ 5 │    Plan phone questionnaire│     1d   │  │
│ │ 6 │    Carry out focus panels  │     1d   │  │
│ │ 7 │    Carry out phone survey  │     1d   │  │
│ │ 8 │    Prepare focus panel report │  1d   │  │
│ │ 9 │    Prepare phone survey report│  1d   │  │
│ │10 │    Present results         │     1d   │  │
│ │11 │ Design phase               │     1d   │  │
│ │12 │ Testing phase              │     1d   │  │
│ │13 │ Manufacturing phase        │     1d   │  │
│ │14 │ Sales phase                │     1d   │  │
│ └───┴────────────────────────────┴──────────┘  │
└──────────────────────────────────────────────┘
```

The detailed tasks are now indented under their summary task, "Investigation phase."

You can continue adding and indenting subordinate tasks where appropriate under each task.

If you do not see the indentation, choose Format Outline and turn on the Name Indentation check box. To turn the check box on or off, press Alt+I or click the check box with the mouse.

Outlining Using the Bottom-up Method. If you have already listed all your tasks, you can create an outline by grouping them, adding the summary tasks, and then demoting the subordinate tasks. To insert space for summary tasks, follow the steps described in the top-down method for adding space for tasks and typing the tasks. Then, again as described in the top-down method, you select and demote the subordinate tasks.

Summary Task Durations. The duration for a summary task is based on the durations of all the subordinate tasks, and is displayed as elapsed time (0.38ed in the previous illustration). Elapsed time is based on the 24-hour clock. Since the task durations are still 1d, except for the milestone task, and all tasks still happen simultaneously, the duration for the summary tasks is also one day. But, since summary task duration is always elapsed duration, it is shown as a portion of a 24-hour day (.38ed), calculated by dividing the elapsed hours between the start time and finish time—9 hours from 8 a.m. to 5 p.m.—by 24 hours in a day. The nine hours is based on the start and finish time for the day in the calendar.

No Outline Icons? Since outline icons show only when the Gantt Chart or Task Sheet is the active view, first confirm you are using one of these views. If you are using the Gantt Chart or Task Sheet and don't see the outline icons, check the following:

- Choose Format Outline and make sure the Summary Tasks check box is turned on

- Choose Options Preferences and check that the Show Icons option is set to Yes

- Choose Format Sort, and then choose the Reset button to put the tasks back in ID number order

Reorganizing Your Outline. Once you have created your outline, it's easy to reorganize your project. When you move a summary task, all its subordinate tasks go with it. If you delete a summary task, all its subordinate tasks are deleted too.

Collapsing and Expanding Your Outline. You can collapse an outline to show just the summary tasks and then expand all or part of the outline to see the desired level of detail. For example, the following illustration shows the outline collapsed to show just the highest level summary tasks, and then the "Investigation phase" task expanded to show one level of subordinate tasks.

	Microsoft Project
▭	File Edit View Table Filter Format
	Investigation phase

ID	Name	Duration
1	Investigation phase	2.38ed
2	Investigation begins	0d
3	Prepare initial product proposal	0.38ed
7	Plan focus panel	0.38ed
16	Plan phone questionnaire	0.38ed
19	Carry out focus panels	1d
20	Carry out phone survey	1d
21	Prepare focus panel report	1d
22	Prepare phone survey report	1d
23	Present results	1d
24	Investigation phase complete	0d
25	Design phase	2.38ed
39	Testing phase	2.38ed
50	Manufacturing phase	2.38ed
60	Sales phase	2.38ed
76		

The outline was collapsed to show just the main phases, and then the "Investigation phase" summary task was selected and expanded.

When you collapse a summary task, its subordinate tasks are hidden. When you expand a summary task, the next level of subordinate tasks is displayed. You can collapse and expand parts of your outline to show exactly the information you want, in as much or as little detail as appropriate.

Select the tasks and then:

To	Press	Click
Collapse selected summary tasks	Alt+Shift+minus on keypad	⊟
Expand selected summary tasks	Alt+Shift+plus on keypad	⊞
Expand all summary tasks	Alt+Shift+asterisk on keypad	ALL

Adding Numbers and Symbols to Your Outline. You can add numbers to your outline as well as plus and minus symbols to indicate if a task is a summary task.

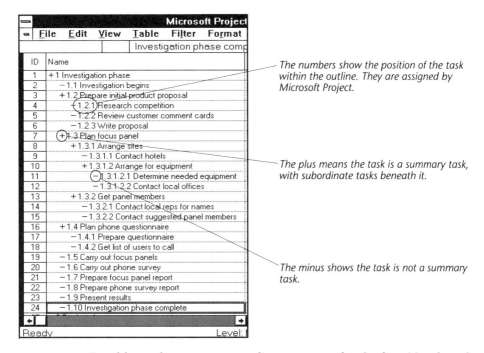

The numbers show the position of the task within the outline. They are assigned by Microsoft Project.

The plus means the task is a summary task, with subordinate tasks beneath it.

The minus shows the task is not a summary task.

To add numbers on your outline, turn on the Outline Number check box in the Format Outline dialog box. To add symbols on the outline, turn on the Outline Symbol check box in the Format Outline dialog box.

Work Breakdown Structure

If you want to enter your project in a work breakdown structure format, use Microsoft Project's outlining feature. Microsoft Project numbers each task and milestone for you when you create an outline, and collapses and expands the outline based on these numbers to allow you to see the various levels of detail.

You can view these outline numbers in the WBS Code box on the Task Form—or in the outline if you have turned on the Outline Number check box in the Format Outline dialog box. If you have a WBS coding system you want to use instead of Microsoft Project's outline numbers, you can replace the number in the WBS Code box on the Task Form. Microsoft Project still retains the outline number it assigned to the tasks, using these numbers to collapse and expand the outline.

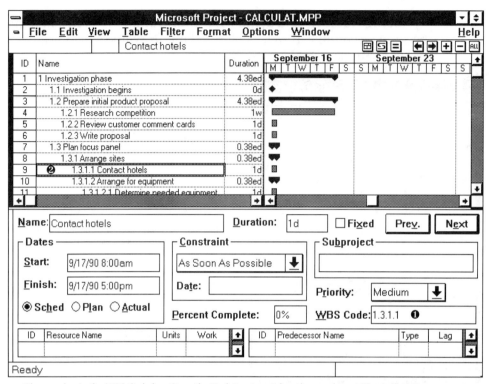

The number in the WBS Code box ❶ on the Task Form matches the number on the outline ❷.
To enter your own WBS code number, type it in the WBS Code box.

You can also enter WBS codes for your tasks by adding the WBS field to the Task Sheet. Type the WBS code in the WBS field as you enter your tasks.

You do not have to create an outline to use a WBS coding system. However, if you want to be able to use the outlining features, such as collapsing and expanding the task list to see the levels of detail, the hierarchy in your WBS coding system should match the outline hierarchy. Despite the WBS number you enter, the tasks must be entered at the appropriate level in the outline. All tasks at the same level in the WBS should be entered at one level in the outline (see the illustration on the following page.

Use the WBS code to sort and filter tasks. For example, you can filter the task list to display only those tasks that have a WBS code for a certain department, or, if your coding system indicates processes, filter the tasks to see all tasks associated with one process.

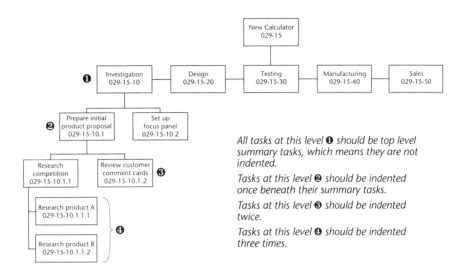

All tasks at this level ❶ should be top level summary tasks, which means they are not indented.

Tasks at this level ❷ should be indented once beneath their summary tasks.

Tasks at this level ❸ should be indented twice.

Tasks at this level ❹ should be indented three times.

Printing Your List of Tasks

To review the information you have entered into Microsoft Project for Windows, print the Task Sheet. If you have included WBS codes and want to check them, use the Table Define Tables command to add the WBS field to the Task Sheet before you print it.

TO PRINT THE TASK SHEET

1. Choose View Task Sheet.
2. Choose File Print.
3. Choose OK.

Before You Print. Be sure the appropriate printer is selected in the File Printer Setup dialog box and that the options for the printer are what you want. For more information, see "Printing and Plotting" in the *Microsoft Project Reference*. You may also want to check and change the settings in the File Page Setup dialog box. These settings control margins, text at the top and bottom of each page, and the style of the text. For more information, see Chapter 10, "Communicating the Plan."

The next step in the planning process is to estimate the duration for each task and enter the durations into Microsoft Project for Windows.

CHAPTER 5

Estimating Time to Perform Tasks

To start molding your list of tasks into a working schedule, your next step is to determine how long each task will take. The more accurately you can estimate this task duration, the better your schedule will be. If your tasks are detailed and precise, estimating time to perform the tasks will be easier and the results more accurate.

Task duration is the time between the start of the task and the finish of the task. Since the schedule calculations and costs are based on these time estimates, they must be as accurate as possible. It takes time to analyze each task, but it saves time down the line because you'll have a better understanding of your schedule—which will help you analyze changes that may occur later.

Since the time estimates for tasks have a tremendous impact on your schedule and on how successfully you meet your end date, encourage those involved in estimating tasks to be realistic. Optimistic estimates can ensure failure because you cannot make the dates. Pessimistic estimates can mean that tasks finish more quickly than expected, causing problems for tasks that follow; supplies, equipment, and other resources may not be scheduled or available because they are not required by the plan until a future time. Pessimistic estimates can also mean not getting contracts because the final dates in your schedule are unacceptable.

While you do your best to come up with accurate estimates based on the information you have about each task, it is important for everyone, including management, to remember that these are estimates. There is a chance that any task will finish either early or late because you can't possibly foresee how each task will actually progress. This is one of the main reasons for including the assumptions you made when estimating durations.

Those who are knowledgeable about a task should estimate task duration. These are the same people who were involved in determining the tasks. For example, you can ask two or three people to estimate how long tasks will take, and then talk to those who will actually perform the tasks. If those who will do the work are uncomfortable about the estimates, meet with all those involved to reach a compromise. Using this method, you avoid an estimate that is either too optimistic because the worker is trying to give you what you want, or too conservative because the worker wants to look good by finishing early.

By having those who do the work involved in estimating the duration, you will have more accurate estimates, more support for the plan (they decided on it), a greater chance of success (they feel responsible to meet the schedule and live up to their own estimates), and higher morale (they feel in control of their work environment).

When you estimate durations, use these guidelines:

Do	Don't
Consider each task independently of other tasks	Consider resource availability when you estimate duration (Microsoft Project will help you take care of this later)
Remember the scope of work described by the task and the assumptions made when the task was included in the task list	Consider the target finish date for the project when figuring task estimates (after seeing the schedule, you can decide what to shorten if your schedule is too long)
Consider the most likely experience level of those who will perform the task	Schedule "tight" to force people to work harder (they generally don't and it hurts morale)
Estimate time in the unit —minutes, hours, days, or weeks—appropriate to the task	Allow managmenet to determine the time estimates (they can't estimate as accurately as those who do the work)
Assume normal working conditions so, if you need to speed up the schedule, you have room to do so	Include extra time for a cushion (estimate as accurately as possible so your duration estimates will be trusted)
Be as realistic as possible, which makes you and the schedule believable	

After you estimate the durations, you enter them into Microsoft Project for Windows and note any assumptions you made for each task duration. You also indicate the scheduling method for each task—either duration should change when you change the number of resources assigned, or it should remain fixed at what you entered.

DETERMINING DURATION

Pinning down the time to perform a task is tricky because you are trying to predict the future based on whatever assumptions about the task you can make today. But, there are three ways which may help you and those who are estimating the durations make more accurate estimates. You can base your estimates on history, on your experience, or on the weighted average of three estimates—an optimistic time, pessimistic time, and most likely time.

Estimating Durations Based on History

The best way to make a good estimate is to look at how long similar tasks took on past projects. When you use historical data, note any differences between the new task and similar tasks in the past. Be sure to take these differences into account when you estimate the duration for the current task.

Keeping task history to use as a basis for future projects is a side benefit of tracking the progress of your projects. If you keep track of every task to the end of a project, you'll have an accurate record of actual task durations, as well as other historical data.

Estimating Durations Based on Your Experience

In this method, you make an estimate based on how long the task would take you to do. If you are very experienced, you can assume it would take the average worker longer to do the task; if you are not experienced, you can assume the task would be done faster by an average worker. Those intimately familiar with the task are the best people to use this method.

Estimating Durations Based on Three Estimates

When you use this method, you estimate three durations—optimistic time, pessimistic time, and most likely time—for each task. The duration you use in the schedule is then calculated based on the formula used in the PERT scheduling method (see boxed note), as follows:

Duration = (O+ 4*L + P)/6

where   O = optimistic time, which occurs 5% of the time

L = most likely time

P = pessimistic time, which occurs 5% of the time

This method can be time-consuming, but may help you estimate time for tasks when you have little or no previous experience.

The PERT Method

The PERT scheduling method was created by Lockheed and the US Navy for projects where there was much uncertainty. This is not the scheduling method used by Microsoft Project for Windows, and is not related to the PERT Chart in Microsoft Project. But, using this equation can help you estimate durations in special cases.

USING MICROSOFT PROJECT FOR WINDOWS

There are three pieces of information you enter into Microsoft Project:

- Duration estimate
- Notes about the assumptions you made when estimating duration
- Scheduling method

Entering Durations

On the Task Entry view, you can type the duration on the Gantt Chart or Task Form. When you type a duration, you type a number followed by the duration unit. You can type the duration in minutes, hours, days, or weeks or elapsed minutes, hours, days, or weeks. If you don't type a unit, Microsoft Project uses the unit specified for the Default Duration Units option in the Options Preferences dialog box. Initially, this is days.

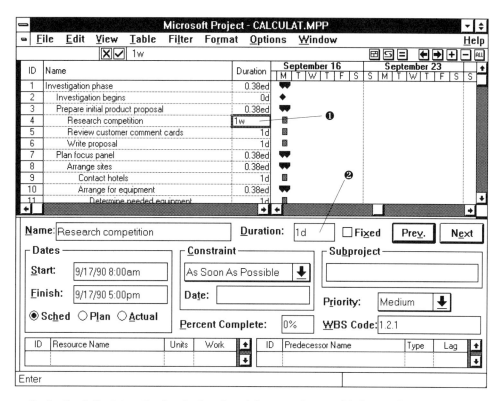

On the Gantt Chart, type the duration here ❶ and then press Enter or click the Enter box (☑).
On the Task Form, type the duration here ❷, and then press Enter or click OK.

If you want to show a duration unit other than the default units (initially days), type one of the following abbreviations after the duration estimate.

Unit	Abbreviation	Elapsed Unit	Abbreviation
Minutes	m	Elapsed minutes	em
Hours	h	Elapsed hours	eh
Days	d	Elapsed days	ed
Weeks	w	Elapsed weeks	ew

Use elapsed time instead of working time when the passing of a certain amount of time is important. For example, use elapsed duration to reflect the number of continuous hours needed for concrete to cure until it is usable.

Elapsed duration is based on 24 hours a day rather than the working hours in a day. A duration of 1d may represent eight working hours (initially the setting for the Default Hours/Day option in the Options Preferences dialog box), while a duration of 1ed represents 24 consecutive hours.

Microsoft Project uses elapsed duration for summary tasks in an outline, where the duration of the summary task runs from the start of the earliest task to the finish of the latest task. It also uses elapsed durations for subprojects, where the duration is the total time the subproject takes.

Using Microsoft Excel to Generate Duration Estimates

If you decide to estimate durations based on the average of three estimates, you can set up a Microsoft Excel worksheet to do the calculations for you. First, use File Save As in Microsoft Project and save your list of project tasks in XLS file format. Open the file in Microsoft Excel, and add columns for the three duration estimates, the average, and the standard deviation. As you enter the estimates, Microsoft Excel calculates the average and standard deviation. Save the file. In Microsoft Project, choose File Open to open the Microsoft Excel file and copy the tasks and average duration into Microsoft Project. For more information, see Chapter 15, "Sharing Information."

Noting Task Assumptions

It's a good idea to keep track of all assumptions you made when estimating durations. In Microsoft Project for Windows, you can include notes for each task in the Notes box on the Task Form. By including the assumptions with each task, they are always handy to refresh your memory about what you expected to happen when you estimated the duration, and to help you analyze why a task is taking more or less time than estimated.

Choose View Task Form. Choose Format Notes. Your screen should look like the illustration on the following page.

When you are finished with the note, and are ready to continue to another task, press Tab and then press Enter twice, or click OK and then click the Next button.

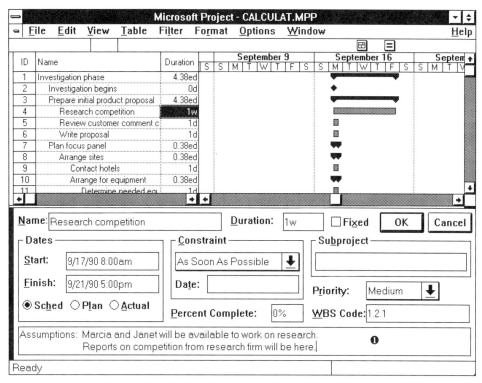

Type notes here ❶ for the task on the form. Press Enter at the end of each line.

Microsoft Project Scheduling Methods

Microsoft Project offers two ways to schedule task duration. One method is called resource-driven scheduling; the duration is recalculated if you change the number of resource units assigned to the task or the amount of work for a group of resources. Use this when you want duration to change with the number of resource units assigned to a task. Microsoft Project uses resource-driven scheduling unless you specify otherwise.

In the other method—fixed-duration scheduling—Microsoft Project does not change the duration regardless of how many resource units you enter. To schedule your project as realistically as possible, use the method best suited to each task.

Use resource-driven scheduling for tasks where adding resources will shorten the duration. For example:

- Three painters might be able to paint a building in one-third the time one painter can
- A landscape crew of four might do twice the work of a crew of two in a day

- If you double the size of the marketing staff, you expect the research on the competition to be finished in half the time

- If you have three teams presenting a new product to clients instead of one team, you can reach all the clients in one-third the time

Use fixed-duration scheduling for those tasks that will not be shorter, no matter how many resources are assigned. For example, you can't speed up concrete curing by assigning resources, nor can you drive from Seattle to Portland any faster. Time you allow reviewers to comment on a marketing plan is also fixed, since regardless of the number of reviewers, they all have the same amount of time, e.g., one week.

If you will not assign resources to tasks, you don't have to pick a scheduling method. Microsoft Project will use the durations you enter and will not recalculate them.

Specifying the Scheduling Method

To change the scheduling method task by task, use the Fixed box on the Task Form. The default scheduling method is resource-driven scheduling, which means the Fixed box is turned off. Specify a scheduling method only if the default method is not what you want for this task.

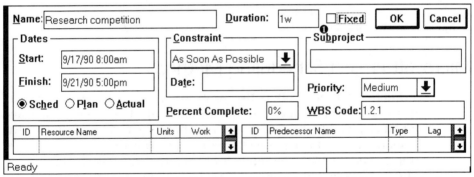

On the Task Form, turn on the Fixed check box ❶ to show fixed-duration scheduling; turn off the check box to use resource-driven scheduling for this task. To turn the check box on or off, press Alt+X, or click the box with the mouse.

You can also add the Fixed field to the Task Sheet. This field contains "Yes" if the task uses fixed-duration scheduling and "No" if the task uses resource-driven scheduling.

Changing the Scheduling Method for Several Tasks. If many of your tasks have fixed durations, you can use the Edit Form dialog box for tasks to simultaneously change them all to fixed. To do this, select all tasks for which you want a fixed duration, and then choose Edit Form or click the form icon (▦). Turn on the Fixed check box and choose OK.

Changing the Default Scheduling Method. If you want to use fixed-duration scheduling for most your tasks, you can change the default method of scheduling using the Options Preferences command. Choose Options Preferences and select Default Duration Type. To see the options for duration type, press Alt+Down Arrow or click the entry bar arrow (▣) with the mouse. Select the default duration type you want. Choose OK.

Changing the Hours per Day and Week Used for Calculations. When Microsoft Project schedules tasks, it converts the durations you enter to hours, using the values in the Default Hours/Day and Default Hours/Week options in the Options Preferences dialog box. Initially, these are set to 8 hours per day and 40 hours per week. If you work 12 hours per day, for example, change the Default Hours/Day option to reflect this so Microsoft Project will schedule the appropriate amount of work each day.

Viewing and Printing the Schedule

Look at the Gantt Chart (choose View Task Entry or View Gantt Chart). All tasks now include the estimated duration and the Gantt bars show those durations.

ID	Name	Duration
1	Investigation phase	25.38ed
2	Investigation begins	0d
3	Prepare initial product proposal	4.38ed
4	Research competition	1w
5	Review customer comment cards	3d
6	Write proposal	1w
7	Plan focus panel	1.38ed
8	Arrange sites	0.38ed
9	Contact hotels	1d
10	Arrange for equipment	0.17ed
11	Determine needed equipment	4h
12	Contact local offices	4h
13	Get panel members	1.38ed
14	Contact local reps for names	1d
15	Contact suggested panel members	2d
16	Plan phone questionnaire	2.38ed
17	Prepare questionnaire	3d
18	Get list of users to call	2h
19	Carry out focus panels	4w
20	Carry out phone survey	1w
21	Prepare focus panel report	2w
22	Prepare phone survey report	1w
23	Present results	4h
24	Investigation phase complete	0d

Microsoft Project - CALCULAT.MPP

File Edit View Table Filter Format Options Window Help

Ready

Because the relationships between tasks have not yet been entered, all tasks are scheduled to start as soon as possible.

If you want to check your list of tasks and the durations, and share this information with others, print the Task Sheet.

TO PRINT THE TASK SHEET

1. Choose View Task Sheet.

2. Choose File Print.

3. Choose OK.

Use this printed information to help determine the order of the tasks and to analyze the relationships between the tasks in the next chapter.

CHAPTER **6**

Making Tasks Happen at the Right Time

You have set your goals, listed the tasks, and estimated how long each task should take. But, all the tasks are still scheduled to start simultaneously. The next step in scheduling your project is to determine the sequence of tasks, how the tasks are related to one another, and if they are tied to certain dates or deadlines. Getting the work done at the right time is just as important as ensuring your task list is complete.

There are four pieces of information you can specify for each task so it will be scheduled at the right time. You can specify:

- Task sequence—which tasks must happen before or after each task
- Task relationship—how tasks are related to other tasks
- Lead or lag time—if you want an overlap or delay between two tasks
- Constraint—that a task must start or finish on, before, or after a certain date

Together, this information is referred to as task "dependencies." When you have decided this information for each task, you enter it into Microsoft Project for Windows.

DECIDING TASK SEQUENCE

The first thing to do is decide the sequence of the tasks. To decide the order of your tasks, answer the following questions for each task or group of tasks.

- What tasks does this task depend on? For example, what tasks must be finished before this task can start?
- What tasks depend on this task? For example, what tasks cannot start until this task is started or finished?

A task that another task depends on—for example, must be finished before another task can start—is called a predecessor task. A task that depends on another task—for example, cannot start until another task is finished—is called a successor task.

When deciding the predecessor tasks, list only those tasks that a task directly depends on. For example, because you must build walls before you can paint them, building walls is a predecessor to painting walls. But, although the building must be designed before the walls can be painted, the design task is not an immediate predecessor to painting. Designing the building is an immediate predecessor to, for example, starting construction. When you list predecessors, think only of those tasks that directly affect the task.

DETERMINING RELATIONSHIPS BETWEEN TASKS

Now that you know the sequence of the tasks, the next step is to decide how tasks are related. Tasks may not have to follow sequentially such that the predecessor finishes before the successor starts. Perhaps two tasks can be worked on simultaneously, either starting or finishing at the same time.

The following list shows the four ways that two tasks can be related. The illustration for each relationship type shows how the bars for that relationship look on the Gantt Chart.

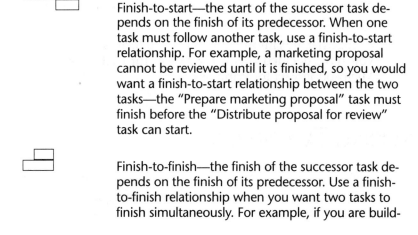

Finish-to-start—the start of the successor task depends on the finish of its predecessor. When one task must follow another task, use a finish-to-start relationship. For example, a marketing proposal cannot be reviewed until it is finished, so you would want a finish-to-start relationship between the two tasks—the "Prepare marketing proposal" task must finish before the "Distribute proposal for review" task can start.

Finish-to-finish—the finish of the successor task depends on the finish of its predecessor. Use a finish-to-finish relationship when you want two tasks to finish simultaneously. For example, if you are building a house and want the landscaping to be finished when the interior decorating is finished, you could use a finish-to-finish relationship between "Decorate interior" and "Landscape exterior."

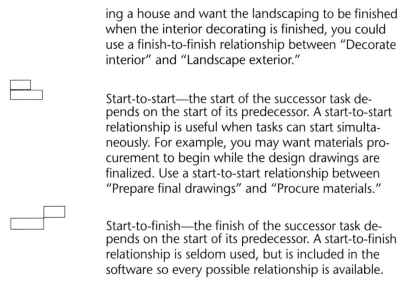

Start-to-start—the start of the successor task depends on the start of its predecessor. A start-to-start relationship is useful when tasks can start simultaneously. For example, you may want materials procurement to begin while the design drawings are finalized. Use a start-to-start relationship between "Prepare final drawings" and "Procure materials."

Start-to-finish—the finish of the successor task depends on the start of its predecessor. A start-to-finish relationship is seldom used, but is included in the software so every possible relationship is available.

Use the relationship that most accurately reflects the way you will do the work. In many projects, tasks do not have to follow one another sequentially using finish-to-start relationships. Finish-to-start relationships may make the schedule longer than necessary and may not use time and resources as efficiently as possible. If two tasks can be worked on simultaneously, be sure you schedule them that way.

INDICATING OVERLAP OR DELAY BETWEEN TASKS

When analyzing task relationships, you might have noticed situations in which, although it was not appropriate to have the two tasks start or finish at the same time, the tasks could be worked on simultaneously. They could be overlapped. Or you might want two tasks to be staggered so there is a delay between the finish of a task and the start of its successor. To show overlap or delay between tasks, use lead or lag time.

Suppose you are conducting a market survey. You start compiling data before all results are in, but you cannot finish until after the completion of the market survey. The most appropriate relationship between the two tasks may be finish-to-start, but with lead time so the successor task "Compile survey results" starts before the predecessor "Conduct market survey" is finished. The Gantt bars would look like this:

Or perhaps, since you do compile results as you go, the best relationship is finish-to-finish, with a one-day lag time between the finish of the predecessor "Conduct market survey" and the successor "Compile survey results" because you know it will take one day after the last survey day to finish compiling results. The Gantt bars would look like this:

Maybe you want to allow time for a mail survey to be returned before you compile results. Here, the most appropriate relationship might again be finish-to-start, but with a one month lag between the end of the predecessor "Mail survey" and the beginning of the successor "Compile survey results." The Gantt bars would look like this:

Suppose you can start painting the walls after half the walls are built. These two tasks would have a finish-to-start relationship, but with a 50 percent overlap or lead time. The Gantt bars would look like this:

Or you might use lag time when you want to wait for the paint to dry before laying carpet. Again, the tasks would have a finish-to-start relationship, but with a one-day waiting period between the finish of "Paint walls" and the start of "Lay carpet." The Gantt bars would look like this:

Using lag and lead time can shorten the schedule and make it more efficient. Check your task list for tasks that can be overlapped to make sure that all tasks are scheduled so time is used most efficiently. Again, think about how tasks will actually be done; if there are tasks that can start before their predecessors are finished, make the schedule reflect this.

SETTING A START OR FINISH DATE FOR A TASK

When you use project scheduling software, tasks are scheduled based on the task sequence and relationships you enter. Sometimes, though, you want a task to happen at a certain time. If you have a task that is tied to a certain start or finish date, you can specify that this date be used instead of the start or finish date calculated by the software.

When you tie a task to a certain date, you are placing a constraint on the task and restricting its start or finish date. This date is a constraint date; it may conflict with dates calculated for the task by the scheduling software, so use constraint dates carefully and not arbitrarily.

For example, if you specify that a task must start on a certain date, and its predecessors are scheduled to finish two weeks earlier, you may end up with two weeks of dead time; conversely, a must start on date may not allow enough time for predecessors to finish before the constraint date.

If a task starting or finishing on a certain date is necessary for a satisfactory outcome of the project, use the constraint, and adjust the scheduling of the predecessors so the schedule will work out; if it is unnecessary, delete the constraint.

The following list shows the types of constraints you can place on a task to control when it starts or finished:

- As soon as possible—a task is scheduled to start as soon as allowed by its predecessors. Unless you specify otherwise, all tasks are scheduled to start as soon as possible.

- As late as possible—a task is scheduled to start as late as possible, but such that its successor tasks can be completed on time.

- Must start on—you specify the date on which the task must start. Use this constraint only when a task absolutely must start on a certain date.

- Must finish on—you specify the date on which the task must finish. Use this constraint only when a task absolutely must finish on a certain date.

- Start no later than—you specify the date on or before which the task must start. Use this constraint when a task must start by a certain date; for example, if a clause in a contract states that you will pay a penalty if a task or project phase has not started by a certain time.

- Finish no later than—you specify the date on or before which the task must finish. Use this constraint when a task must finish by a certain date; for example, if a clause in a contract states that you will pay a penalty if a task or project phase has not finished by a certain time.

- Start no earlier than—you specify the date on or after which the task must start.

- Finish no earlier than—you specify the date on or after which the task must finish.

Generally, you want tasks to start as soon as possible. This allows the most flexibility in your schedule. Use the other constraints only when starting or finishing a task by a specific time is important to the outcome of the project.

For example, use a constraint date with the following situations:

- Your contract states that you will be penalized for not starting or finishing by a certain date, or that you will receive a bonus for finishing early.

- You can decrease costs on a project. Suppose your contract states that grass must be established on a playing field by May 1. You can either sow seed in October of the previous year, or lay sod in April, which increases costs. You could use a Start No Later Than constraint on the "Sow grass seed" task to make sure the predecessor tasks are scheduled to allow you to sow seed in October.

- You want to make a go/no go decision on getting a new product to market. Suppose a new computer game must be finished by September to be available for the Christmas shopping season; if you are not ready by September, you want to wait until the next spring. Use a Finish No Later Than constraint on the "Second prototype completed" milestone so, if you make the milestone, you can decide to proceed with the product; if you miss the milestone, you can decide to delay the product.

- Your project depends on certain weather conditions. Suppose you are to build a new ski lift. Certain things you can do during the winter, but you want the actual building to occur during the summer. You might place a Start No Earlier Than constraint date of May 1 at the beginning of the building phase.

USING MICROSOFT PROJECT FOR WINDOWS

Having decided the order, relationship, lead or lag time, and constraints—all the task "dependencies"—enter this information into Microsoft Project, which uses this information to calculate your schedule.

If most of your tasks have a finish-to-start relationship, you can quickly link them with one command. Then you can add lead or lag time between the tasks as appropriate, or add a constraint date if needed. If you have a more complex schedule, with a variety of relationships, and lead and lag time, enter the predecessors, relationships, and lead and lag time individually for each task.

Linking Several Tasks with a Finish-to-Start Relationship

If all or most of your tasks have finish-to-start relationships with other tasks, Microsoft Project includes a quick way for you to "link" all the tasks. First, on the Gantt Chart or Task Sheet, select the tasks you want to link. Then choose Edit Link.

When you select the tasks, the tasks do not have to be adjacent. You can select all tasks that logically follow one another in finish-to-start relationships, skipping those not appropriate.

If you are using outlining, you may find it easier to hide summary tasks when you are selecting the tasks to link. To hide the summary tasks, choose Format Outline, and turn off the Summary Tasks check box. In the following two illustrations, the summary tasks are hidden.

In the first of the next two illustrations, the tasks chosen follow one another logically in a finish-to-start relationship. Tasks 5, 9, and 14 through 18 are not selected because they do not follow tasks 4, 6, and 12. Tasks 5, 9, and 14 can all follow task 2 because they are not dependent on preceding tasks and can start as early as resources are available to work on them. If you selected all tasks at once, tasks 5, 9, and 14 would not have the correct predecessors.

You could make a second pass, however, selecting tasks 2 and 5 to establish finish-to-start relationships between these tasks, and so on.

Choose View Gantt Chart.

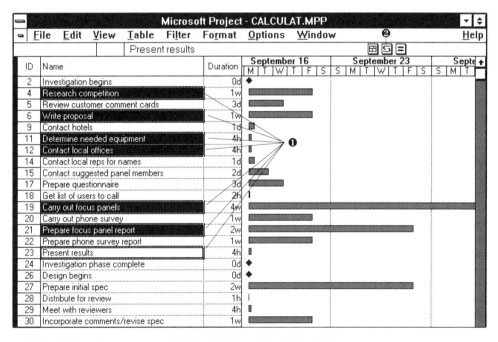

Select all the tasks you want to link with a finish-to-start relationship ❶.

To select adjacent tasks, either hold down Shift and press the Up or Down Arrow key, or drag the mouse over the tasks.

To select non-adjacent tasks, press F8, select the first group of tasks, press Shift+F8, move to the next group of tasks, and repeat the sequence. With the mouse, hold down Ctrl to choose additional tasks.

Choose Edit Link or click the link icon ❷.

After choosing Edit Link, you see the bars representing the task durations spread out on the Gantt Chart.

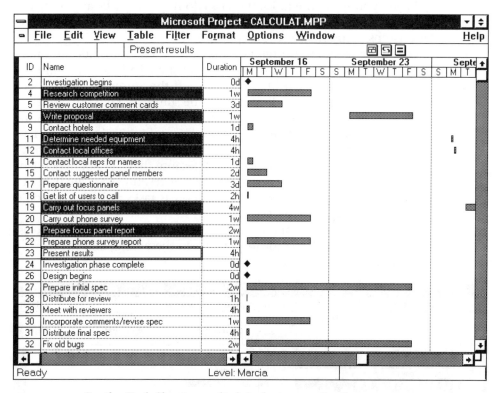

On the Task Sheet, you link tasks in exactly the same way.

Removing Relationships Between Tasks

If you want to remove all the relationships from a group of tasks, use the Edit Unlink command. The Edit Unlink command appears on the Edit menu only if you hold down Shift when you select the Edit menu. First, select the tasks to be unlinked. Then hold down Shift and choose Edit Unlink.

Entering a Predecessor, Relationship, and Lead or Lag Time

The Task Entry view is probably the easiest for entering predecessors, relationships, and lead or lag time because it has a separate box for each type of information.

Entering a Predecessor

When you enter a predecessor, you can either type the task number or you can click the predecessor task with the mouse.

Choose View Task Entry.

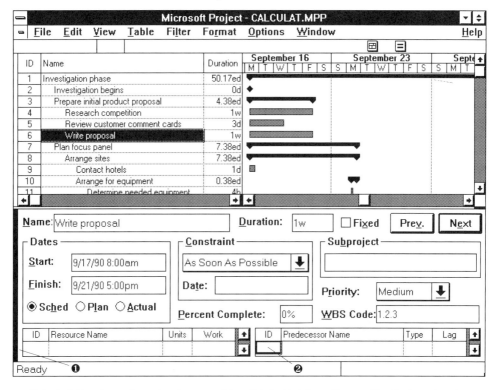

If the Task Form is not the active view, press F6 or click the Task Form. You can identify the active view by the dark, bar on the left side of the screen ❶.

Press Alt+2 to go to the predecessors fields or click the ID field ❷.

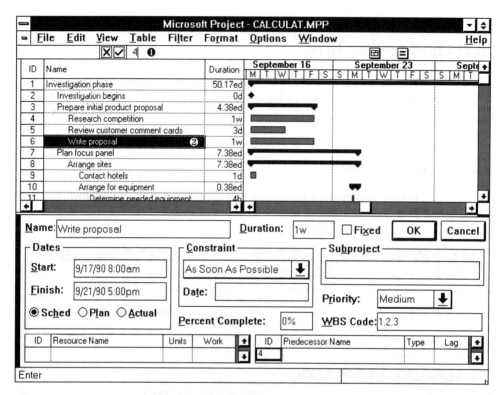

Keys: *Type the ID number of the task that is a predecessor to the selected task.*

Mouse: *Click the entry bar ❶; the Cancel box (☒), Enter box (☑), and insertion point appear. Click the task that is the predecessor task ❷.*

Press enter *or click the Enter box.*

Entering a Relationship

Microsoft Project assigns a finish-to-start relationship automatically. If you want to change the relationship, move to the Type field on the Task Form, and then type or select the relationship. The relationship abbreviations correspond to the following relationship types:

Abbreviation	Relationship Type
FF	Finish-to-finish
FS	Finish-to start
SF	Start-to-finish
SS	Start-to-start

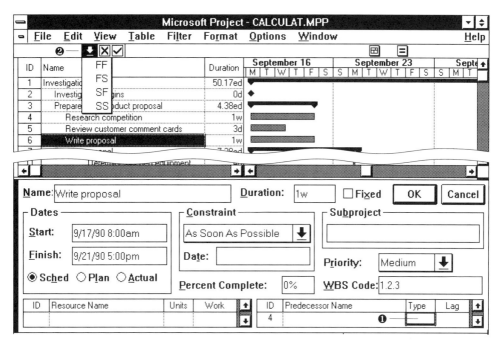

If the two tasks have a relationship other than finish-to-start (FS), press the Right Arrow key to move to the Type field ❶ or click the field.

To display the list of relationships in the entry bar, press Alt+Down Arrow or click the entry bar arrow ([↓]) ❷. Select the relationship you want.

Press enter or click the Enter box.

Entering Lead or Lag Time

In Microsoft Project for Windows, you indicate lead or lag time as:

- Number of minutes, hours, days, or weeks
- Elapsed minutes, hours, days, or weeks
- Percentage of the duration of the predecessor task
- Elapsed percentage of the duration of the predecessor task

Lead time is shown by a minus sign; lag is denoted by a plus sign. To enter the exact time, use the same abbreviations as for durations:

Unit	Abbreviation	Elapsed Unit	Abbreviation
Minutes	m	Elapsed minutes	em
Hours	h	Elapsed hours	eh
Days	d	Elapsed days	ed
Weeks	w	Elapsed weeks	ew

To indicate a two-day lead time between two tasks, type "-2d"; to indicate a four-hour lag, type "4h". Use elapsed time when you want consecutive 24-hour periods, e.g., to allow time for paint to dry. Type "2ed" to indicate a two-elapsed-day lag (48 hour) between two tasks.

To enter lead or lag as a percentage, type the percentage of the predecessor task by which the successor will be delayed or overlapped. Type "-25%" to show a 25% lead time between a task and its predecessor or type "50%" for a 50% lag time. To enter elapsed percentage, type an e before the %, such as "25e%".

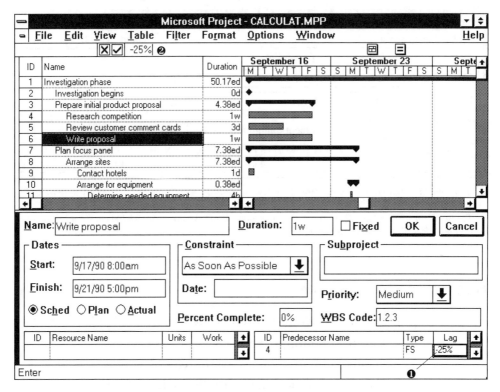

Press the Right Arrow key to move to the Lag field or click the field ❶.

Type the lead or lag time ❷ and then press Enter or click the Enter box (☑).

Deleting a Relationship on the Task Form. If you want to delete a relationship on the Task Form, select the Predecessor Name or ID field, and then press the Del key.

Entering Successor Tasks. If you want to enter successor tasks instead of predecessor tasks, you do so in exactly the same way. On the Task Form, choose Format Resources & Successors to display the successors fields in place of the predecessors fields at the bottom of the

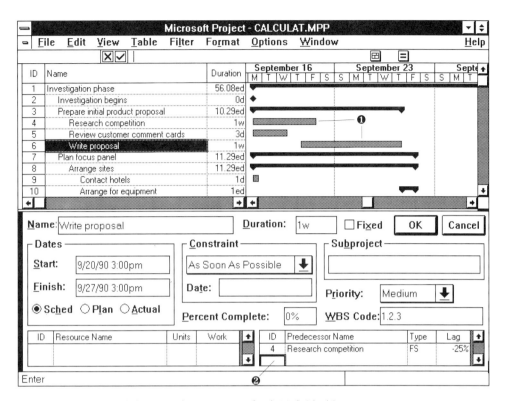

Task 6 is now scheduled to start after 75 percent of task 4 is finished ❶.

To add another predecessor, press the direction keys to move to the next ID field or click the field ❷.

Task Form. Or, to look at and enter predecessors and successors at the same time, choose Format Predecessors & Successors. You do not have to enter both predecessors and successors for each task, however. Microsoft Project determines the successors based on the predecessors you enter, and vice versa.

Entering Dependencies on the Task Sheet

You can also enter the predecessor, relationship, and lead or lag time on the Task Sheet, in the Predecessors field. Again, when you enter a predecessor, you can either type the task number or you can click the predecessor task with the mouse.

Choose View Task Sheet.

ID	Name	Duration	Scheduled Start	Scheduled Finish	Predecessors	Res
1	Investigation phase	25.38ed	9/17/90 8:00am	10/12/90 5:00pm		
2	Investigation begins	0d	9/17/90 8:00am	9/17/90 8:00am		
3	Prepare initial product proposal	4.38ed	9/17/90 8:00am	9/21/90 5:00pm		
4	Research competition ❸	1w	9/17/90 8:00am	9/21/90 5:00pm		
5	Review customer comment cards	3d	9/17/90 8:00am	9/19/90 5:00pm		
6	Write proposal	1w	9/17/90 8:00am	9/21/90 5:00pm	4 ❶	
7	Plan focus panel	1.38ed	9/17/90 8:00am	9/18/90 5:00pm		

Press the direction keys to select the Predecessors field for the task or click the field ❶.
Keys: Type the predecessor task ID number.
Mouse: Click the entry bar ❷. Click the predecessor task ❸. Click the Enter box (☑).

ID	Name	Duration	Scheduled Start	Scheduled Finish	Predecessors	Res
1	Investigation phase	25.38ed	9/17/90 8:00am	10/12/90 5:00pm		
2	Investigation begins	0d	9/17/90 8:00am	9/17/90 8:00am		
3	Prepare initial product proposal	4.38ed	9/17/90 8:00am	9/21/90 5:00pm		
4	Research competition	1w	9/17/90 8:00am	9/21/90 5:00pm		
5	Review customer comment cards	3d	9/17/90 8:00am	9/19/90 5:00pm		
6	Write proposal	1w	9/17/90 8:00am	9/21/90 5:00pm	4fs-25%	
7	Plan focus panel	1.38ed	9/17/90 8:00am	9/18/90 5:00pm		

If the task has a relationship other than finish-to-start (FS) or has a lead or lag time, type the relationship abbreviation after the predecessor ID, followed by the lead or lag time ❶.

Use the following relationship abbreviations:

Abbreviation	Relationship Type
FF	Finish-to-finish
FS	Finish-to-start
SF	Start-to-finish
SS	Start-to-start

You Can Enter as Many Predecessors as the Task Has

ID	Name		Duration	Scheduled Start	Scheduled Finish	Predecessors	Res
	Microsoft Project - CALCULAT.MPP						
	File **Edit** **View** **Table** **Filter** **Format** **Options** **Window**						Help
	☒☑ 4fs-25%,5						
ID	Name	❶	Duration	Scheduled Start	Scheduled Finish	Predecessors	Res
1	Investigation phase		25.38ed	9/17/90 8:00am	10/12/90 5:00pm		
2	Investigation begins		0d	9/17/90 8:00am	9/17/90 8:00am		
3	Prepare initial product proposal		4.38ed	9/17/90 8:00am	9/21/90 5:00pm		
4	Research competition		1w	9/17/90 8:00am	9/21/90 5:00pm		
5	Review customer comment cards ❷		3d	9/17/90 8:00am	9/19/90 5:00pm		

Keys: Type a comma and the next predecessor ❶.

Mouse: Click the next predecessor ❷.

Type the relationship and lead or lag time only if necessary. You can type as many as 20 predecessors for each task.

Press Enter or click the Enter box (☑).

Using the List Separator

Use the list separator character specified in the List Separator option in the Options Preferences dialog box. Initially, this is a comma in the U.S. The list separator character may change if you change the international settings for Microsoft Project.

Adding the Successors Column. You can change the Task Sheet to show the Successors column instead of the Predecessors column. Or you can show both columns. Use the Table Define Tables command to change the columns shown on the Task Sheet.

Deleting a Relationship on the Task Sheet. On the Task Sheet select the field containing the relationship you want to delete. Press F2 to activate the entry bar, and then press Del to delete the whole entry. Or press the direction keys to pick the part of the entry you want to delete, and then press Del.

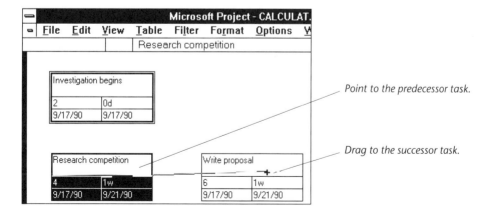

Point to the predecessor task.

Drag to the successor task.

Specifying Task Sequence on the PERT Chart

You can also set predecessors on the PERT Chart either after or while you enter the tasks. You must have a mouse to use this method.

Choose View PERT Chart.

Microsoft Project applies a finish-to-start relationship between the two tasks, with no lead or lag time.

Adding a New Task. To add a new task on the PERT Chart, with a finish-to-start relationship to its predecessor, point to the predecessor, and drag outside the task node. The new node is formed when you release the mouse button. Type the task name and duration in the node.

Changing the Relationship. If you want to change the relationship, or add lead or lag time, you can either replace one of the fields in the PERT Chart node with the Predecessors field or place the Task Form below the PERT Chart and enter details about the new task on it.

Placing the Task Form Below the PERT Chart. If you are using a full-screen PERT Chart, and want to create a combination view with the Task Form below it, do one of the following: Press Shift+F6, press the direction keys to move the split bar to the middle of the view, and press Enter; or drag the split box at the bottom of the vertical scroll bar to the middle of the view. The Task Form is automatically placed below.

If you are already using a combination view, press F6 to choose the bottom view or click the view, and then choose View Task Form.

Deleting a Relationship. You can also delete relationships on the PERT Chart. Point to the predecessor task and drag to the successor task. Microsoft Project asks for verification of the deletion.

Entering a Constraint

Constraints other than As Soon As Possible must be used carefully as you do not want to introduce unnecessary scheduling factors. They may restrict your flexibility later when rescheduling tasks. If you do not indicate a constraint, Microsoft Project uses As Soon As Possible.

Constraint dates may override the dates calculated by Microsoft Project for the task. For example, suppose the "Landscape exterior" task has a two-week duration, and you include a Must Finish On constraint date of May 25. When Microsoft Project calculates the schedule, the predecessor to "Landscape exterior" is scheduled to finish on May 18. Without the constraint date, Microsoft Project would schedule the "Landscape exterior" task to finish two weeks later, on June 1. Because of the constraint date, Microsoft Project is restricted to scheduling the task to finish on May 25, and indicates the problem by displaying a message that the task is scheduled to finish after the late finish date of May 25. The message lets you know there is "negative slack" in your schedule, i.e., there is not enough time to complete the predecessor task and the "Landscape exterior" task by the Must Finish On constraint date.

You can see that if the constraint date shows an important deadline in your project, the information Microsoft Project gives you is most useful. It lets you know that as the schedule is now, you will not make the dates. If the constraint date is not an important deadline, however, it places needless restrictions on your project.

When you have a group of tasks that must be finished by a certain date, enter a milestone at the end of the tasks, and use a Finish No Later Than constraint on the milestone. Microsoft Project will display the message that the scheduled finish is after the late finish date if the schedule slips and there is insufficient time to complete the predecessors to the milestone. When you see the message, you know that you have to take some action to correct the slippage and make the milestone date.

Changing the Constraint Type

Choose View Task Entry. On the Gantt Chart, select the task. On the Task Form, select the constraint.

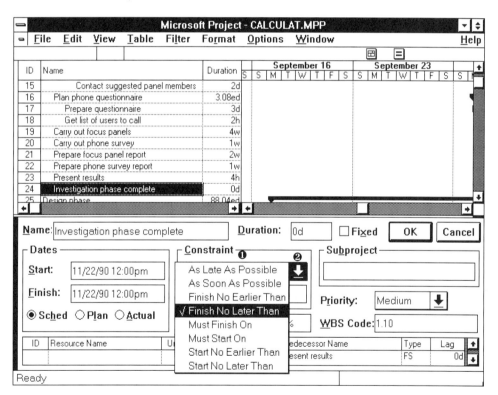

To select the Constraint box, press Alt+C or click the box ❶.

To see the list of constraints, press Alt+Down Arrow or click the Constraint arrow (▼) ❷.

To select a constraint, press the Up Arrow or Down Arrow key and press Enter, or click the constraint.

Typing a Constraint Date

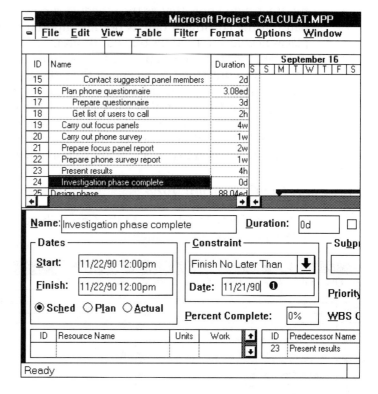

If you selected a constraint other than As Soon As Possible or As Late As Possible, press Tab to move to the Date box or click the box ❶.

Type the constraint date and time.

Press Enter or click OK.

If you do not type a constraint date for those constraints requiring a date, Microsoft Project for Windows uses the current date. If you do not type a time, Microsoft Project adds the default time of 8:00 a.m. for a constraint on the start of a task and a time at the end of the day for a constraint on the finish of a task.

If you type a start or finish date for a task in the Start or Finish box on the Task Form, Microsoft Project sets a Must Start On or Must Finish On constraint for that task, using the date you typed as the constraint date. The same thing happens if you move a task bar on the Gantt Chart with the mouse such that the start or finish date changes.

You can also enter constraints on the Task Sheet by applying the Constraint Dates table. This table includes columns for Constraint Type and Constraint Date. Of course, you can add the Constraint Type and Constraint Date fields to the Entry table, or create a new table with just those columns you use when you enter new task information. Use the Table Define Tables command to change the Entry table or to create a new table. For more information, see Chapter 16, "Using Microsoft Project Tools."

> **Date and Time Hints**
>
> When you type a date in the current year, all you have to type is the month and day, such as 1/20 for January 20. Microsoft Project fills in the rest. If the date is in another year, you do have to type the year. When you type the month, you can type the full name (January), an abbreviation (Jan), or a number (1). To separate the day, month, and year, you can use any separator character—for example, a space, hyphen, slash, or comma.
>
> If you are using the 12-hour clock (set it with the Time Format option in Options Preferences—it is initially set to 12 Hour), and you do not specify a.m. or p.m., Microsoft Project assumes: a.m. if the time you type is between 7:00 and 11:59; p.m. for any other.
>
> When you do not type a time, Microsoft Project uses 8:00 a.m. as the default time except on "finish" constraints. To change the default, choose Options Preferences, select Default Time, and type the time you want. Press Enter.

Printing the Schedule

To print a record of what you have entered so far and to share this information with others on the team, you can print the following views:

To See	Print
List of tasks, durations, predecessors, relationships, and lead or lag time	Task Sheet, with the Entry table applied
List of tasks and constraints	Task Sheet with the Constraint Dates table applied
List of tasks and durations, and their task bars shown over time	Gantt Chart
Task relationships	PERT Chart

TO PRINT YOUR SCHEDULE

1. Choose the view you want to print
2. Choose File Print
3. Choose OK
4. If you are printing the Gantt Chart, choose OK again

Next, you will enter the resources needed to complete the tasks.

CHAPTER 7

Assigning People, Equipment, and Costs to Tasks

Now that you have entered the predecessors, relationships, lead and lag time, and constraints, you have a first pass of your schedule. But, your project plan is still incomplete. Next, you need to plan the project resources—the people and equipment—that will do the work on the tasks, and determine the costs for these resources.

Of course, it is not mandatory that you assign resources or enter cost information, if your current project does not require you keep track of resources and costs. However, the more tasks in the project and the longer the project, the more likely it is that you will want to track resources and costs, because this improves your ability to control the project.

Including resources in your plan accomplishes several things. It shows:

- Who will do the tasks
- When resources are needed during the project
- If resources are assigned to too many or too few tasks so you can plan future resource requirements

Be sure to plan your staff carefully. How well you plan the resources can make or break your project. If you plan well, your project has another plus going for it; if you do not plan well, do not have the appropriate staff available, or fail to assign the necessary resources to the tasks, you are almost guaranteeing failure.

Including cost information gives you a preliminary budget for your project, allowing you to estimate cash flow needs over the life of the project.

To complete this step, you need to estimate the type and quantity of resources needed for each task. If you want to track cost information, you also need to determine the cost for each resource.

In Microsoft Project for Windows, you can enter resources, costs for resources, and costs for those tasks that do not have resources assigned. You also can control the days and times when each resource is available to work using the resource calendars.

ESTIMATING RESOURCE NEEDS

When you estimate the resources needed for each task, remember the duration and scope of each task. Ask yourself the following questions for each task as you assign the resources.

- What type of people resources are needed for the task? What level of skill must each person have? Can any skilled worker work on the task, or is there only one person able to do this task?

- How many resources do you need to get the task finished in the time allotted? For example, if the task is "Frame walls" and the resource is "Carpenters," how many carpenters do you need to assign to the task to finish on time?

- What other resources do you need? What equipment or computer time, for example.

One way to analyze resource requirements for a task is to check similar tasks in past projects. Be sure to consider any differences between the two tasks and make the appropriate adjustments so your resource estimate is as accurate as possible. For example, if you are comparing two design tasks, and the current task is for a space 30 percent larger than the previous task, factor in this increase in task scope as you estimate resource needs. Or if the experience level of the workers available to you now is considerably different from a previous task, assign more or fewer resources as appropriate to compensate for the experience levels.

As always, have those who know the task best estimate resources. They can estimate most accurately.

You may find as you estimate resource needs that breaking a task into smaller tasks improves your ability to predict more accurately the resources and work for the task. If so, repeat the steps to enter the task, estimate duration, and add the appropriate relationships with other tasks so the new tasks fit into the schedule.

ESTIMATING COSTS

In many projects, the most important parameter is cost. Cost controls how quickly tasks are performed and how resources are used by allowing, or not allowing, additional expenses to accelerate the schedule—for example, by adding overtime work or hiring additional staff. Most of the costs for completing a project are directly associated with the execution of the tasks. The project budget is based on these task and resource costs. To develop a project budget, you assign a cost to each resource, and then calculate the cost for each task.

By planning your costs, you can:

- Check the anticipated cash flow, so you know how much money you will spend and when you will spend it.

- Experiment with juggling resources to cut costs. For example, can you substitute two less costly resources for one expensive resource and possibly decrease the cost to complete the task?

- Assign cost responsibility to a manager or department, whose responsibility is to see that the phases of a project can be costed, monitored, and kept on budget. This may be required on some contracts.

- Generate more accurate bid proposals. By setting up your schedule and including costs for resources, you have an estimate for the project cost and can bid accordingly. You can use this initial schedule to look for ways to cut costs to ensure your bid is as low as possible, yet reasonable and realistic.

For all resources you will be using in your project, you need to know:

- How much the resource costs per time period

- If there is a cost per use for the resource, such as a flat rate every time you use the main computer, in addition to the per time period rate

For tasks that do not have resources assigned—perhaps because they are being performed by an outside contractor at a fixed rate, or because you choose not to track resources—you need to know the estimated cost of the task.

USING MICROSOFT PROJECT FOR WINDOWS

There are two basic approaches you can use when entering new resources into Microsoft Project for Windows. You can:

- Enter all the resources at one time and then assign them to tasks later
- Enter new resources as you assign them to tasks

All resource information is stored in a "resource pool." Microsoft Project stores the resource pool with your project unless you choose to use a resource pool in another project. If the same resources work on multiple projects, use a shared resource pool to keep track of the resource use and requirements for all projects.

Of course, before you can share a resource pool, you must have one to share. If this is your first project in Microsoft Project for Windows, you obviously do not have a resource pool, so this is not an option. If this is not your first project, and you want to use the resource pool in another project, you can. For more information, see Chapter 14, "Managing Multiple Projects."

When you enter resources, you can also enter costs for each resource; from these individual resource costs, the task, resource, and project costs are calculated. If none of your resources are assigned to work on a task, you can enter the cost for the task. For example, you might enter a task cost when you are using a contractor to do a task for a set fee.

If you have salary information in a Microsoft Excel spreadsheet, you can import this information into Microsoft Project. As salary information changes over time, you can update your project with the new information from Microsoft Excel instead of entering the information in Microsoft Project. For more information, see Chapter 15, "Sharing Information."

You use resource calendars to control when a resource is available to work. Each resource has its own calendar. Here, you enter working information specific to the resource, such as vacation time or part-time hours. The initial working days and hours in each new resource calendar match the information in the base calendar.

How Microsoft Project for Windows Schedules Resources

When you assign resources to a task, you enter a resource and the number of units that will work on the task. Microsoft Project calculates the work load of each resource group on the task using the following formula:

$$work = duration * resource\ units$$

Work is the total work for all the units of a resource assigned to the task. For example, if duration is 40h for the "Prepare market plan" task, and you enter the following resources and units, the work is calculated by Microsoft Project as follows:

Resource You Assign	Units You Assign	Work Microsoft Project Calculates
Marcia	1	40h
Marketing staff	3	120h
Cheryl	0.25	10h

All resources are assigned to work for the duration of the task; each resource group will take the same amount of time (the full duration) to complete the task. Cheryl works on the task one-quarter of each day, while the other two resources work full days on the task.

When you estimated duration for each task, you chose a scheduling method—either resource-driven scheduling or fixed-duration scheduling. If you now change the work or units, Microsoft Project recalculates the duration if you are using resource-driven scheduling, but not if you are using fixed-duration scheduling.

Resource-driven Scheduling

If you change duration, work, or units for a task that uses resource-driven scheduling, Microsoft Project does the following:

If You Change	Microsoft Project Recalculates
Duration for the task	Work for each resource
Work for a resource	Duration for the resource; if this is the resource finishing last on the task, changes task duration
Units	Duration for the resource; if this is the resource finishing last on the task, changes task duration

For example, if you change the work for Marcia to 50 hours, Marcia's duration is recalculated to 50 hours (50 hours divided by 1 unit); the duration for the task is also changed to 50 hours because Marcia's work on the task will take the longest. The work for the other two resources is not changed.

If you decrease to two the number of Marketing staff assigned to the task, the duration is recalculated by dividing the work (120 hours) by the units (2). The new duration for the resource is 60 hours. The duration for the task will also increase because the Marketing staff's finish date is the latest because their work on the task will take the longest—60 hours, as opposed to 50 hours for Marcia.

Resource	Units	Work	Resource Duration
Marcia	1	50h	50h
Marketing staff	3	120h	60h
Cheryl	0.25	10h	40h

The duration for each resource does not appear anywhere in Microsoft Project. You can calculate it by dividing work by the number of resource units; you can also look at the scheduled start and finish dates for the resource on the Task Form by choosing Format Resource Schedule.

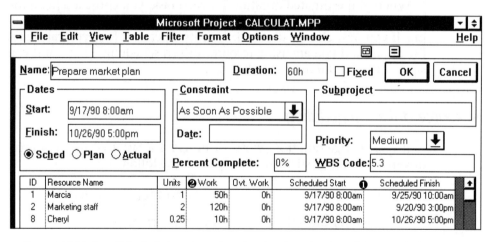

Start and finish dates ❶ for each resource group assigned to the task. Microsoft Project calculates these dates.

Total work ❷ for each resource. You can change the value that Microsoft Project calculates.

Whenever you assign more than one resource to a task, the resource with the latest finish date on the task is the one that controls the duration for the task. If you change the units or the work for a resource, this may or may not change the duration of the task. In the simplest case, if you add a resource unit, duration decreases; if you take away a resource unit, duration increases.

Fixed-duration Scheduling

When a task uses fixed-duration scheduling, Microsoft Project does the following:

If You Change	Microsoft Project
Duration for the task	Recalculates work for each resource
Work for a resource	Does not change duration for the task, but does change the scheduled start and finish date for the resource on the task; if this resource is now scheduled to finish after the task finish date, Microsoft Project tells you so, but does not change duration
Units	Does not change duration for the task, but does recalculate the work for the resource by multiplying duration times units

With fixed-duration scheduling, the task duration you enter does not change no matter how many resource units you assign to the task or what the work is.

Entering New Resources

If you have a list of new resources for the project, you may find it quickest to enter all resource information at one time using the Resource Sheet, and then assign the resources to the tasks by selecting the appropriate resource name from a list on the Task Sheet or Task Entry view. You can also enter new resources on the Resource Form, which shows one resource at a time.

When you enter new resources, you need to know the following:

- Resource name
- Maximum number of resource units available
- Base calendar for the resource, if you are using more than one in the project

Resources can be individuals (Tom, Mary, John) or groups (carpenters, machinists, engineers). Use resource groups if the members of a group are interchangeable on a job. If the workers are not interchangeable, list each resource individually.

If you are interested in tracking costs, you also need to know:

- Standard rate of pay per minute, hour, day, week, or year for the resource
- Overtime rate per minute, hour, day, week, or year for the resource, if applicable
- Per-use rate that you pay each time you use the resource, if applicable
- When these costs are accrued—at the time the task starts, when the resource finishes work on the task, or prorated as the task progresses

When you enter costs, type a number, and then a slash (/) and the unit of time. For example, type 10/h for $10 per hour. Use the following abbreviations for the time:

Rate of Pay Per	Abbreviation
Minute	m
Hour	h
Day	d
Week	w
Year	y

If you know a monthly rate, change it to weekly or yearly; Microsoft Project for Windows uses the abbreviation m for minutes, not months.

Notes on the Currency Symbol

The currency symbol depends on the international settings for Microsoft Project, and on the Currency Symbol setting in the Options Preferences dialog box. You can change this setting as appropriate. Initially, this is a dollar sign for software in the United States.

You can also enter a group and code for each resource, such as the department that employs the resource or an accounting code. Based on this group and code information, you can sort or filter the resources to show all resources by department, or only resources that have a certain code.

Entering Resources on the Resource Sheet

The Resource Sheet looks like a spreadsheet, with rows and columns; all the resources are listed down the left side of the sheet.

To see the Resource Sheet, choose View Resource Sheet.

Microsoft Project - CALCULAT.MPP									▼ ♦	
File	**Edit**	**View❷ Table**	**Filter**	**Format**	**Options**	**Window**				**Help**
		☒ ☑	Marcia					田	⊟	
ID	Name	Initials	Group	Max. Units	Std. Rate	Ovt. Rate	Cost/Use	Accrue At	Code	♦
1	Marcia ❶									
2										
3										

In the Name field, type the resource name ❶.
Press Enter or click the Enter box (☑) ❷.

When you type a name on the Resource Sheet, information is entered into several fields. Check their values and change them as appropriate.

Microsoft Project - CALCULAT.MPP									▼ ♦	
File	**Edit**	**View**	**Table**	**Filter**	**Format**	**Options**	**Window**			**Help**
	❷ ↓		Prorated					田	⊟	
ID	Name	Initials	Group	Max. Units	Std. Rate	Ovt. Rate	Cost/Use	Accrue At	Code	♦
1	Marcia	M		1	$0.00/h	$0.00/h	$0.00	Prorated	❶	
2										
3										

To move to the field you want to change, press the direction keys or click the field.

If you want to change the accrual method, select the Accrue At field ❶, and then press Alt+Down Arrow or click the entry bar arrow (▣) ❷ to see the list of accrual methods. There are three accrual methods. Start means that all costs for the resource accrue as soon as the resource starts work on the task. Finish means that all costs for the resource accrue when the resource finishes work on the task; costs are zero as long as the resource's work on the task is less than 100 percent complete. Prorated means that as the percent complete or work changes on the task, the costs change in proportion to the percent complete.

Changing Resource Information Simultaneously. If several resources should have the same information in a field, such as the same standard rate or accrual method, or if you want to assign a code or group to several resources, you can change that information for all the selected resources simultaneously. Select all the resources you want to change, and then choose Edit Form or click the form icon (田). In the Edit Form dialog box for resource, change the information that is common to all the selected resources and choose OK.

Changing the Default Standard Rate or Overtime Rate. If many of your resources have the same standard rate or overtime rate, you can set this rate so it is automatically entered when you enter a new resource. Initially, Microsoft Project enters rates of 0 (zero). Choose Options Preferences. To change the standard rate entered automatically, select Default Standard Rate and type the value you want; to change the overtime rate entered automatically, select Default Overtime Rate and type the value you want. Choose OK.

Entering a Skill Level for Resources or the Person Responsible. Microsoft Project for Windows includes "custom" fields that you can use however you want. When you add a custom field to a table, you can name the column to represent the information it will contain. There are two custom text fields you can add to a resource table—Text1 and Text2. For example, if you wanted to note the skill level of each resource or the manager responsible for each resource, you would use the Table Define Tables command to add the Text1 or Text2 field to the Entry table (or any table you want). Then, in the Title column in the table definition dialog box, you would type "Skill Level" or "Manager" for the title. You can sort and filter on the information in a custom field, just as on any field. Using sorting, for example, you could sort so all those with a skill level of 1 are together, and so on. Or filter so only those resources reporting to a certain manager are displayed. For more information about creating tables, see Chapter 16, "Using Microsoft Project Tools."

Entering Resources on the Resource Form

To see the Resource Form, choose View Resource Form.

You can also enter new resources on the Resource Form, one resource at a time.

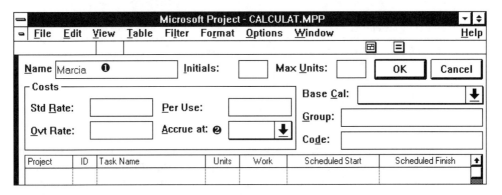

Type the resource name here ❶.

To move to a box you want to change, press Tab or click the box.

If you want to change the accrual method ❷, press Alt+A and then press Alt+Down Arrow, or click the Accrue At arrow (▣) to see the list of accrual methods.

Press Enter or click OK when you finish changing information for this resource. Press Enter again or click the Next button to go to a blank form to enter the next resource.

Assigning Resources to Tasks

You assign resources to tasks on any of the task views. When you assign a resource to a task, you do not have to type the resource name if the resource is already in the resource pool; in the entry bar list, Microsoft Project displays the list of resources in the resource pool. If you do type a resource name, Microsoft Project checks the resource pool for the resource name you typed; if the resource does not exist, you can add it to the resource pool and enter additional information about the resource, such as the maximum units and cost information.

When you assign resources to tasks, you need to know certain information for each task.

- What resources do you want to assign to the task?

- How many units of each resource do you want to assign to the task? You can assign less than one unit if a resource will work part-time on a task.

- What is the amount of work (man-hours) each resource will do on the task, if it is less than the full duration of the task?

Assigning Resources on the Task Entry View

Use the Task Entry view to enter resources when you want to see and change the work amounts for the resources.

Choose View Task Entry.

To make the Task Form the active view, press F6 or click the view. You can identify the active view by the bar on the left side of the screen.

To go to the Resource Name field, press Alt+1 and then press the Right Arrow key, or click the field.

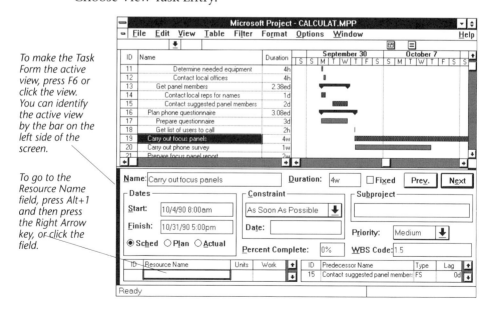

Microsoft Project automatically assigns one unit of the resource to the task. If you want to assign more or less than one unit, type the number in the Units field. To assign less than one unit, type a fraction representing the time the resource is assign to the task. For example, type "[.5]" if the resource is assigned half-time.

If the resource is already part of the resource pool, press Alt+Down Arrow or click the entry bar arrow (⬆) to display the list of resources.

To select the resource name, press the Up or Down Arrow key and press Enter, or click the resource name.

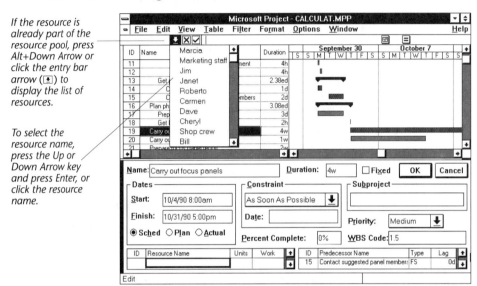

To add another resource, press the direction keys to go to the next Resource Name field or click the field.

When you are finished assigning resources for the selected task, press Enter or click OK. Now check the values in the Work fields. Work for each resource is calculated by multiplying the duration by the number of units of each resource assigned to the task. If the work is not what you want, change it. For example, if one of the resources will work for a few hours at the beginning of the task, and then not be involved for the remainder of the task, change the work amount for that resource.

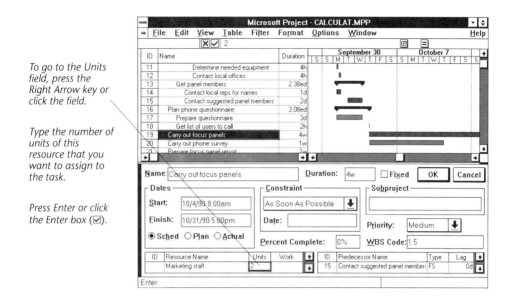

To go to the Units field, press the Right Arrow key or click the field.

Type the number of units of this resource that you want to assign to the task.

Press Enter or click the Enter box (☑).

Changing the Work

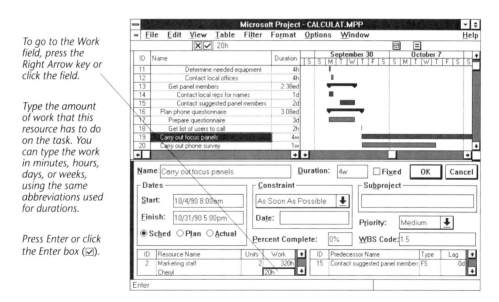

To go to the Work field, press the Right Arrow key or click the field.

Type the amount of work that this resource has to do on the task. You can type the work in minutes, hours, days, or weeks, using the same abbreviations used for durations.

Press Enter or click the Enter box (☑).

Assigning Resources on the Task Sheet

Resources can also be assigned on the Task Sheet in the Resource Names field. You can enter the units of the resource after the resource name, but you cannot enter work on the Task Sheet. To enter work, use the Task Form.

Choose View Task Sheet.

ID	Name		Duration	Scheduled Start	Scheduled Finish	Predecess(	Resource N
		Marcia					
1	Investigatic	Marketing staff	66.17ed	9/17/90 8:00am	11/22/90 12:00pm		
2	Investig	Jim	0d	9/17/90 8:00am	9/17/90 8:00am		
3	Prepare	Janet ❸	11.38ed	9/17/90 8:00am	9/28/90 5:00pm		
4	Rese	Roberto	1w	9/17/90 8:00am	9/21/90 5:00pm		Marcia ❶
5	Rev	Carmen	3d	9/17/90 8:00am	9/19/90 5:00pm		
6	Write	Dave	1w	9/24/90 8:00am	9/28/90 5:00pm	4,5FS-25%	
7	Plan foc	Cheryl	2.38ed	10/1/90 8:00am	10/3/90 5:00pm		
8	Arrar	Shop crew	0.38ed	10/1/90 8:00am	10/1/90 5:00pm		
9	C	Bill	1d	10/1/90 8:00am	10/1/90 5:00pm	6	
10	A	Contact local offices	0.38ed	10/1/90 8:00am	10/1/90 5:00pm		
11		ment	4h	10/1/90 8:00am	10/1/90 12:00pm	6	
12			4h	10/1/90 1:00pm	10/1/90 5:00pm	11	

Select the Resource Names field ❶ for the task to which you want to assign resources.

To display the names in the resource pool, press Alt+Down Arrow or click the entry bar arrow (▣) ❷.

To select the resource you want ❸, press the Up or Down Arrow key and press Enter, or click the resource name.

Microsoft Project automatically assigns one unit of the resource to the task. If you want to assign more or less than one unit, type the number in square brackets after the resource name. To assign less than one unit, type a fraction representing the time that the resource is assigned to the task. For example, type "[.5]" if the resource is assigned half-time.

ID	Name	Duration	Scheduled Start	Scheduled Finish	Predecess(	Resource N
1	Investigation phase	66.17ed	9/17/90 8:00am	11/22/90 12:00pm		
2	Investigation begins	0d	9/17/90 8:00am	9/17/90 8:00am		
3	Prepare initial product proposal	11.38ed	9/17/90 8:00am	9/28/90 5:00pm		
4	Research competition	1w	9/17/90 8:00am	9/21/90 5:00pm		Marcia
5	Review customer comment cards	3d	9/17/90 8:00am	9/19/90 5:00pm		Marketing s
6	Write proposal	1w	9/24/90 8:00am	9/28/90 5:00pm	4,5FS-25%	
7	Plan focus panel	2.38ed	10/1/90 8:00am	10/3/90 5:00pm		

Entry bar: Marketing staff[3] ❶

If you want to assign more or less than one unit of this resource, type the number of units in square brackets after the resource name ❶.

Level Message. As you assign resources to tasks, you may see a message in the status bar that a resource needs to be leveled. This means that the resource is overallocated—that is, more than its maximum units are assigned to tasks. For example, if you have three marketing staff available, but have assigned five marketing staff to tasks on a certain day, you will see a message to level marketing staff. You can take care of this now or later, either by shifting tasks or resources yourself, or using Microsoft

Project's leveling feature to move tasks around. Leveling resources is discussed in Chapter 9, "Refining the Schedule and Freezing the Baseline."

Assigning the Same Resources to Several Tasks. If several tasks use the same resources, you can enter the resources for all the tasks simultaneously. First, on the Task Entry view or Task Sheet, select the tasks that will use the same resource. Then choose Edit Form or click the form icon (🖻). In the Resources box, type the resources to be assigned to these tasks. If you are assigning other than one unit, enter the units in square brackets. For example, type "plumbers[3],supervisor[.5]" to assign three plumbers and half of a supervisor's time.

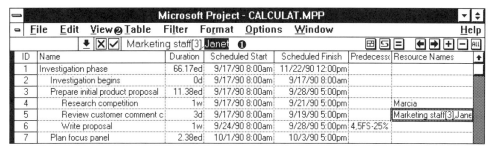

To assign another resource to this task, type a comma, and then choose or type another resource name ❶ *and the number of units.*

When you finish entering the resources for this task, press Enter or click the Enter box (☑) ❷.

Using the List Separator Character

Use the list separator character specified in the List Separator option in the Options Preferences dialog box. Initially, this is a comma for software in the United States. The list separator character may change if you change the international settings for Microsoft Project.

Assigning a New Resource to a Task

As you are assigning resources to a task, you may want to assign a resource that is not in the resource pool. Or perhaps you would rather not create the resource pool first. You can just start assigning resources on either the Task Entry view or the Task Sheet without having any resources in the resource pool. As you assign the resources to tasks, you create the resource pool.

If you assign a resource that does not exist in the resource pool, Microsoft Project asks you if you want to add this resource to the resource pool. If you choose the Yes button, Microsoft Project displays the Edit Form dialog box for resources so you can enter additional information about the resource. If you think that this resource already exists, choose the No button, and then check the entry bar list for the resource.

The Edit Form dialog box for resources looks and works like the Resource Form.

The resource name you typed is in the Name box ❶.
To move to a box you want to change, press Tab or click the box.
When you finish, press Enter or click OK ❷.

If you are assigning many new resources and do not want to enter additional information about them as they are entered, Microsoft Project can add them to the resource pool automatically for you. To do this, choose Options Preferences, select Auto Add Resources, and select Yes. Later, you can enter additional information about each resource using the Resource Sheet, Resource Form, or Edit Form dialog box for resources.

Changing a Resource Calendar

Every resource has a resource calendar. This calendar is created by Microsoft Project and matches the settings in the base calendar you created in Chapter 3. If you are using more than one base calendar—for example, one for day shift, one for swing shift, and one for graveyard shift—you can specify the base calendar for the resource when you first enter the resource or when you change the resource calendar.

The base calendar you choose controls the initial working days, working hours, and holidays for the resource. All settings in the base calendar are transferred to the resource calendar. You can change these to reflect the resource's actual working habits, adding to the resource calendar vacation time, part-time hours, or other exceptions to the base calendar.

For example, the resource Jim works the swing shift, so his resource calendar has the settings from the Swing Shift base calendar. In his resource calendar, you add his vacation time. Jim will be scheduled to work the days and hours in the Swing Shift base calendar, but not scheduled to work during his vacation time.

When Microsoft Project for Windows schedules the resource, it uses the resource calendar settings to determine when the resource is available. Changes you make to the base calendar are also made in the resource calendar; if settings in the resource calendar conflict with those in the base calendar, the resource calendar settings are used.

If you are using fixed-duration scheduling for any tasks, the settings in the resource calendar are ignored when these tasks are scheduled.

Changing a Resource's Base Calendar

If you have created more than one base calendar in your project, such as Day, Swing, and Graveyard for three shifts, be sure the appropriate base calendar is used by each resource. The base calendar can be changed when you create resources or when you change the resource calendar. When creating a new resource, you can select the base calendar in the Base Cal box on the Resource Form or the Edit Form dialog box for resources. When you change a resource's calendar, you can select the base calendar in the Base box in the Options Resource Calendar dialog box.

Changing Working Days or Hours for a Resource

You change a resource calendar to indicate when the working days or hours for this resource differ from its base calendar—for example, you would show vacation days, or part-time hours in the resource calendar.

To change a resource calendar, select the resource whose calendar you want to change. Then choose Options Resource Calendar.

The name of the resource appears in the upper-left corner ❶.

The name of the base calendar is listed here ❷. *You can select a different one if you want.*

Change the working days and hours in the resource calendar ❸ *just as you change the days and hours in a base calendar.*

When you finish, press Enter or click OK ❹.

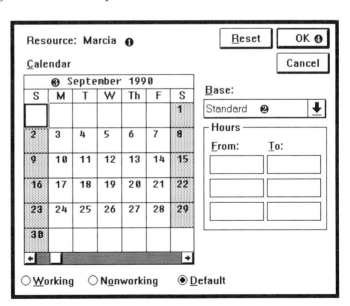

If you have changed the working days or hours in the resource calendar, you can use the Default option to change them back to the original setting in the base calendar or to match the other settings for that day in the resource calendar. For example, if you have changed the hours on Fridays for the resource calendar to half days and want to change them to match the base calendar, select the Friday title, and then select the Default option.

Entering a Task Cost

A task cost can be entered only when you have not assigned resources to a task. If you have assigned resources to a task, Microsoft Project calculates the task cost by summing all the resource costs. This cost will replace a cost you enter.

Enter task costs if you are not using Microsoft Project to assign resources to the tasks in this project, but you have cost estimates for the tasks based on past experience. Or maybe a task in your project is being performed by an outside contractor who has given you a bid for the work. You will not assign resources to this task because your resources will not work on the task; the contractor will take care of resources. You can enter this task cost so Microsoft Project will include this cost when calculating total cost for the project.

To enter a task cost, use the Task Sheet with the Cost table applied. Choose View Task Sheet. Choose Table Cost.

ID	Name	Cost	Planned Cost	Variance	Actual Cost	Rem. Cost
17	Prepare questionnaire	$0.00	$0.00	$0.00	$0.00	$0.00
18	Get list of users to call	$0.00	$0.00	$0.00	$0.00	$0.00
19	Carry out focus panels	$5,076.93	$0.00	$5,076.93	$0.00	$5,076.93
20	Carry out phone survey	10000 ❶	$0.00	$10,000.00	$0.00	$10,000.00
21	Prepare focus panel report	$0.00	$0.00	$0.00	$0.00	$0.00

Select the Cost field for the task to which you want to assign a cost ❶.

Type the cost.

Press Enter or click the Enter box (☑).

Printing the Resources and Schedule

All the project information is now entered into Microsoft Project for Windows. To review this information and share it with others, there are several views you can print.

To See	Print This View
List of resources in the resource pool, and information about each resource	Resource Sheet
List of tasks, including resources assigned to each task	Task Sheet
Summary of work and cost for each resource	Resource Sheet, with the Summary table applied
Current schedule	Gantt Chart

TO PRINT A VIEW

1. Choose the view you want to print.
2. Choose File Print.
3. Choose OK.
4. If you are printing the Gantt Chart, choose OK again.

In Part 3, you will review all the information you have entered to help you decide where to optimize the schedule.

REFINING AND COMMUNICATING THE PLAN

You now have an initial schedule for your project. But chances are excellent that this schedule won't cut it. Maybe it takes too long—or costs too much. Or maybe you just want to optimize the schedule so that all resources are used as efficiently as possible, and so the project is finished as soon as possible at the lowest cost. Perhaps you get a bonus for finishing early, or need to move people or equipment to other projects.

So, how do you make the schedule fit your needs? The next steps in the process are:

- Evaluate the schedule using Microsoft Project's views, tables, and filters to check dates, critical tasks, slack time, task order, resources, and costs (Chapter 8).

- Refine the schedule by adding and reassigning resources, adding overtime work, breaking up tasks, reducing the scope of the project, changing task sequence and constraints, and changing durations until you have the best schedule for your needs on this project (Chapter 9).

- When you are comfortable with the schedule, save the baseline schedule (Chapter 9). You will use the baseline schedule when you are tracking the project in Part 4.

- Communicate the plan to the project team and management (Chapter 10).

You repeat the first two steps until you solve all areas of concern in the project plan.

CHAPTER 8

Evaluating
the Schedule

As you entered the information about tasks, durations, relationships, and resources, Microsoft Project calculated the schedule. Now you need to look at this schedule and evaluate it to make sure it fits your needs.

The purpose of evaluating your schedule is to find errors, inconsistencies, and areas for improvement. For example, when you evaluate the schedule, you may find tasks that still start at the beginning of the project instead of later because you neglected to indicate their predecessors. You may find tasks or resources entered or ordered incorrectly, or resources assigned to the wrong tasks. This is your chance to review everything you have entered just to make sure it reflects your intentions.

In addition to looking for mistakes made when entering the project information, check the schedule itself. Check that the project is finishing when you need it to finish, within budget, meeting the requirements of the client, customer, or management, and that resources are available as needed for all tasks. You may have to find ways to speed up the schedule, move tasks or resources around so resources are available as needed, lower costs to meet budget constraints, and so on.

This chapter explains how to check your schedule to decide which parts are okay and which parts need some help. Once you know which parts of the schedule you need to concentrate on, the next chapter lists ways to change and improve your schedule so it meets your needs.

When you evaluate the schedule, you look at six major areas:

- Project finish date and task dates
- Critical tasks and the critical path
- Slack time
- Task sequence, relationships, and constraints
- Resources
- Costs

Now that you can see their impact on the schedule, keep your assumptions in mind as you review each area. Note any assumptions that have changed so you can make appropriate adjustments to the schedule. Make sure, too, that all the project objectives have been satisfied.

PROJECT DATES

The first date you want to check is the project finish date to see if it is acceptable. This shows you how much, if any, you need to shorten the critical path so the project finishes on time.

You also want to look over the task bars on the Gantt Chart or task nodes on the PERT Chart, just to check for anything that is out of place. For example, you may see a task linked to the wrong task, or to no task at all such that it starts at the beginning of the project instead of the appropriate time during the project.

CRITICAL TASKS

The tasks on the critical path determine the project finish date. The critical path is that sequence of tasks adding up to the longest total time required to complete the project. The duration of the project is the total duration of these critical tasks. To shorten the project duration, focus on the critical path. You can shorten the critical path by changing dependencies between tasks and by shortening critical tasks.

In the critical path method of scheduling, the critical path is determined by calculating the schedule twice. First, a forward pass is made from the start date of the project. This pass determines the earliest start and finish dates for each task. For example, if you have three tasks, each one day long and occurring on consecutive days, the forward pass might look like this:

Monday	Tuesday	Wednesday	Thursday	Friday
Task A	Task B	Task C		

The early start and finish dates are summarized in the following table:

	Early Start	**Early Finish**
Task A	Monday, 8 a.m.	Monday, 5 p.m.
Task B	Tuesday, 8 a.m.	Tuesday, 5 p.m.
Task C	Wednesday, 8 a.m.	Wednesday, 5 p.m.

Then a backward pass is made, calculated from either a finish date you enter, or from the date computed in the first pass. This pass determines the latest start and finish dates for each task. For example, if the latest finish date for the Task C is Friday, the backward pass would look something like this:

Monday	Tuesday	Wednesday	Thursday	Friday
		Task A	Task B	Task C

The late start and finish dates are summarized in the following table:

	Late Start	**Late Finish**
Task A	Wednesday, 8 a.m.	Wednesday, 5 p.m.
Task B	Thursday, 8 a.m.	Thursday, 5 p.m.
Task C	Friday, 8 a.m.	Friday, 5 p.m.

The difference between the two sets of dates is the slack time. The three tasks in the example each have two days of slack time, from their early start date (for example, for Task A, Monday, 8 a.m.) to their late start date (for Task A, Wednesday, 8 a.m.).

The critical path is that path that has no slack time from project start to project finish. There may even be more than one critical path through the project if different phases of the project are worked on simultaneously. For critical tasks, the early and late start dates are the same, as are the early and late finish dates.

Aside from identifying the critical path, the critical path method of scheduling tells you:

- Earliest and latest start and finish dates for all tasks. Use this information to move tasks around to level resources.

- Which tasks cannot slip if the project completion date is to be maintained. If a critical task does slip, you must adjust the remaining tasks on the critical path, maybe by working on critical tasks simultaneously, or by adding resources to critical tasks, to meet the project end date.

The critical path is recalculated every time you change task data, so it is constantly changing. A critical task may become noncritical and a noncritical task critical as you move resources, change dependencies, and so on. For example, if you find a way to shorten a critical task, perhaps by adding resources to accomplish the task faster, this task may no longer be critical, but another task may become critical. The time you save on the first task might not reflect fully in the end date of the project because of the changing critical path.

In the following illustration, Tasks B, C, and D are on the critical path. The finish date for Task D and the project is Friday, 8/31, at 5 p.m.

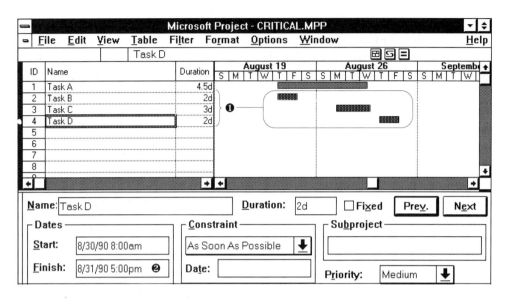

These three tasks form the critical path ❶.

The finish date for Task D and the project is 8/31 at 5 p.m. ❷.

If you find a way to shorten Task C from 3 days to 1.5 days, saving 1.5 days, the finish date changes to Friday at noon, a savings of only half a day. Tasks B and C are no longer critical, but Task A is now critical.

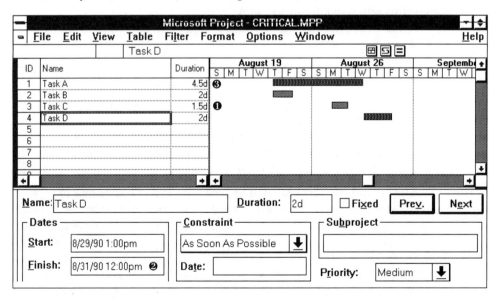

Task C is now 1.5 days long instead of 3 days, and is no longer critical ❶.

The finish date for Task D and the project is 8/31 at 12 noon ❷, a savings of half a day.

Task A is now critical ❸. Tasks A and D now form the critical path.

SLACK TIME AND NONCRITICAL TASKS

When the schedule is calculated, slack time is also calculated. Slack is how much time a task can be delayed without delaying project end date. You can also look at slack time as the difference between the critical path duration and the duration of any other path. Noncritical tasks have slack time; critical tasks do not. Noncritical tasks can start and/or finish later than their scheduled dates, up to the available slack time, without affecting the project finish date.

There are two kinds of slack time: total slack and free slack.

- Total slack time is the amount of time a task can be delayed without delaying the end date of the project. It is the difference between the date a task is scheduled to start and the late start date for the task calculated by the backward pass. Total slack includes all the slack between this task and the end of the project. If you use all the total slack on one task, those tasks dependent on this task have no more slack and become critical.

  When the duration for a task is longer than the time allowed by the scheduled dates, total slack is negative instead of positive. Negative slack in your schedule tells you that, as currently scheduled, there is not enough time for some tasks.

- Free slack is the amount of time a task can be delayed without delaying any other task.

Looking at the amount of slack time tasks have helps you decide how to best use resources. Shift tasks with slack time to even out resource use.

TASK ORDER, RELATIONSHIPS, AND CONSTRAINTS

When you looked at the critical path, you identified those tasks whose durations you want to shorten. Now that you know which tasks you need to concentrate on, check the task dependencies—task sequence, the relationships between the tasks, and the constraints. Be sure you have not imposed a sequence or relationship that is not absolutely necessary nor added unnecessary constraints. You may find that by changing the task sequence, overlapping tasks, or removing constraints, you can shorten project duration.

RESOURCES

Next, check that you have sufficient resources at the right times to do the work. Where there are overallocated resources—resources assigned to more tasks than the resource can do simultaneously—adjust the tasks and resources to resolve the problems.

Look also at how resources are used over the life of the project. You want to use resources evenly throughout the project, with as few peaks and valleys as possible. To achieve this, you may want to move tasks around within their slack time.

COST

Check the total project cost. If it is unacceptable, look at the individual task and resource costs to determine what you can do to lower costs. For example, can you use a less costly resource on a task? Or maybe request additional bids for a task to be performed by an outside contractor to lower the cost of the task?

USING MICROSOFT PROJECT FOR WINDOWS

When you evaluate the schedule, use Microsoft Project views, tables, and filters to see exactly the information you need. You can check:

- Project finish date
- Critical path and all the tasks on the critical path
- Slack time and noncritical tasks
- Relationships and constraints
- How resources are assigned to tasks and used over time
- Project, task, and resource costs

The following table lists a few of the many ways to evaluate the schedule in Microsoft Project.

To See	Use
When the project is scheduled to finish	Options Project Info
Critical path and tasks on the critical path	Gantt Chart PERT Chart Task Sheet with Critical filter applied
Slack time to determine how you can shift tasks to use resources more efficiently	Task Sheet with Schedule table applied Gantt Chart with slack bars
Relationships between tasks, to decide if any can be changed to occur simultaneously to speed up the schedule, or sequentially to use overallocated resources more efficiently	Gantt Chart over the Task PERT Chart
Constraints, to verify all are necessary	Task Sheet with Constraint Dates table applied and Constrained filter applied
All resources, their cost and work, plus peak usage	Resource Sheet with Summary table applied
Level of resource use over the life of the project	Resource Usage View
When resources are scheduled to work on tasks	Resource Form with schedule fields displayed
Highs and lows in peak resource usage	Resource Histogram
If project costs are within budget	Options Project Info
Task costs to decide what to cut	Task Sheet with Cost table applied, over the Task Form with resource cost fields displayed

Checking the Project Finish Date and Project Costs

Use the Options Project Info command to check the project finish date and the total costs for the project.

For example, in the calculator project, one of your goals is to have a new calculator ready for the back-to-school promotion. If this is scheduled to occur in August, finishing the project on August 29 will be too late.

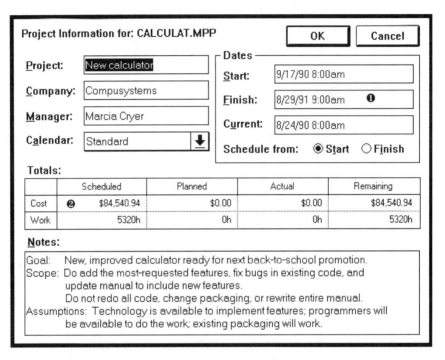

Check the project finish date here ❶.
Check the total costs for the project here ❷.

If the project finish date is too late, the next step is to look at the critical path and the tasks on the critical path to see how you can speed things up. If the costs are too high, you need to look at individual task and resource costs to find costs to reduce.

Checking Critical Tasks

By identifying the critical tasks, you know which tasks to accelerate if you need to finish the project earlier than currently scheduled. In Microsoft Project, you can look at the critical path and critical tasks on the Gantt Chart or PERT Chart. You can also look at a list of critical tasks and milestones on the Task Sheet. In Microsoft Project, tasks with the Must Start On and Must Finish On constraints are always critical.

Changing the Amount of Time that Makes a Task Critical. Initially, Microsoft Project considers any task with zero total slack time a critical task. But, you can change this. Use the Options Preferences command to specify the amount of slack a task can have and be considered critical. For example, if you have a two-year project, you may want any task with slack of less than one week to be considered a critical task.

To change the amount of time that makes a task critical, choose Options Preferences. Select the Show As Critical If Slack <= option, and type the number of elapsed days of slack time a task can have and still be critical. For example, type "7" if you want tasks with one week (seven elapsed days) of slack time to be critical tasks. Press Enter or click the Enter box (☑).

Critical Path on the Gantt Chart

The Gantt Chart graphically shows the critical path through the project. Critical task bars are a different pattern or color from noncritical tasks so it is easy to identify the critical path.

To display the Gantt Chart, choose View Gantt Chart.

The darker pattern bars ❶ are critical tasks. (These are red on a color monitor or printer.)

The lighter pattern bars ❷ are noncritical tasks. (These are blue on a color monitor or printer.)

These tasks are critical and are part of the critical path ❸. This is one area where you can look for ways to accelerate the tasks.

Critical Path on the PERT Chart

On the PERT Chart, the node borders and the lines connecting the nodes identify the critical tasks and critical path.

By following the bold critical path through the PERT Chart, you'll see which tasks you need to concentrate on if you need to bring in the finish date.

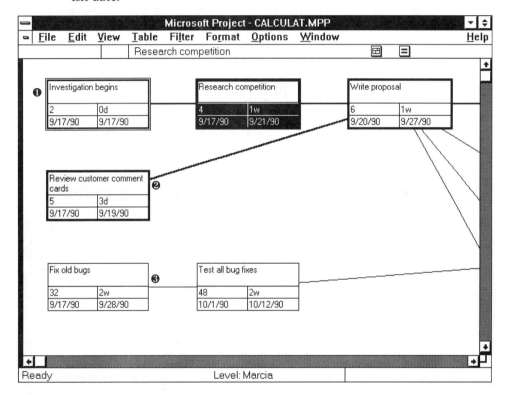

Milestones have double borders: bold if they are critical ❶, thin if they are not. (Critical milestones are red on a color monitor; noncritical milestones are black.)

Critical tasks have a bold border and the critical path is bold ❷. (These are red on a color monitor or printer.)

Noncritical tasks have a thin border and the noncritical path is a thin line ❸. (These are black on a color monitor or printer.)

Critical Tasks on the Task Sheet

There are several ways to look at critical tasks on the Task Sheet. One way to pick out critical tasks from the rest of the tasks is to change the color or style of critical task names. To do this, choose Format Text.

Select Critical Tasks ❶.

To make critical tasks bold, turn on the Bold check box ❷.

To make critical tasks red, select Red in the Color box ❸.

Choose OK ❹.

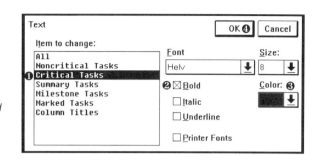

If you want to see a list of critical tasks only, apply the Critical filter to the Task Sheet. When the Critical filter is applied, only those tasks and milestones that are critical are displayed in the view.

Apply the Critical filter by choosing Filter Critical.

ID	Name	Duration	Scheduled Start	Scheduled Finish	Predecess	Resource Names
1	Investigation phase	58.08ed	9/17/90 8:00am	11/14/90 10:00am		
2	Investigation begins	0d	9/17/90 8:00am	9/17/90 8:00am		
3	Prepare initial product proposal	10.29ed	9/17/90 8:00am	9/27/90 3:00pm		
4	Research competition	1w	9/17/90 8:00am	9/21/90 5:00pm	2	Marcia,Marketing staf
5	Review customer comment ca	3d	9/17/90 8:00am	9/19/90 5:00pm		Marketing staff[3],Jan
6	Write proposal	1w	9/20/90 3:00pm	9/27/90 3:00pm	4FS-25%,5	Marcia,Janet
7	Plan focus panel	5ed	9/27/90 3:00pm	10/2/90 3:00pm		
13	Get panel members	5ed	9/27/90 3:00pm	10/2/90 3:00pm		
14	Contact local reps for name	1d	9/27/90 3:00pm	9/28/90 3:00pm	6	Marketing staff
15	Contact suggested panel m	2d	9/28/90 3:00pm	10/2/90 3:00pm	14	
19	Carry out focus panels	4w	10/2/90 3:00pm	10/30/90 3:00pm	15	Marcia,Marketing staf
21	Prepare focus panel report	2w	10/30/90 3:00pm	11/13/90 3:00pm	19	Marcia[0.1],Marketing
23	Present results	4h	11/13/90 3:00pm	11/14/90 10:00am	21,22	Marcia
24	Investigation phase complete	0d	10/31/90 5:00pm	10/31/90 5:00pm	23	
27	Prepare initial spec	2w	11/1/90 8:00am	11/14/90 5:00pm	26	Dave,Bill,Marcia[0.1],
29	Meet with reviewers	4h	11/22/90 8:00am	11/22/90 12:00pm	27FS+1w	Dave,Bill
30	Incorporate comments/revise spe	1w	11/22/90 1:00pm	11/29/90 12:00pm	29	Dave,Bill,Terri[0.2]
31	Distribute final spec	1h	11/29/90 1:00pm	11/29/90 2:00pm	30	Terri
33	Code new features	28ed	11/29/90 2:00pm	12/27/90 2:00pm		
34	Code clock feature	4w	11/29/90 2:00pm	12/27/90 2:00pm	31	Design staff[2]
35	Code notes feature	4w	11/29/90 2:00pm	12/27/90 2:00pm	31	Design staff
44	Test new features	21ed	12/13/90 2:00pm	1/3/91 2:00pm		
45	Test clock	3w	12/13/90 2:00pm	1/3/91 2:00pm	43,34FF+1	Testing staff
46	Test notes	2w	12/20/90 2:00pm	1/3/91 2:00pm	43,35FF+1	Testing staff
49	Final testing pass	2w	1/3/91 2:00pm	1/17/91 2:00pm	45,46,47,4	Testing staff[2]

Microsoft Project - CALCULAT.MPP

File   Edit   View   Table   Filter   Format   Options   Window   Help

Investigation phase

Ready   Level: Marcia

All the tasks now displayed on the Task Sheet are critical tasks. Note that the list of ID numbers is no longer complete. For example, tasks 8 through 12 are missing, which means they are not critical tasks ❶.

If you also sort the tasks by duration, the critical tasks will be in order from the longest to the shortest. This helps you see where to put your efforts in shortening tasks.

Choose Format Sort.

1. *In the 1st Key box, select Duration ❶.*
2. *Select the Descending option ❷.*
3. *Choose OK ❸.*

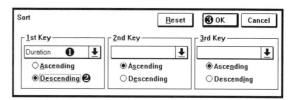

The longest critical task is now at the top of the list. The shortest critical task is at the bottom.

ID	Name	Duration	Scheduled Start	Scheduled Finish	Predecess	Resource Names
62	Sales phase	125.79ed	4/25/91 2:00pm	8/29/91 9:00am		
52	Manufacturing phase	91ed	1/24/91 2:00pm	4/25/91 2:00pm		
1	Investigation phase	58.08ed	9/17/90 8:00am	11/14/90 10:00am		
33	Code new features	28ed	11/29/90 2:00pm	12/27/90 2:00pm		
44	Test new features	21ed	12/13/90 2:00pm	1/3/91 2:00pm		
3	Prepare initial product proposal	10.29ed	9/17/90 8:00am	9/27/90 3:00pm		
19	Carry out focus panels	4w	10/2/90 3:00pm	10/30/90 3:00pm	15,9,12	Marcia,Marketing staf
34	Code clock feature	4w	11/29/90 2:00pm	12/27/90 2:00pm	31	Design staff[2]
35	Code notes feature	4w	11/29/90 2:00pm	12/27/90 2:00pm	31	Design staff
72	Prepare marketing materials	4w	6/5/91 9:00am	7/3/91 9:00am	71	Marcia[0.2],Marketing
76	Support sales force	4w	8/1/91 9:00am	8/29/91 9:00am	75	Sales engineers
7	Plan focus panel	5ed	9/27/90 3:00pm	10/2/90 3:00pm		
13	Get panel members	5ed	9/27/90 3:00pm	10/2/90 3:00pm		
45	Test clock	3w	12/13/90 2:00pm	1/3/91 2:00pm	43,34FF+1	Testing staff
56	Plan production line changes	3w	2/7/91 2:00pm	2/28/91 2:00pm	55	
57	Set up production test	3w	2/28/91 2:00pm	3/21/91 2:00pm	56	Production team,Prod
58	Test production	3w	3/21/91 2:00pm	4/11/91 2:00pm	57	Production team[3]
21	Prepare focus panel report	2w	10/30/90 3:00pm	11/13/90 3:00pm	19	Marcia[0.1],Marketing
27	Prepare initial spec	2w	11/1/90 8:00am	11/14/90 5:00pm	26	Dave,Bill,Marcia[0.1]
46	Test notes	2w	12/20/90 2:00pm	1/3/91 2:00pm	43,35FF+1	Testing staff
49	Final testing pass	2w	1/3/91 2:00pm	1/17/91 2:00pm	45,46,47,4	Testing staff[2],Marilyn
60	Pass production function to Singapor	2w	4/11/91 2:00pm	4/25/91 2:00pm	59	Nancy
73	Prepare packaging	2w	7/3/91 9:00am	7/17/91 9:00am	72	

To return to ID number order, choose Format Sort, choose the Reset button, and then choose OK.

To display all the tasks again, choose Filter All Tasks.

If you want to see the status of all tasks in the project, add the Critical column to the table. If a task or milestone is critical, this field contains Yes; if the task or milestone is not critical, the field contains No.

Checking Slack Time

Another way to analyze your schedule is to look at the amount of slack time the tasks have. By minimizing slack time, you make your schedule as efficient as it can be and use resources more effectively. You can look at slack time on the Task Sheet or Gantt Chart.

Microsoft Project for Windows tells you when a task has negative total slack, which means the task is scheduled to take longer than its predecessors and successors allow.

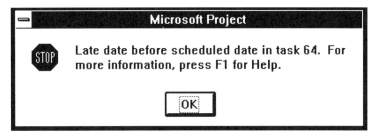

The message tells you that the task is scheduled to finish after the date calculated by Microsoft Project as the late finish date.

Negative slack appears as a negative number in the Total Slack column on the Task Sheet when you have the Schedule table applied.

> **Turning Off the Scheduling Message for Negative Slack**
>
> When a task has negative slack, Microsoft Project tells you so every time it recalculates the schedule, which, if Microsoft Project is recalculating automatically, is every time you change something. If you don't want to deal with a scheduling problem now, and you don't want to keep getting the message, you can turn it off. To do this, choose Options Preferences, select the Scheduling Messages option, and then select No. Press Enter or click the Enter box (☑).
>
> **Turning Off Automatic Calculation**
>
> You can also turn off automatic calculation. Microsoft Project then calculates the schedule only when you tell it to. To turn off automatic calculation, choose Options Calculation. Select the Manual option, and then choose OK. When you are ready to calculate the schedule, choose Options Calculate Now or click the calculate icon (▤).

Slack Time on the Task Sheet

To see the free slack time and total slack time for each task, apply the Schedule table to the Task Sheet.

Choose View Task Sheet and then choose Table Schedule (see the illustration on the following page).

| □ | | | Microsoft Project - CALCULAT.MPP | | | | ▼ | ♦ |

| ▭ | **File** | **Edit** | **View** | **Table** | **Filter** | **Format** | **Options** | **Window** | **Help** |

| | | | Investigation phase | ❶ | | ❷ | ❸ | 田 S ≡ | ← → + − ALL |

ID	Scheduled Start	Scheduled Finish	Late Start	Late Finish	Free Slack	Total Slack ❹	
1	9/17/90 8:00am	11/14/90 10:00am	9/3/90 3:00pm	8/29/91 9:00am	0ed	❺ -13.71ed
2	9/17/90 8:00am	9/17/90 8:00am	9/3/90 3:00pm	9/3/90 3:00pm	0ed	-13.71ed
3	9/17/90 8:00am	9/27/90 3:00pm	9/3/90 3:00pm	9/14/90 12:00pm	0ed	-13.71ed
4	9/17/90 8:00am	9/21/90 5:00pm	9/3/90 3:00pm	9/10/90 3:00pm	0ed	-13.71ed
5	9/17/90 8:00am	9/19/90 5:00pm	9/4/90 1:00pm	9/7/90 12:00pm	0ed	-12.79ed
6	9/20/90 3:00pm	9/27/90 3:00pm	9/7/90 1:00pm	9/14/90 12:00pm	0ed	-13.13ed
7	9/27/90 3:00pm	10/2/90 3:00pm	9/14/90 1:00pm	8/29/91 9:00am	0ed	-13.08ed
8	9/27/90 3:00pm	9/28/90 3:00pm	8/28/91 9:00am	8/29/91 9:00am	0ed	❻ 334.75ed
9	9/27/90 3:00pm	9/28/90 3:00pm	8/28/91 9:00am	8/29/91 9:00am	334.75ed	334.75ed
10	9/27/90 3:00pm	9/28/90 3:00pm	8/28/91 9:00am	8/29/91 9:00am	0ed	334.75ed
11	9/27/90 3:00pm	9/28/90 10:00am	8/28/91 9:00am	8/28/91 2:00pm	0ed	334.17ed
12	9/28/90 10:00am	9/28/90 3:00pm	8/28/91 9:00am	8/29/91 9:00am	334.17ed	334.17ed
13	9/27/90 3:00pm	10/2/90 3:00pm	9/14/90 1:00pm	9/19/90 12:00pm	0ed	-13.13ed
14	9/27/90 3:00pm	9/28/90 3:00pm	9/14/90 1:00pm	9/17/90 12:00pm	0ed	-13.08ed
15	9/28/90 3:00pm	10/2/90 3:00pm	9/17/90 1:00pm	9/19/90 12:00pm	0ed	-13.13ed
16	9/27/90 3:00pm	10/2/90 3:00pm	10/17/90 8:00am	10/19/90 5:00pm	0ed	17.08ed
17	9/27/90 3:00pm	10/2/90 3:00pm	10/17/90 8:00am	10/19/90 5:00pm	0ed	17.08ed
18	10/2/90 1:00pm	10/2/90 3:00pm	10/19/90 3:00pm	10/19/90 5:00pm	0ed	17.08ed
19	10/2/90 3:00pm	10/30/90 3:00pm	9/19/90 1:00pm	10/17/90 12:00pm	0ed	-13.13ed
20	10/2/90 3:00pm	10/9/90 3:00pm	10/22/90 8:00am	10/26/90 5:00pm	0ed	17.08ed
21	10/30/90 3:00pm	11/13/90 3:00pm	10/17/90 1:00pm	10/31/90 12:00pm	0ed	-13.13ed
22	10/9/90 3:00pm	10/12/90 10:00am	10/29/90 8:00am	10/31/90 12:00pm	19.08ed	19.08ed
23	11/13/90 3:00pm	11/14/90 10:00am	10/31/90 1:00pm	10/31/90 5:00pm	0ed	-13.71ed
24	10/31/90 5:00pm	10/31/90 5:00pm	10/31/90 5:00pm	10/31/90 5:00pm	0ed	❼ 0ed
25	9/17/90 8:00am	2/7/91 9:00am	11/1/90 8:00am	8/29/91 9:00am	0ed	45ed

| ← | ▢ | | | Level: Marcia | | → |
| Ready | | | | | | |

Late start ❶ and finish ❷ dates are included in this table. Use these dates to decide how to shift tasks and resources.

Free slack ❸ and total slack ❹ are listed for each task.

Negative slack is indicated with a minus sign before the total slack ❺.

When you see a slack amount that is the length of the project ❻, it indicates that the task is not linked to any other tasks, and that you need to check its predecessors and successors.

Zero total slack ❼ indicates a critical task.

Slack is always indicated in elapsed time. Elapsed time is the total amount of time, including nonworking time, between the early start date and the late start date. For more information about elapsed time, see "Entering Durations" in Chapter 5, "Estimating Time to Perform Tasks."

Slack Time on the Gantt Chart

To see the slack time graphically for each task, add slack bars to the Gantt Chart. Use the Format Palette command to add these bars.

For instructions on adding slack bars, see Chapter 16, "Using Microsoft Project Tools."

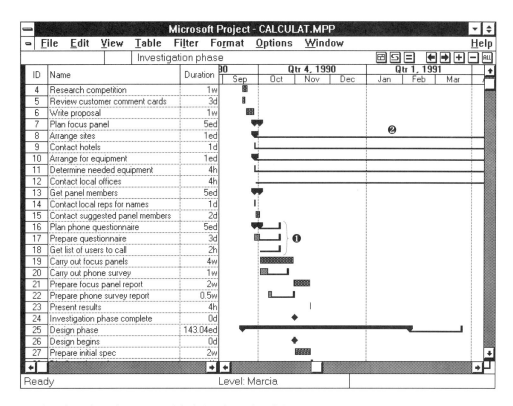

These bars show the amount of slack time for each task ❶.

Again, look for tasks with large amounts of slack ❷ because they may be missing predecessors and successors.

Checking Relationships and Constraints

The purpose of checking relationships and constraints is to make sure you haven't imposed a relationship or constraint that isn't absolutely necessary. For example, see if you can accelerate the schedule by changing the relationship between tasks so the tasks overlap, or try adding lag between tasks to better use overallocated resources. Overallocated resources are those assigned to more tasks than there are resources available to work on the tasks.

Check for constraints that force a task to start or finish on a certain date. Such constraints may be causing scheduling problems. Replacing Must Start On, for example, with As Soon As Possible, or even changing it to Start No Earlier Than or Start No Later Than as appropriate, may give you more flexibility in solving scheduling problems. Remember that Must Start On and Must Finish On constraints always make a task critical, so use them sparingly.

Checking Relationships

To review the relationships between tasks, use the Gantt Chart to see graphically how tasks are related now. By placing the Task PERT Chart below the Gantt Chart, you see the immediate predecessors and successors to the task selected on the Gantt Chart and the relationships between the tasks. This will help you find tasks that could be performed in a different order to either save time or free up resources.

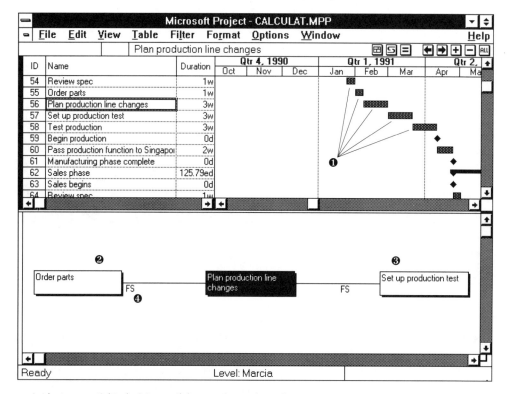

Look at sequential tasks ❶ to see if they can be overlapped.

Look at predecessors ❷ and successors ❸ on the Task PERT Chart to check that relationships reflect how you plan to perform the tasks.

The relationship ❹ between each pair of tasks is shown between the tasks.

Checking Constraints

Check the constraints to make sure all constraints other than As Soon As Possible are necessary. To check constraints on all tasks, apply the Constraint Dates table to the Task Sheet. To see a list of tasks that have a constraint other than As Soon As Possible, apply the Constrained filter to the Task Sheet.

Choose View Task Sheet. To apply the Constraint Dates table, choose Table Define Tables, select Constraint Dates in the Tables box, and then press Enter or click the Set button.

ID	Name	Duration	Constraint Type	Constraint Date
21	Prepare focus panel report	2w	As Soon As Possible	
22	Prepare phone survey repo	0.5w	As Soon As Possible	
23	Present results	4h	As Soon As Possible	
24	Investigation phase comple	0d ❶ Finish No Later Than		10/31/90 5:00pm
25	Design phase	143.04ed	As Soon As Possible	
26	Design begins	0d	As Soon As Possible	
27	Prepare initial spec	2w	As Soon As Possible	
28	Distribute for review	1h	As Soon As Possible	
29	Meet with reviewers	4h	As Soon As Possible	

By looking at the Task Sheet with the Constraint Dates table applied, you can check that constraints other than As Soon As Possible are necessary ❶.

If you want to see only those tasks that have a constraint other than As Soon As Possible, apply the Constrained filter. To do this, choose Filter Define Filters. In the Filters box, select Constrained, and press Enter or click the Set button. To display all the tasks again, choose Filter All Tasks.

When you check constraints, you may find Must Start On constraints that you don't remember entering. Any time you enter a scheduled start date for a task, for example on the Task Form in the Start field with the Sched option selected, or by changing the start date with the mouse on the Gantt Chart, Microsoft Project will enter a constraint of Must Start On. Microsoft Project assumes if you are entering a start date, you mean that the task must start on that date. Change any constraint that is unnecessary or is inappropriate.

Checking Resources

Use the four resource views to check the resource pool, see which resources are overallocated (assigned too many tasks), check when resources are scheduled to work on tasks, and look for highs and lows in resource use. Checking for overallocated and underallocated resources is important because it shows problem areas in your project. For example, it might be warning you that the same person is assigned to two full-time tasks on the same day. Obviously, one person can't do both tasks, so you'll either need to move the tasks around or assign someone else to one of the tasks. In Chapter 9, you'll see various ways to take care of overallocated resources.

Reviewing a List of Resources

To see a list of all resources in the resource pool, plus information about peak usage, apply the Summary table to the Resource Sheet. Choose View Resource Sheet and then Table Summary.

ID	Name	Group	Max. Units	Peak	Std. Rate	Ovt. Rate	Cost	Work
1	Marcia ❹	Marketing	1	❸ 2	$50,000.00/y	$0.00/h	$8,509.61	354h
2	Marketing staff	Marketing	3	6	$32,000.00/y	$0.00/h	$12,615.38	820h
3	Jim	Marketing	1	1	$32,500.00/y	$0.00/h	$1,375.00	88h
4	Janet	Marketing	1	1	$47,500.00/y	$0.00/h	$5,115.39	224h
5	Roberto	Marketing	1	1	$30,000.00/y	$0.00/h	$2,653.84	184h
6	Carmen	Marketing	1	0	$60,000.00/y	$0.00/h	$0.00	0h
7	Dave	Design	1	1	$30,000.00/y	$0.00/h	$1,788.46	124h
8	Cheryl	Marketing	1	1	$16,000.00/y	$11.50/h	$430.77	56h
9	Shop crew	Production	1	0	$15.00/h	$22.50/h	$0.00	0h
10	Bill	Design	1	1	$25,000.00/y	$0.00/h	$1,586.54	132h
11	Computer time	MIS	1	0.1	$60.00/h	$0.00/h	$245.00	4h
12	Research Inc.	Vendor	1	1.25	$500.00/d	$0.00/h	$6,250.00	100h
13	Terri	Design	1	1	$6.50/h	$9.75/h	$169.00	26h
14	Design staff	Design	3	5	$25,000.00/y	$0.00/h	$12,019.24	1000h
15	Documentation dept	Documentat	1	1	$20.00/h	$0.00/h	$9,600.00	480h
16	Testing staff	Testing	3	2	$25,000.00/y	$0.00/h	$9,134.63	760h
17	Marilynn	Testing	1	0.75	$32,500.00/y	$0.00/h	$750.00	48h
18	Nancy	Production	1	1	$32,500.00/y	$0.00/h	$1,875.00	120h
19	Production team	Production	3	3	$25,000.00/y	$0.00/h	$6,730.77	560h
20	Jeff	Sales	1	1	$29,000.00/y	$0.00/h	$557.69	40h
21	Karen	Sales	1	1	$35,000.00/y	$0.00/h	$673.08	40h
22	Sales engineers	Sales	3	1	$32,000.00/y	$0.00/h	$2,461.54	160h
23	Rick	Sales	1	0	$10.00/h	$15.00/h	$0.00	0h
24	Bob	Production	1	0	$8.00/h	$12.00/h	$0.00	0h
25	Mary	Sales	1	0	$20,000.00/y	$0.00/h	$0.00	0h

Microsoft Project - CALCULAT.MPP

Marcia ❷ ❶

Ready   Level: Marcia ❺

The Peak column ❶ shows the highest number of units of the resource allocated to tasks at any one time.

When the number in the Peak column is greater than the number in the Max. Units column ❷, it means that the resource is overallocated because more units are assigned to tasks than there are units available ❸.

Overallocated resources are in bold or red ❹.

When a resource is overallocated, Microsoft Project tells you by displaying "Level" at the bottom of the screen ❺. If more than one resource is overallocated, the name of the first overallocated resource in the list is displayed.

If you want to see only those resources that are overallocated, apply the Overallocated filter. To do this, choose Filter Overallocated. To display all the resources again, choose Filter All Resources.

You can also sort this list according to the cost of using a resource on the project. If you must cut costs, you may want to look at the high end and decide how to decrease your use of the most expensive resources.

If you create a combination view with the Task Sheet over the Resource Form showing the schedule fields, you can see the tasks to which the selected resource is assigned, and then decide how you can reduce this resource's participation on tasks.

To Sort Resources by Cost	To Return to ID Number Order
1. Choose Format Sort	1. Choose Format Sort
2. In the first Key box, select Cost	2. Choose the Reset button
3. Select the Descending option	3. Choose OK
4. Choose OK	
The most costly resource will now be on top and the least costly on the bottom	

Checking Resource Usage

The Resource Usage view shows you all resources in a spreadsheet format and their usage during each time period. Use the Resource Usage view to check work allocation for all resources in your project. This information will help you decide which resources have too much work (overallocated) and which need more work (underallocated). In Chapter 9, as you are refining your schedule, this information will help you decide which resources you can shift to accelerate tasks or to solve overallocation.

The Resource Usage view shows four types of information:

- Work during each period for each resource
- Work each resource is overallocated during each period
- Percentage of allocation for each resource during each period
- Cost of using each resource during each period

To see the amount of work each resource has during each period, choose View Resource Usage (see the illustration on the following page).

ID	Name		S	M	T	W	T	F	S	S	M	T	W	T
				September 23							September 30			
1	**Marcia** ❶			❷ 8h	8h	8h	6h					2h	8h	8h
2	**Marketing staff**						4h	8h				4h	16h	16h
3	Jim													
4	Janet			8h	8h	8h	6h					2h	8h	8h
5	Roberto						2h	8h			8h	8h	8h	8h
6	Carmen													
7	Dave													
8	Cheryl						2h	6h						
9	Shop crew													
10	Bill			0.8h	0.8h	0.8h	0.8h	0.8h						
11	Computer time											0.2h	0.8h	0.8h
12	**Research Inc.**											2.5h ❸10h	10h	
13	Terri													
14	**Design staff**			16h	16h	16h	16h	16h						
15	Documentation dept													
16	Testing staff										16h	16h	16h	16h
17	Marilynn													
18	Nancy													
19	Production team													
20	Jeff													
21	Karen													
22	Sales engineers													
23	Rick													
24	Bob													

Microsoft Project - CALCULAT.MPP
File   Edit   View   Table   Filter   Format   Options   Window   Help
Marcia

Ready   Level: Marcia

Resources that are overallocated are in bold ❶ (red on a color monitor).
Each box ❷ shows the amount of work the resource is to do for the period indicated on the timescale.
When a resource is overallocated during a period on the timescale, the amount of work is in bold ❸.

To change the type of information in the boxes, use the Format commands. For example, to see the percentage of total capacity that each resource is allocated during the period, choose Format Percent Allocation.

In the following illustration, Research Inc. is scheduled to work 125 percent. The other three overallocated resources—Marcia, Marketing staff, and Design staff—are not overallocated during the period shown on the timescale because all their percentages are 100 or less.

To resolve overallocated resources, you may be able to shift one of the tasks such that it occurs earlier or later, or assign other resources to the task to reduce the number of units required of the overallocated resource.

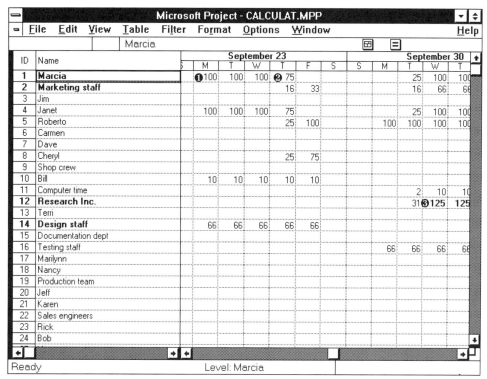

ID	Name	September 23							September 30			
		M	T	W	T	F	S	S	M	T	W	T
1	**Marcia**	❶100	100	100	❷ 75					25	100	100
2	**Marketing staff**				16	33				16	66	66
3	Jim											
4	Janet	100	100	100	75					25	100	100
5	Roberto				25	100			100	100	100	100
6	Carmen											
7	Dave											
8	Cheryl				25	75						
9	Shop crew											
10	Bill	10	10	10	10	10						
11	Computer time									2	10	10
12	**Research Inc.**									31❸125	125	
13	Terri											
14	**Design staff**	66	66	66	66	66						
15	Documentation dept											
16	Testing staff								66	66	66	66
17	Marilynn											
18	Nancy											
19	Production team											
20	Jeff											
21	Karen											
22	Sales engineers											
23	Rick											
24	Bob											

The percentage allocated to each resource during the period on the timescale is indicated in each box ❶.

A percentage less than 100 ❷ indicates the resource is underallocated during the period on the timescale.

A percentage greater than 100 ❸ indicates the resource is overallocated during the period on the timescale.

Changing the Timescale

You can change the timescale so the usage boxes cover as much or as little time as you want. Choose the Format Timescale command to change the major timescale (the upper dates) or the minor timescale (the lower units). You can also double-click the timescale with the mouse to choose the Format Timescale command.

Using the keyboard, press Ctrl+* (asterisk on the keypad) to show a larger time unit on the timescale, or press Ctrl+/ (slash on the keypad) to show a smaller time unit on the timescale.

Changing Work Units

Initially, the units on the Resource Usage view are hours. You can change these units to minutes, days, or weeks by changing the Default Work Units in the Options Preferences dialog box. To do this, choose Options Preferences. Select Default Work Units, select the units you want, and then press Enter or click the Enter box (☑).

Checking Resource Task Assignments

On the Resource Form, you can see the list of tasks to which each resource is assigned. This will help you decide how to change assignments for tasks with overallocated resources and where you might be able to find additional resources to work on tasks you want to accelerate.

Choose View Resource Form and then Format Schedule.

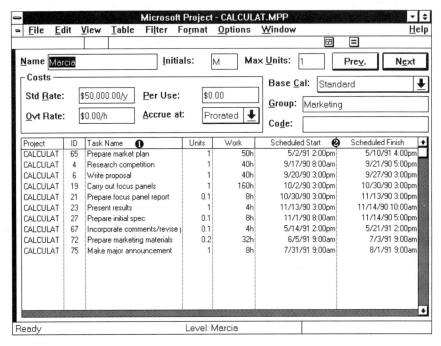

The list of tasks to which this resource is assigned shows in the schedule fields at the bottom of the form ❶.

You can check the dates the resource is schedule to start and finish work on each task ❷.

Checking the Usage Graph for One Resource

The Resource Histogram shows a graph of the peak use of one resource at a time. This is the peak use that occurs at one moment during the period indicated on the timescale. For example, in the following illustration, five units of Marketing staff are assigned to work on Tuesday through Thursday. They may not all be assigned to full-day tasks each day, but during some part of those three days, five Marketing staff are needed.

To see the Resource Histogram, choose View Resource Histogram.

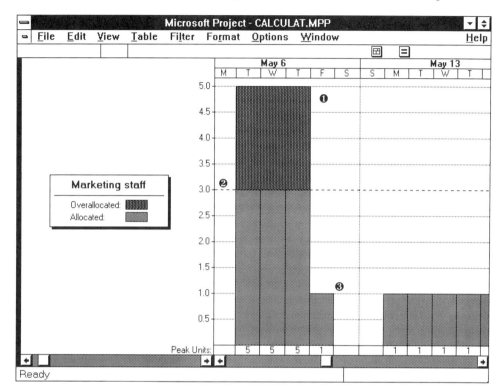

Marketing staff is overallocated during these three days ❶.

The capacity line at three units ❷ shows that a maximum of three Marketing staff are available at one time.

Marketing staff is underallocated during the rest of the time on the histogram ❸.

To see more or less detail, change the timescale.

Use the Resource Histogram to help decide how to move tasks around so resources are not overallocated. By combining this view with another view, such as the Gantt Chart, you see the tasks causing the overallocation as well as the period during which a resource is overallocated.

Checking Costs

To look at costs for each task, apply the Cost table to the Task Sheet. Choose View Task Sheet and then Table Cost (see the illustration on the following page).

—			Microsoft Project - CALCULAT.MPP					▼ ◆
▫	**File** **Edit** **View** **Table** **Filter** **Format** **Options** **Window**							**Help**
			Investigation phase				⊞ ⑤ ☰	← → + − AL
ID	Name		Cost	Planned Cost	Variance	Actual Cost	Rem. Cost	◆
1	Investigation phase		$26,137.31	$0.00	$26,137.31	$0.00	$26,137.31	
2	Investigation begins		$0.00	$0.00	$0.00	$0.00	$0.00	
3	Prepare initial product proposal		$6,338.46	$0.00	$6,338.46	$0.00	$6,338.46	
4	Research competition		$2,807.69	$0.00	$2,807.69	$0.00	$2,807.69	
5	Review customer comment cards		$1,655.77	$0.00	$1,655.77	$0.00	$1,655.77	
6	Write proposal		$1,875.00	$0.00	$1,875.00	$0.00	$1,875.00	
7	Plan focus panel		$246.16	$0.00	$246.16	$0.00	$246.16	
8	Arrange sites		$123.08	$0.00	$123.08	$0.00	$123.08	
9	Contact hotels		$61.54	$0.00	$61.54	$0.00	$61.54	
10	Arrange for equipment		$61.54	$0.00	$61.54	$0.00	$61.54	
11	Determine needed equipment		$61.54	$0.00	$61.54	$0.00	$61.54	
12	Contact local offices		$0.00	$0.00	$0.00	$0.00	$0.00	
13	Get panel members		$123.08	$0.00	$123.08	$0.00	$123.08	
14	Contact local reps for names		$123.08	$0.00	$123.08	$0.00	$123.08	
15	Contact suggested panel member		$0.00	$0.00	$0.00	$0.00	$0.00	
16	Plan phone questionnaire		$346.15	$0.00	$346.15	$0.00	$346.15	
17	Prepare questionnaire		$346.15	$0.00	$346.15	$0.00	$346.15	
18	Get list of users to call		$0.00	$0.00	$0.00	$0.00	$0.00	
19	Carry out focus panels		$13,538.46	$0.00	$13,538.46	$0.00	$13,538.46	
20	Carry out phone survey		$2,745.00	$0.00	$2,745.00	$0.00	$2,745.00	
21	Prepare focus panel report		$1,576.93	$0.00	$1,576.93	$0.00	$1,576.93	
22	Prepare phone survey report		$1,250.00	$0.00	$1,250.00	$0.00	$1,250.00	
23	Present results		$96.15	$0.00	$96.15	$0.00	$96.15	
24	Investigation phase complete		$0.00	$0.00	$0.00	$0.00	$0.00	
25	Design phase		$25,355.55	$0.00	$25,355.55	$0.00	$25,355.55	◆
←								→ □
Ready			Level: Marcia					

The Cost table shows the cost of each task.

There are no values in the Planned Cost fields yet because you have not saved the baseline schedule. When you save the baseline schedule, the values in the Cost fields are copied into the Planned Cost fields. There are no values in the Actual Cost fields yet because you have not incurred any costs. When you enter information about progress on tasks, Microsoft Project calculates actual costs based on the work performed on each task.

To look at the individual resource costs that make up the task cost, use a combination view with the Task Sheet on top and, on the bottom, the Task Form showing resource cost fields (choose Format Resource Cost).

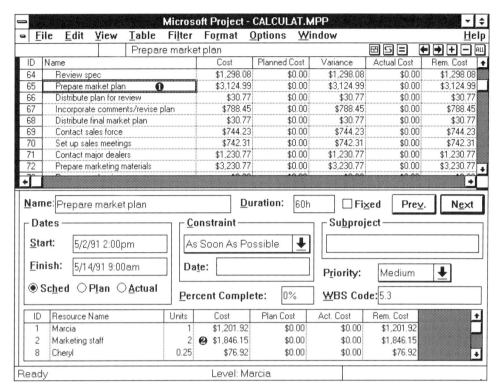

Select the task whose costs you are interested in ❶.

The resource cost fields at the bottom of the Task Form ❷ *show the cost of using each resource on the selected task.*

The next chapter shows you how to take what you learned as you evaluated your schedule and use it to refine the schedule until it fits your needs.

CHAPTER 9

Refining the Schedule and Freezing the Baseline

In the last chapter, you identified areas in the schedule that need adjusting—critical tasks that need to be shortened, resources that are overallocated, and so on. Your goal now is to adjust the schedule until it is satisfactory.

This step may take some time and several passes until you determine the best schedule for the situation. This exercise will help you understand your project and the schedule, and be conscious of the compromises you are making to meet your goals.

When the schedule meets your needs, you save or "freeze" this schedule as your plan, or baseline. By freezing the baseline, you have a record of your original schedule information. Later, when the project is underway, you can compare progress to this baseline.

REFINING THE SCHEDULE

When you evaluated your schedule, you probably found areas that could be improved. Now, you need to try out possible solutions to the scheduling problems. One of the major advantages of using project management software is that you can try a solution—for example, add resources to a critical task and then look at the impact on the project in terms of time, cost, and resource usage. If the first solution you try does not work, you can continue experimenting until you come up with the best solution for this project. This is often called "what-if" analysis. For instance, what if you added resources to a task on the critical path. How would this shorten the critical path and how would it change the project and task costs?

The following lists offer some ideas for shortening the project, reducing cost, and resolving resource conflicts.

If the project finish date is too late, look for ways to shorten the critical path. You could:

- Add resources to critical tasks to shorten their duration, either by hiring new resources or by shifting resources to critical tasks from tasks with slack.

- Work overtime on critical tasks or add another shift.

- Change task sequence, add lead or lag time, or remove unnecessary constraints.

- Change the scope of tasks in the project if the finish date is a higher priority than the scope. For example, if a manual must be ready to ship by the time the software is ready, and writing the manual is a critical task causing the manual to be ready after the software, you could reduce the pages in the manual to a number you can write in the shorter time allowed.

- Reduce the scope of the project so you can delete some of the tasks. For example, suppose you have a list of features you want to add to a new calculator product, and your goal is to introduce the new product in time for the biggest sales period of the year. Lacking time to implement all the new features and make the target date, you could reduce the scope by cutting features until you feel confident you can introduce the new product on time.

If the costs are too high, you could:

- Assign the most costly resources to fewer tasks and replace them with less costly resources.

- Get additional bids for tasks performed for a contracted rate by an outside contractor.

- For resources that have a per-use charge, move tasks around so you can perform all tasks using that resource at once. For example, if you need a crane to do work on a building and also to hang a sign, consider installing the sign when you have the crane on site to do the other work, even though the "Hang sign" task doesn't have to be done until later in the project.

- Reduce task or project scope so you need fewer resources to complete the tasks in the project. For example, if your budget for designing the new calculator is less than the cost indicated in the current schedule, you can cut features so the design phase will take less time, and therefore fewer resources and less money to complete.

If there are conflicts for the resources, you could:

- Shift tasks to level out resource usage.
- Shift underallocated resources to tasks whose resources are overallocated.
- Hire additional resources.
- Work longer hours or additional shifts.
- Break tasks into smaller tasks to give you more flexibility in scheduling resources.

Be sure you involve the project team in any major changes you propose to the schedule. You want everyone to know about, be involved in deciding on, and approve of any change that affects their area.

FREEZING THE SCHEDULE

When you are satisfied with the schedule, you save, or freeze, this schedule so you can use it for tracking progress after the project is under way. This original schedule is called the baseline. The baseline schedule is a record of the original task dates, and resource and cost information. You can track and control your project only if you have the original schedule to compare what actually happens against what you planned for the project.

USING MICROSOFT PROJECT FOR WINDOWS

At this stage of the planning process, you use Microsoft Project for Windows to experiment with adjustments to the schedule. You add resources, change work, adjust calendars, and so on, entering the new information in the same way you entered the original information into Microsoft Project.

Each time you change the schedule, check the Options Project Info dialog box to see how the changes affect the project finish date and project costs. Check the schedule as you did in Chapter 8 to review the critical path, slack time, dependencies, constraints, resources, and costs. If you don't like the change, you can undo it and try something else.

If you are not making the final decisions, but are providing information to others, you can keep track of the most likely alternatives and then share these options. This gives management the data to make an informed decision about how the project should be carried out. For example, if your project is over budget, you can present two options: one showing the cost and schedule for implementing the full scope, and a second showing what would have to be cut to meet the original budget.

When you finish adjusting the schedule, use the Options Set Plan command to save the baseline. If you are waiting for a decision from management or a client about which schedule alternative is acceptable, save the baseline after you have that decision and have made the schedule match it. Just make sure to save the baseline before the project gets underway and before you begin entering progress information.

Experimenting with the Schedule

As you experiment with your schedule, Microsoft Project for Windows helps you decide which changes best fit your needs. Microsoft Project calculates the new schedule and costs; you decide if the change is for the better. For example, if you add resources to a task to speed it up, you can compare the shorter time with the higher cost and decide if this is a compromise you want to make. By trying different solutions, you can see how the schedule is affected by each solution and how the costs change, until you find the best compromise between time and cost.

The following tables list ideas for experimenting with the schedule, how you do it in Microsoft Project, and the possible effects on the schedule.

TO DECREASE PROJECT DURATION

Option	In Microsoft Project, Use	Effect on Schedule
Add resources to critical tasks to shorten their duration or shift resources from noncritical tasks to critical tasks	Task Form, resources fields; Task Sheet or Gantt Chart, Resources field	May decrease task duration if the task uses resource-driven scheduling; may increase duration of tasks that lose resources
Add overtime work for the resources with the latest finish date on critical tasks	Task Form, Ovt. Work field (Format Resource Work); Resource Form, Ovt. Work field (Format Work)	Decrease task duration if the task uses resource-driven scheduling
Change the project calendar or resource calendars to increase working hours or add additional shifts	Options Base Calendars; Options Resource Calendar	Decrease duration of project because scheduled finish dates for tasks will be sooner
Change the order of tasks, add lead or lag time, or remove unnecessary constraints	Task Form, predecessors fields; Task Sheet or Gantt Chart, Predecessors field	Lead and lag time can decrease project duration by overlapping tasks; constraints can reduce scheduling flexibility
Reduce the scope of critical tasks	Task Entry view, Duration field	Decrease duration of tasks to reflect the decrease in scope
Reduce the scope of the project	Task Sheet; Gantt Chart	Decrease project duration by deleting the tasks that are no longer included in the scope

TO REDUCE COSTS

Option	In Microsoft Project, Use	Lowers Costs If
Replace costly resources with less costly ones	Task Entry view, resources fields	The less costly resources do not cause work to increase such that task cost is not decreased
Get additional bids for flat rate tasks	Task Sheet with Cost table applied	New bids are lower
Reduce per-use charge by changing task sequence such that tasks using certain resources can be completed simultaneously	Task Entry view, predecessors fields; Resource Form to change per-use rate	You have fewer per-use charges
Reduce task or project scope	Task Entry view to delete tasks or change resources on tasks with reduced scope	You need fewer resources for the reduced scope

TO RESOLVE RESOURCE CONFLICTS

Option	In Microsoft Project, Use	Effect on Schedule
Shift underallocated resources to tasks whose resources are overallocated	Gantt Chart or Task Sheet over Resource Usage view showing percentages	On resource-driven tasks, may decrease duration of tasks that get additional resources; may increase duration of tasks that lose resources
Hire additional resources	Task Form, resources fields; Task Sheet or Gantt Chart, Resources field; Edit Form dialog box for resources to change Max Units	On resource-driven tasks, may decrease duration of tasks that get additional resources; will increase cost
Add overtime work for overallocated resources	Task Form, Ovt. Work field (Format Resource Work) Resource Form, Ovt. Work field (Format Work)	Decrease task duration if the task uses resource-driven scheduling
Work longer hours or additional shifts	Options Base Calendars; Options Resource Calendar	On resource-driven tasks, may make tasks that get additional resources finish sooner
Break tasks into smaller tasks to change the order of parts of tasks to use resources better	Task Sheet; Gantt Chart	May resolve over-allocations by shifting parts of tasks to times when resources are available
Shift tasks to level out resource usage	Gantt Chart over Resource Usage view	May change project duration

To help you decide which schedule changes are best, look at the Options Project Info dialog box to check the effect the change has on the project finish date and project cost.

| Project Information for: CALCULAT.MPP | | OK | Cancel |

Project: New calculator

Company: Compusystems

Manager: Marcia Cryer

Calendar: Standard

Dates

Start: 9/17/90 8:00am

Finish: 8/29/91 9:00am ❶

Current: 8/24/90 8:00am

Schedule from: ◉ Start ○ Finish

Totals:

		Scheduled	Planned	Actual	Remaining
Cost	❷	$84,540.94	$0.00	$0.00	$84,540.94
Work		5320h	0h	0h	5320h

Notes:

Goal: New, improved calculator ready for next back-to-school promotion.
Scope: Do add the most-requested features, fix bugs in existing code, and
          update manual to include new features.
          Do not redo all code, change packaging, or rewrite entire manual.
Assumptions: Technology is available to implement features; programmers will
          be available to do the work; existing packaging will work.

Check for changes in the finish date here ❶.
Check for changes in the cost here ❷.

Decreasing Project Duration

There are several approaches you can use to shorten a project and change the project finish date, from adding resources to changing the scope of the project or tasks in the project. Naturally, when you are trying to finish a project sooner, the tasks of interest to you are those on the critical path. Adding resources to noncritical tasks or changing the scope of noncritical tasks won't decrease project duration. Use one or several of the approaches, depending on how radical a change you need to make and what other constraints you have, such as the budget and limited resources.

The time you save on a critical task may not be reflected in the project duration. For example, suppose you add resources to accelerate a critical task, which changes its duration from three weeks to two and makes it noncritical; another task that was previously noncritical may now become critical, resulting in, perhaps, a savings of only two days in the project duration. Or if your project has more than one critical path, you'll need to shorten critical tasks on all critical paths, not on just one.

Assigning More Resources

One way to complete critical tasks faster is to assign more resources—if the tasks use resource-driven scheduling. You can move the resources from other projects, from other tasks—tasks with slack, for example—or hire additional resources. Adding resources to a task using fixed-duration scheduling won't change task duration.

For task duration to decrease, you must increase resource units for the resource whose scheduled finish date is the latest on the task. For example, in the following illustration, the Marketing staff is scheduled to finish the "Prepare marketing plan" last, on 5/14.

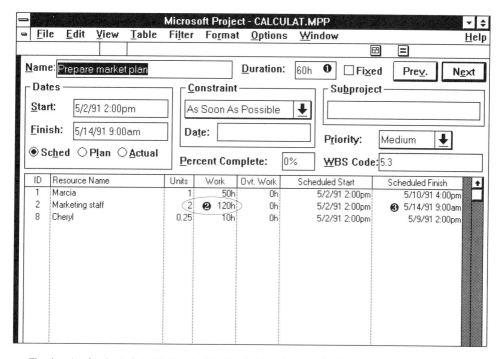

The duration for the task is 60h ❶, calculated by dividing the work for the Marketing staff (120h) by 2 Marketing staff units ❷.

The Marketing staff is scheduled to finish last on the task so this is the resource to which you add units ❸.

To decrease task duration, you must add additional Marketing staff units. If you add one unit, for a total of three, the finish date for the resource changes to 5/9, 2:00 p.m. The duration for the task changes to 50 hours, however, because Marcia's finish date is now the latest on the task, driving the task duration.

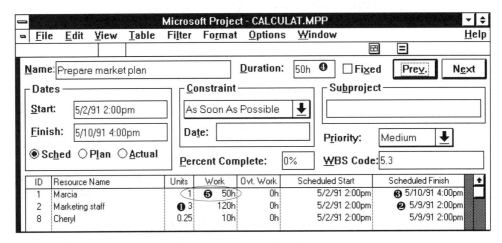

Add one unit to Marketing staff, for a total of three ❶.
The finish date for Marketing staff on the task changes to 5/9/91 ❷.
Marcia now drives the duration for the task because her finish date is the latest ❸.
The new duration for the task is 50h ❹, calculated by dividing the work for Marcia (50h) by one unit ❺.

If you are using resource-driven scheduling, Microsoft Project will calculate a new finish date and duration for the task. Enter the new resources just as you entered the original resources. Either increase the units or add new resource names, as appropriate.

If you add new resource names instead of changing units, however, you must change the work for the existing resources to make the task duration decrease. For example, suppose you add a new resource, Jane, to help Marcia. Jane will do 20 hours of Marcia's work. But Microsoft Project has no way of knowing that Jane is doing Marcia's work, so you must change Marcia's work to 30 hours.

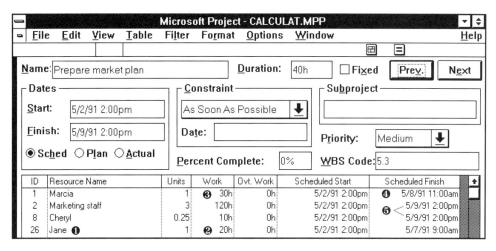

Add the resource Jane ❶, with 20 hours of work ❷.

Reduce Marcia's hours by 20 hours ❸ since Jane is completing 20 hours of Marcia's work.

The finish date for Marcia is now earlier ❹.

Both the Marketing staff and Cheryl are the driving resources now because they both finish last on the task ❺.

If you have not used Microsoft Project to enter and assign resources to the tasks in your project, you have to determine how the task will be shortened if you add additional resources. It's up to you to make assumptions about the working speed of the resources, and then estimate a new duration for the task. Enter the new duration just as you entered the original duration—in the Duration field on the Gantt Chart or Task Sheet, or in the Duration box on the Task Form.

Working Longer Hours on Resource-driven Tasks

If certain resources are in short supply, you can specify longer work hours for a resource. Longer hours can be specified in two ways:

- If you want a resource to work extra time on a specific task at an overtime rate, you indicate overtime work for the task in the Ovt. Work field on the Task Form or Resource Form.

- If you want a resource to work longer hours on all tasks during a certain period at a standard rate, you extend the working hours on its resource calendar.

If you are using resource-driven scheduling, Microsoft Project recalculates the finish date for a resource when you add overtime work or lengthen the working hours.

The resource with the latest scheduled finish date on the task is the one that must work longer hours. Otherwise, task duration does not decrease.

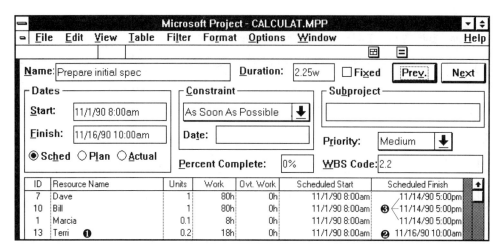

Change the working hours for this resource ❶ because this resource is scheduled to finish last on the task ❷.

Adding longer hours for these resources ❸ will not decrease task duration nor change the scheduled finish date for the task.

ADDING OVERTIME WORK

If you want to add overtime work on a specific task or tasks, and you want this overtime work to be paid for at the overtime rate, enter the additional hours in the Ovt. Work field on the Task Form or Resource Form. You enter an overtime rate of pay on the Resource Form, Resource Sheet, or the Edit Form dialog box for resources.

When you enter overtime work, Microsoft Project subtracts the value in the Ovt. Work field from the value in the Work field, before calculating duration:

$$duration = (work - ovt.\ work) / units$$

If this resource is the one scheduled to finish last on the task and is thus the resource driving the duration on the task, adding overtime work reduces the amount of work, and thus the duration. Do not change the calendar for this resource to reflect the extra time.

To enter overtime work on the Task Form, choose Format Resource Schedule or Format Resource Work.

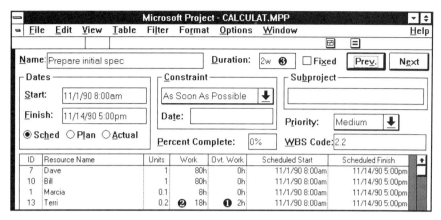

Type the amount of overtime work in this field ❶.

The value in the Ovt. Work field ❶ is subtracted from the value in the Work field ❷ before duration is calculated.

Duration is now two weeks ❸.

To add a rate for overtime work, select the resource, and then choose Edit Form or click the form icon (⊞).

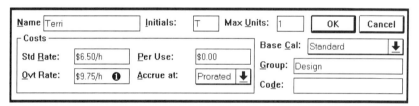

Type the rate in the Ovt Rate field ❶.

To enter overtime work on the Resource Form, choose Format Work.

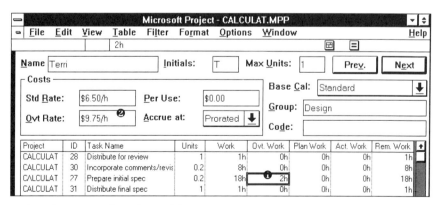

Type the amount of overtime work here ❶.

Type the overtime rate here ❷.

CHANGING THE CALENDAR

If you want to add longer hours for one or more resources for certain periods during a project, or for the whole project, you can change the work hours and days for those resources on their resource calendars. You can also change the working days and hours on the project calendar to increase working time for all resources. If this is a feasible solution for your resources and you are using resource-driven scheduling, the tasks will be completed in a shorter time.

When you lengthen working hours, these additional hours are paid at the standard rate, not the overtime rate. If you want the hours billed at the overtime rate, you must enter the time as overtime work on individual tasks.

To change a resource calendar, select the resource whose calendar you want to change. Then choose Options Resource Calendar.

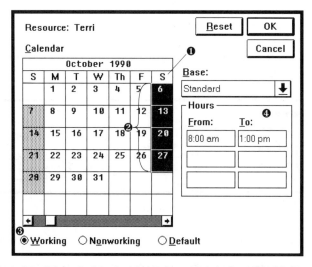

To add Saturday work for the length of the project, select the Saturday title ❶.

If you want to work Saturdays for a limited time, select all Saturdays that you want to work ❷ instead of selecting the Saturday title.

To change the Saturdays to working days, select Working ❸.

If the hours will be different on Saturday, type the hours here ❹.

If you want to lengthen the working hours for weekdays, select the day titles and then type the new working hours under Hours. To lengthen working hours for certain days, just select the days. Tasks that this resource is assigned to during the period with longer working hours will finish sooner, if the resource was the driving resource scheduled to finish last on the task.

Check the task finish date on the Task Form to see the change. Even though the finish dates for tasks using this resource may be earlier than the original finish date, the duration shown in the Duration box won't change because of how duration is calculated. Duration is always calculated by dividing the work by the units, and work hasn't changed.

Adding Another Shift

Another way to decrease project duration is to add another shift of resources to critical tasks. For example, if you have additional resources you can assign to tasks, but don't have the equipment for all resources to use at once, you can add another shift. To add another shift, you do three things:

- Assign this new shift to the tasks on the Task Entry view or Task Sheet. For example, on the "Set up production test" task, you might have assigned "Production team." Now you want to finish this task faster, so you decide to add the Production team swing shift. In the Resource Name field on the Task Form, type "Production team-- swing".

- Reduce the work for the existing resources to reflect the amount of work to be done by the new resources. For example, reduce the work for the Production team day shift by the amount of work that will be done by the swing shift.

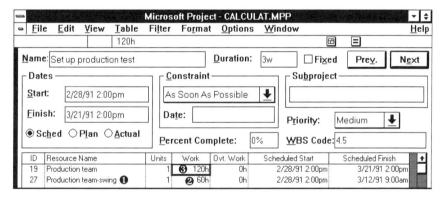

Type the new resource name ❶ and work ❷.

Because the existing resource now has to do only half the work on the task, change the work for the existing resource from 120h to 60h ❸.

- Change the resource calendar for Production team-swing to reflect the night hours.

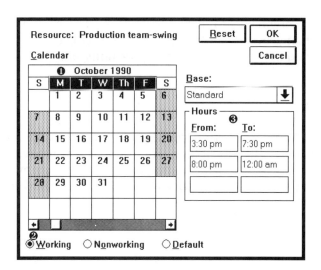

Select the working days ❶.
Select Working ❷.
Type the hours this shift will work ❸.

If you have many resources that work shifts, create a base calendar for each shift. Then select the appropriate base calendar for each resource as you add new resources to the resource pool or assign new resources to tasks. You can specify a base calendar on the Resource Form or in the Edit Form dialog box for resources. For example, suppose you have resources working three shifts—day, swing, and graveyard—and you have created a base calendar for each shift reflecting their working hours. Make sure you select the appropriate base calendar for each new resource so it will have the correct working hours in its resource calendar. For more information, see Chapter 16, "Using Microsoft Project Tools."

Indicating Hours When Your Shift Works Overnight

When a shift works day hours, such as 8 to 5, every day has the same hours. When a shift works overnight, however, the hours on the first day and the last day are different from the rest of the work days. For example, if the work hours are 6 p.m. to 6 a.m., Sunday through Thursday, you enter the information as follows:

- Select Sundays. Under Hours, type "6:00 pm" to "12:00 am"

- Select Monday, Tuesday, and Wednesday. Under Hours, type "12:00 am" to "6:00 am", and "6:00 pm" to "12:00 am"

- Select Thursdays. Under Hours, type "12:00 am" to "6:00 am"

Changing Task Dependencies

One way to bring in the finish date is to overlap the tasks on the critical path and to find critical tasks that can be performed earlier in the schedule, perhaps simultaneously with other critical tasks. Be creative. For example, while you can't review a market plan before it is written, perhaps you can have the first part reviewed while the second part is being written. By having the review cycle start after half the writing task is complete, you can perhaps cut time off the project duration.

To change the task dependencies, use the Task Entry view. You can change the task predecessors, change the relationship between tasks, and add lead or lag time. Use the same procedures as those you used when entering the values originally. For more information, see Chapter 6, "Making Tasks Happen at the Right Time."

Think carefully about all constraints and look for Must Start On or Must Finish On constraints to eliminate. When you use a "must" date, it limits the flexibility of the schedule since Microsoft Project must use these dates instead of the dates it calculates.

Make sure you mean to have the constraints that are there. It's easy to accidently enter a "must" constraint by changing the start date of a task on the Gantt Chart with the mouse. A "must" constraint is also entered whenever you type a scheduled start date for a task. If you discover a constraint that you don't need, change the constraint in the Constraint box on the Task Form.

Decreasing Task Scope

By decreasing the scope of a critical task, you can shorten its duration, and reduce the duration of the project by at least a portion of the reduction on the task. For example, suppose in your investigation phase for a new product, you planned to spend five weeks studying five competitors' products. When you see the schedule, however, you realize that this task is on the critical path; since the schedule needs to be shortened, perhaps you can be less thorough than originally planned. You may decide not to study two of the products at all because their market share is so small, thus saving up to two weeks on the task. Or you may decide to do an abbreviated study on these two products, perhaps half a week each, thus saving up to one week on the task. Whatever you decide about changing the scope of the task, be sure every one involved understands the new scope and its affect on the project overall.

Once you have decided what the new scope is, determine the new duration with help from the project team. Enter the new duration on the Task Entry view.

Changing Project Scope

If you decide that a project must be finished by a certain date, no matter what, you may have to reduce the scope of the project as a whole to make this date. This decision must be made with the support of the project team, your client, and management. You can generate a series of options and their finish dates to help others decide the best compromise.

For example, on the new calculator project, if you cut features A, B, and C, you may save three weeks; if you cut four other features, you may save two weeks. How do you decide which group of features to cut and what the time savings will be? You can generate a list of all the features in order of importance, along with the duration of the task to implement each feature. Use a custom field to enter an "importance" ranking for each feature, and then sort on this custom field so the most important features are at the top of the list. If you know how much time you need to save, you can use this list to determine which features to cut.

Be sure you get the agreement of the project team and management that decreasing scope is an acceptable solution. You can prepare a presentation showing the schedule with the full scope—too long and too costly, based on the original goals—and the schedule with the new scope, to show management or a client the effect of changing scope. This will give them the data they need to choose between the greater scope, later date, and higher cost, or the more limited scope, shorter time, and lower cost.

In Microsoft Project, you indicate a change in project scope by deleting tasks that will no longer be performed. You can do this on the Task Entry view or Task Sheet. After you delete tasks, review the dependencies on the remaining tasks to make sure they are correct.

Reducing Costs

You can use several approaches to reduce costs, from changing the resources assigned to tasks to decreasing the scope of the project or tasks. Use one or a combination of approaches, depending on how much you need to cut and how critical the budget is. If the budget is more important on this project than other factors, you may decide to cut the scope or allow the project to finish later than originally planned, to keep costs in line.

Changing Resource Assignments

While resources may not be interchangeable, there may be ways to use a less costly resource on a task. For example, perhaps you can assign apprentice-level workers to certain tasks currently assigned to more skilled workers. Be sure to reconsider duration, however, because the less-skilled resources may take longer to perform the task.

To change resources, use the Task Entry view or the Task Sheet. If the task uses resource-driven scheduling, be sure to change the work for the resource if you expect it to be different than originally planned.

Changing Task Cost

Usually, Microsoft Project calculates task costs for you, based on the cost of the resources assigned. Until a task is complete, you can enter the cost for a task only when you have assigned no resources to the task. To change cost for an unfinished task that has resources assigned, use the other methods in this section; to change cost for a task that has no re-sources assigned—perhaps because the task is being performed by an outside contractor—try getting additional bids for the task. For example, if you are planning to hire an outside research firm to conduct a phone survey of your customers, you can request bids from other companies to find a lower bid.

Change a cost for a task on the Task Sheet, with the Cost table applied. Choose View Task Sheet, and then Table Cost.

ID	Name	Cost	Planned Cost	Variance	Actual Cost	Rem. Cost
17	Prepare questionnaire	$0.00	$0.00	$0.00	$0.00	$0.00
18	Get list of users to call	$0.00	$0.00	$0.00	$0.00	$0.00
19	Carry out focus panels	$5,076.93	$0.00	$5,076.93	$0.00	$5,076.93
20	Carry out phone survey	9000 ❶	$0.00	$10,000.00	$0.00	$10,000.00
21	Prepare focus panel report	$0.00	$0.00	$0.00	$0.00	$0.00
22	Prepare phone survey repo	$0.00	$0.00	$0.00	$0.00	$0.00
23	Present results	$0.00	$0.00	$0.00	$0.00	$0.00
24	Investigation phase comple	$0.00	$0.00	$0.00	$0.00	$0.00

Select the Cost field for the task whose cost you want to change ❶. Type the new cost.

Remember, if you change the cost of a task with assigned resources and the task is not a completed task, Microsoft Project replaces the cost you entered with the cost it calculates.

Changing Task Relationships to Reduce Per-Use Cost

You may have some resources in your project for which you pay a fee for every use, in addition to an hourly rate. If you use the resource at different times during the project, you'll have to pay this per-use fee for every task using the resource. See if any of the tasks can be performed at the same time to avoid paying this per-use fee repeatedly.

One way to do this is to put either a start-to-start relationship or a finish-to-finish relationship between the two tasks so they will be scheduled simultaneously. If one of the tasks is moved earlier or later in the project, be sure to remove the original predecessors and successors that are no longer appropriate so you don't force later parts of the schedule to occur out of order.

For example, suppose the "Hang sign" task requires a crane and was scheduled at the end of the project, with "Final site cleanup" task as its successor. When you move the sign task to be concurrent with the building tasks that also use the crane, you do not want the cleanup task to be moved up in the schedule too. Delete the relationship between the two tasks, and link the cleanup task to the original predecessor of the sign task.

To prevent Microsoft Project from charging the per-use fee every time it finds the resource assigned to a task, do one of the following:

- Divide the per-use fee by the number of tasks using the resource, and enter this value as the per-use fee. For example, if you plan to use a resource, such as a crane, on three tasks during the project, but have arranged the schedule such that all three tasks occur at the same time, you will, in reality, incur only one per-use fee rather than three. The per-use charge you enter into Microsoft Project for the resource would be one-third of the actual per-use charge because the charge is divided among the three tasks. Use this method when you are able to complete at the same time all tasks to which the resource is assigned.

- Name the resource in two ways and include a per-use fee on one and not on the other. For each group of tasks that use the resource and will be performed simultaneously, assign the resource with the per-use fee to one of the tasks and the resource without the per-use fee to the rest of the tasks. For example, you could have Crane1 with the per-use fee and Crane2 without. If you have three tasks using the crane at the same time, assign Crane1 to one of the tasks and Crane2 to the other two. If, later in the schedule, you have four tasks occurring simultaneous and using the crane, assign Crane1 to one task, and Crane2 to the other three. Use this method when you cannot complete at the same time all tasks that use the resource.

Enter the per-use fee in the Per Use box on the Resource Form or Edit Form dialog box for resources.

Microsoft Project - Project1	▼ ‖ ♦

□ **<u>F</u>ile <u>E</u>dit <u>V</u>iew <u>T</u>able Fi<u>l</u>ter Fo<u>r</u>mat <u>O</u>ptions <u>W</u>indow** **<u>H</u>elp**

⊞   ▣

<u>N</u>ame `Crane` **Initials:** `C` **Max <u>U</u>nits:** `1` **OK** **Cancel**

┌─ **Costs** ──────────────────────────────

Std <u>R</u>ate: `$100.00/h` **<u>P</u>er Use:** `$500` ❶

O<u>v</u>t Rate: `$0.00/h` **<u>A</u>ccrue at:** `Prorated ↓`

Base <u>C</u>al: `Standard` ↓

<u>G</u>roup:

Co<u>d</u>e:

Type the per-use fee in the Per Use box ❶.

Decreasing Scope to Lower Cost

Just as you can reduce scope to shorten project duration, you can reduce scope to lower costs. If cost is the most important factor on this project, use trial and error to decide how much of the project you must cut to meet the cost limits.

Since cost is almost always reduced when work is reduced, you know you can lower costs by reducing work. You can either cut the scope of the project by deleting tasks or cut the scope of some of the tasks in the project. For example, if you are preparing a marketing brochure, you may decide to lower costs by reducing the size of the brochure and using two colors instead of four. When you cut tasks, delete them on the Task Entry view or Task Sheet. If you change the scope of tasks, change the work and/or duration for the tasks to reflect their new scope.

Resolving Resource Conflicts

There are several ways to resolve resource conflicts, such as leveling resources by moving tasks, moving underallocated resources to tasks needing additional resources, or working longer hours. Again, use the approach or approaches that fit your needs for this project. For example, if the project finish date is more important than cost, you may be able to hire many additional resources to complete the tasks that have overallocated resources assigned. Or perhaps you have no need for additional resources after this project; in this case, it would be more appropriate for resources to work longer hours. The best solution depends on the time and budget parameters for the project.

Leveling Resources

When you assigned resources to tasks, you might have seen a message at the bottom of the screen that a resource needed to be leveled. And when you checked for tasks with overallocated resources in Chapter 8, you probably found several. You may have one resource used on several tasks that occur at the same time (overallocated); this same resource may be working at only 20 percent capacity later in the project (underallocated). In the best interests of the project and the resources, you want to use all resources as evenly as possible, with no one overworked and no one idle.

Microsoft Project shows you how your resources are used—where the peaks and valleys are—and helps you even out resource use. Once you have established that a resource is overallocated or underallocated, you can move tasks or resources around; or Microsoft Project can move tasks around for you. This is called "resource leveling." The goal of leveling resources is to have resources available as needed for critical tasks.

HAVING MICROSOFT PROJECT LEVEL RESOURCES

Microsoft Project for Windows levels resources by moving tasks such that tasks requiring the same resources are no longer scheduled at the same time. It accomplishes this by delaying certain tasks so they start later than originally scheduled.

Initially, Microsoft Project levels resources only when you choose the Options Level Now command. You can control when it levels, how it delays tasks, and how it picks which tasks to delay by using the Options Leveling command.

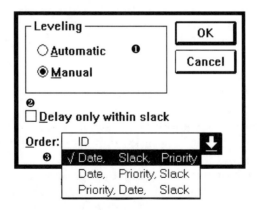

Specify when resources should be leveled here ❶—*automatically when a resource is overallocated or only when you say.*

If you want tasks to be delayed only within slack time, turn on this check box ❷.

Specify how the tasks should be leveled here ❸. *This tells Microsoft Project how to pick the tasks to delay.*

Options to Control Leveling	Description
Automatic	Select if you want Microsoft Project to level resources automatically any time it finds an overallocated resource.
Manual	Select if you want Microsoft Project to level resources only when you tell it to by choosing Options Level Now.
Delay Only Within Slack	This option tells Microsoft Project if it can slip the end date to level resources. Turn on this check box when the finish date must not be changed; turn off the check box when it is acceptable for the finish date to be slipped out.
Order	In this box, you select what Microsoft Project should look at first, second, and third when it levels the resources.
ID	The task with the higher ID is delayed.
Date, Slack, Priority	Microsoft Project delays the task with the later date, then with the greater slack, and then with the lower priority.
Date, Priority, Slack	Microsoft Project delays the task with the later date, then with the lower priority, and then with the greater slack.
Priority, Date, Slack	Microsoft Project delays the task with the lower priority, then the later date, and then the greater slack.

Priority is a task ranking you assign on the Task Form or Edit Form dialog box for tasks. There are five choices, from Lowest to Highest. Until you change the priority, Microsoft Project assigns Medium priority. Tasks with the priority of Highest will not be delayed. Use Priority to control leveling—if certain tasks must not be leveled, assign Highest to these tasks. To assign a certain priority to several tasks at once, select the tasks, choose Edit Form or click the form icon (🖿), select the priority you want in the Priority box, and then choose OK.

When Microsoft Project levels, it adds delay to tasks so that resources are available as needed on other tasks. You can see the delay by adding the Delay field to the Task Sheet.

ID	Name	Duration	Delay		Scheduled Start	Scheduled Finish	Predecess	Resourc
2	Investigation begins	0d	0ed		9/17/90 8:00am	9/17/90 8:00am		
4	Research competition	1w	0ed		9/17/90 8:00am	9/21/90 5:00pm	2	Marcia,N
5	Review customer comment cards	3d	5ed	❷	9/24/90 8:00am	9/26/90 5:00pm		Marketir
6	Write proposal	1w	2ed		10/1/90 8:00am	10/5/90 5:00pm	4FS-25%,5	Marcia,ト
9	Contact hotels	1d	0ed		10/8/90 8:00am	10/8/90 5:00pm	6	Cheryl
11	Determine needed equipment	4h	0ed		10/8/90 8:00am	10/8/90 12:00pm	6	Marketir
12	Contact local offices	4h	0ed		10/8/90 1:00pm	10/8/90 5:00pm	11	
14	Contact local reps for names	1d	0ed		10/8/90 8:00am	10/8/90 5:00pm	6	Marketir
15	Contact suggested panel members	2d	0ed		10/9/90 8:00am	10/10/90 5:00pm	14	
17	Prepare questionnaire	3d	0ed		10/8/90 8:00am	10/10/90 5:00pm	6	Roberto
18	Get list of users to call	2h	0ed		10/10/90 3:00pm	10/10/90 5:00pm	17FF	
19	Carry out focus panels	4w	0ed		10/11/90 8:00am	11/7/90 5:00pm	15	Marcia,N
20	Carry out phone survey	1w	28ed		11/8/90 8:00am	11/14/90 5:00pm	18	Researc
21	Prepare focus panel report	2w	0ed		11/8/90 8:00am	11/21/90 5:00pm	19	Marcia[C
22	Prepare phone survey report	0.5w	0ed		11/15/90 8:00am	11/19/90 12:00pm	20	Researc
23	Present results	4h	0ed		11/22/90 8:00am	11/22/90 12:00pm	21,22	Marcia
24	Investigation phase complete	0d	0ed		10/31/90 5:00pm	10/31/90 5:00pm	23	
26	Design begins	0d	0ed		10/31/90 5:00pm	10/31/90 5:00pm	24	
27	Prepare initial spec	2w	7ed		11/8/90 8:00am	11/21/90 5:00pm	26	Dave,Bi
28	Distribute for review	1h	0ed		11/22/90 8:00am	11/22/90 9:00am	27	Terri
29	Meet with reviewers	4h	0ed		11/29/90 8:00am	11/29/90 12:00pm	27FS+1w	Dave,Bi
30	Incorporate comments/revise spec	1w	0ed		11/29/90 1:00pm	12/6/90 12:00pm	29	Dave,Bi
31	Distribute final spec	1h	0ed		12/6/90 1:00pm	12/6/90 2:00pm	30	Terri
32	Fix old bugs	2w	0ed		9/17/90 8:00am	9/28/90 5:00pm		Bill[0.1],
34	Code clock feature	4w	0ed		12/6/90 2:00pm	1/3/91 2:00pm	31	Design

Add the Delay field ❶ to the Task Sheet using the Table Define Tables command.

The Delay field shows which tasks Microsoft Project has moved and by how much so that resources are available as needed ❷.

You can remove the delay Microsoft Project added by choosing the Options Remove Delay command. If you like some of the changes Microsoft Project made, but not others, select those tasks from which you want to remove the delay before you choose the command.

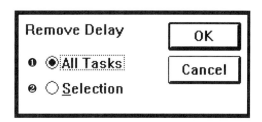

To remove all the delay added by Microsoft Project, and thus undo all the leveling, select the All Tasks option **❶**.

To remove delay from certain tasks, select the tasks before you choose the command, and then select the Selection option **❷**.

LEVELING RESOURCES YOURSELF

To level an overallocated resource yourself, you can:

- Move a task to which the overallocated resource is assigned elsewhere in the project. To move a task, change the predecessors and successors or add lead or lag time to the task so that the task occurs at a different time in the schedule.

- Add delay to the task such that it occurs when resources are available. To enter delay, add the Delay field to the Task Sheet. Type the amount of delay in elapsed minutes, hours, days, or weeks in the Delay field. If you don't want to change the project end date, be sure to add delay only to tasks with slack time; don't add more delay time than the task has slack time. Add the Slack column to the Task Sheet so you can see how much slack tasks have to help you decide which tasks to delay.

- Increase the duration of resource-driven tasks to which the overallocated resource is assigned by decreasing the percentage of time the resource spends on each task, leaving time for the resource to work on other tasks. To change the percentage of time a resource spends on a task, change the value in the Units field on the Task Form. For example, if you want an individual resource to work half-time on a task, change the value in the Units field from 1 to 0.5. On a resource-driven task that has one resource, the duration will double.

Assigning Additional Resources

If a task has overallocated resources assigned, you can hire additional resources, shift resources from other tasks, or add another shift. For more information, see "Assigning More Resources" and "Adding Another Shift" in "Decreasing Project Duration" earlier in this chapter.

Working Longer Hours

Another way to take care of overallocated resources is to have the resource work longer hours or work overtime. This is the same approach discussed earlier in this chapter. For more information, see "Working Longer Hours on Resource-driven Tasks" in "Decreasing Project Duration."

Breaking Tasks into Smaller Tasks to Shift Resources

If a task uses several different resources, you may find some resources are not available when the task is scheduled. One way around this is to break the task into smaller tasks such that resources are needed at different times instead of being scheduled all at once.

For example, if, on the "Prepare market plan" task, Cheryl, who is to type the plan, is not available to work on the task, you could break the task into "Write market plan" and "Type market plan." The typing task could then be scheduled when Cheryl is available, but the rest of the task, now "Write market plan," can occur as originally scheduled.

Freezing the Baseline Schedule

Once the schedule is acceptable, you want to save it so you'll have a baseline against which to compare progress as the project unfolds. To freeze the baseline schedule, you use the Options Set Plan command. This command copies the start and finish dates, work, cost, and durations into the Planned fields. The only way you can track your project is by saving this record of your original schedule.

Choose Options Set Plan.

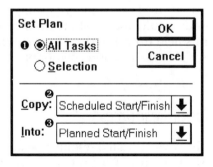

Select All Tasks ❶*.*
Copy the scheduled information ❷ *into the planned fields* ❸*.*

Saving Other Sets of Start and Finish Dates

In the Options Set Plan dialog box, you have a choice of the information you copy and a choice of the fields into which you copy the information. If you want to save another set of dates, such as at a milestone along the way, you can copy dates that you have entered in the Start1/Finish1, Start2/Finish2, or Start3/Finish3 custom fields. When you copy these other dates, only the start and finish dates are saved, not the cost and work information.

Once you have set the baseline, you can review all planned information by applying the Planned table to the Task Sheet.

Choose View Task Sheet. Choose Table Define Table, select Plan in the Tables box, and then press Enter or click the Set button.

ID	Name	Plan Dur.	Plan Start	Plan Finish	Plan Work	Plan Cost
1	Investigation phase	58.08ed	9/17/90 8:00am	11/14/90 10:00am	1156h	$26,137.31
2	Investigation begins	0d	9/17/90 8:00am	9/17/90 8:00am	0h	$0.00
3	Prepare initial product prop	10.29ed	9/17/90 8:00am	9/27/90 3:00pm	336h	$6,338.46
4	Research competition	1w	9/17/90 8:00am	9/21/90 5:00pm	160h	$2,807.69
5	Review customer comm	3d	9/17/90 8:00am	9/19/90 5:00pm	96h	$1,655.77
6	Write proposal	1w	9/20/90 3:00pm	9/27/90 3:00pm	80h	$1,875.00
7	Plan focus panel	5ed	9/27/90 3:00pm	10/2/90 3:00pm	20h	$246.16
8	Arrange sites	1ed	9/27/90 3:00pm	9/28/90 3:00pm	12h	$123.08
9	Contact hotels	1d	9/27/90 3:00pm	9/28/90 3:00pm	8h	$61.54
10	Arrange for equipmer	1ed	9/27/90 3:00pm	9/28/90 3:00pm	4h	$61.54
11	Determine needer	4h	9/27/90 3:00pm	9/28/90 10:00am	4h	$61.54
12	Contact local offic	4h	9/28/90 10:00am	9/28/90 3:00pm	0h	$0.00
13	Get panel members	5ed	9/27/90 3:00pm	10/2/90 3:00pm	8h	$123.08
14	Contact local reps for	1d	9/27/90 3:00pm	9/28/90 3:00pm	8h	$123.08
15	Contact suggested p	2d	9/28/90 3:00pm	10/2/90 3:00pm	0h	$0.00
16	Plan phone questionnaire	5ed	9/27/90 3:00pm	10/2/90 3:00pm	24h	$346.15
17	Prepare questionnaire	3d	9/27/90 3:00pm	10/2/90 3:00pm	24h	$346.15
18	Get list of users to call	2h	10/2/90 1:00pm	10/2/90 3:00pm	0h	$0.00
19	Carry out focus panels	4w	10/2/90 3:00pm	10/30/90 3:00pm	600h	$13,538.46
20	Carry out phone survey	1w	10/2/90 3:00pm	10/9/90 3:00pm	44h	$2,745.00
21	Prepare focus panel report	2w	10/30/90 3:00pm	11/13/90 3:00pm	108h	$1,576.93
22	Prepare phone survey repo	0.5w	10/9/90 3:00pm	10/12/90 10:00am	20h	$1,250.00
23	Present results	4h	11/13/90 3:00pm	11/14/90 10:00am	4h	$96.15
24	Investigation phase comple	0d	10/31/90 5:00pm	10/31/90 5:00pm	0h	$0.00
25	Design phase	143.04ed	9/17/90 8:00am	2/7/91 9:00am	1772h	$25,375.05

The Plan table shows the plan duration, the plan start and finish date for each task, the plan work, and the plan cost.

In the next chapter, you'll learn how to generate reports for your presentation of the project. Using Microsoft Project, you can create a variety of reports that show the schedule now, and how it can be changed, with costs and benefits of each possible schedule.

CHAPTER 10

Communicating the Plan

You and your planning team have spent a lot of time creating the perfect plan and schedule for this project. Now you are ready to share that plan. You want to show management or a client exactly how you will make this project happen. Or perhaps you want to get support from management for the project goals, timing, and expenditures. And you want everyone involved in executing the project tasks to know what is planned and what their involvement is.

At this stage, you report on the schedule, the planned resource use, and the projected costs. By sharing this information with all members of the team, you gain support for the project. Everyone feels a part of the team, sees the big picture, and knows at the outset what they are trying to accomplish and for whom and why.

DIFFERENT REPORTS FOR DIFFERENT PEOPLE

One big advantage of using project management software is that once you have entered all the project information, you can create many reports, each including only the information and detail appropriate for the recipients. For example, you can create summary level reports for management, projected cost reports for the accounting department, and individual task-level reports for each supervisor. Since all reports are based on the same core of information, it is easy and quick to give people what they need. You can be selective about the data in each report. Do not send all information to everyone. They may end up reading none of it, thus missing what is relevant to them.

At one extreme, you have the reports you prepare for top management in which you include more summary information than details. It is unnecessary, for example, to send top management the breakdown of every single task; they do not have time to review the plan at that level of detail. Send them a summary of major milestones, dates, and costs, plus the project goals.

At the other extreme are the reports you generate for the task supervisors, which contain maximum detail. Supervisors can use these to manage the actual work because all the tasks they are involved in are listed, with schedule information, resources used, and notes about each task.

Using Microsoft Project for Windows

Since Microsoft Project now contains all project information, you can generate any report appropriate for your audience. For example, if you have outlined your project, you can collapse the outline to only show top-level summary tasks, and then print the Gantt Chart to show when these major phases will occur. This, along with the Project Summary report showing project dates, costs, and other project-wide statistics, is a good report for management and others who do not want details. Or you can collapse the project, and then expand only those summary tasks relevant for each supervisor. All supervisors then have a picture of the whole, plus the details for their groups.

Basically, there are two ways to print information in Microsoft Project. You can print:

- Six of the views that come with Microsoft Project for Windows, plus views you create based on these six views. These views are the Gantt Chart, PERT Chart, Task Sheet, Resource Sheet, Resource Histogram, and Resource Usage view.

- Five reports that come with Microsoft Project, plus reports you create based on these reports. You print these reports by choosing the File Print Report command.

The following table lists common types of reports, and what you use to generate the report in Microsoft Project for Windows.

You use tables, filtering, and sorting to change the information in the views; you use the Format commands to change the way the information looks in the views. You have similar control over the information and the way the information looks in reports.

To Show	In Microsoft Project, Use
Summary of the project, including number of tasks and resources, costs, start and finish dates, and project notes	Project Summary report
Summary of major phases, with bar chart showing the start and finish dates	Gantt Chart, with outline collapsed
List of tasks and durations, plus bar chart of tasks and critical path	Gantt Chart
What tasks will be performed and in what sequence	PERT Chart
List of tasks, start and finish dates, and assigned resources	Task Sheet with Entry table applied
Tasks and notes	Task report
Task work, cost, and totals	Task Sheet or Task report with Summary table applied
Task schedule—list of tasks scheduled during a time period	Periodic Task report
List of all resources assigned to work on the project	Resource Sheet or Resource report
Level of resource use during each period (day, week, month, quarter, or year)	Resource Usage view
Forecast of resource costs—how much money needed and when	Resource Usage view, choose Format Cost
Resource schedule—list of resources scheduled to work on tasks during a time period	Periodic Resource report

To change the information in a view and adjust the width and titles of table columns, apply a different table using the Table commands. To filter information so that only certain related information appears (such as critical tasks only), apply a filter using the Filter commands. To sort the tasks or resources so they appear in the order of your choosing, instead of ID number order, use the Format Sort command.

To change the information in a report, use the File Print Report command. After selecting the type of report you want to print, you can edit the report to change the table or filter applied and sort the information however you like. The tables and filters available with the File Print Report command are the same as those used with the views. By creating custom tables and filters, you can print a report that shows exactly what you want.

When you create a new view or report by changing the table, filter, sort order, text, and so on, you name it so that you can use it over and over. Views and reports are automatically saved in a file, as are the tables and filters you create. Microsoft Project saves them for you when you exit the program. The next time you want to use the same report format with new data, just select that report or view. For more information about the file that contains the views, tables, filters, and reports, and about creating tables and filters, see Chapter 16, "Using Microsoft Project Tools."

In the next sections, you'll see how to set up the page and print a view and a report. This information is followed by several examples of printed views and reports, plus the instructions for creating each one. These reports are also available on the companion disk to this book, available from Editorial Services. To purchase the disk, use the order form at the back of this book.

Setting Up the Page

Before you print anything, you need to make sure the page is set up the way you want. To do this, you use the File Page Setup command. You can have a different page setup for each of the following: Gantt Views, PERT Views, Resource Usage Views, Resource Histogram Views, Sheet Views (Task Sheet, Resource Sheet), and Reports.

If You Do Not Want to Use Inches for Your Margins...

You can specify centimeters in the WINPROJ.INI file. The Metric setting in this file matches your country's unit of measure. If you want to use centimeters instead of inches, change the Metric setting to Yes; if you want to use inches instead of centimeters, change the Metric setting to No.

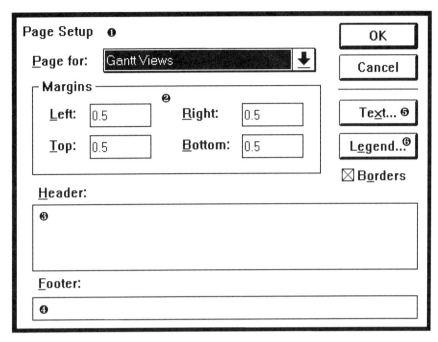

Select the type of view, or select Reports to indicate what this setup is for ❶.

Type the margins here ❷, *in inches from the edge of the paper.*

Type information that goes at the top of each page here ❸, *up to three lines. Press Enter at the end of each line. You can use codes to indicate what project information to include and how to align the information.*

Type information here ❹ *that goes at the bottom of each page. Include codes as appropriate.*

Specify how text should be formatted for the header, footer, and legend by choosing this button ❺.

Specify legend placement and information for Gantt Views or PERT Views by choosing this button ❻.

CODES FOR HEADERS, FOOTERS, AND LEGENDS

The special codes for creating the reports you want are detailed on the tables below and on the next page.

To	Type This Code
Align following characters at left margin	&L
Center following characters	&C
Align following characters at right margin	&R

To Print	Type This Code	To Print	Type This Code
Report date	&D	Report time	&T
Page number	&P	Project filename	&F
Project start	&s	Project finish	&f
Name of view	&v	Name of report	&r
Project name	&p	Company name	&c
Manager's name	&m	Current date	&d

Printing

The instructions in this section show how to print views and reports using the File Print and File Print Report commands.

Before You Print...

Before you can print, you must choose File Printer Setup to set up your printer for printing. In this dialog box, you specify such things as the printer, paper, resolution, fonts, and orientation of output. For more information about using a printer with Microsoft Windows and Microsoft Project for Windows, see your Windows documentation, and "Printing and Plotting" in the *Microsoft Project Reference*.

Printing a View

To print a view, first make the view look the way you want and contain the information you want. For example, apply a different table or filter, sort the tasks or resources, or format the text or gridlines. Then choose File Print. If you are printing a view that includes a timescale (Gantt Chart, Resource Histogram, or Resource Usage view), specify a start date and finish date to indicate the span of time you want printed.

Print Timescale ❺ OK

From: 9/17/90 8:00am ❶

Cancel

To: 8/29/91 9:00am ❷

❸ ☐ One page wide
❹ ☐ Print all sheet columns

Type the date you want at the left edge of the timescale ❶.

Type the end date for the period you want to print ❷.

If you want to print only one page width of the chart, turn on this check box ❸.

For the Gantt Chart and Resource Usage view, there may be more columns in the table applied to the view than are showing on the screen. To print all the columns, turn on this check box ❹.

Choose OK ❺.

For all views, specify the number of copies and the pages to print.

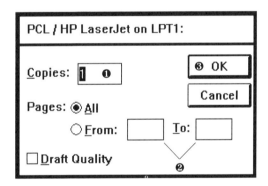

PCL / HP LaserJet on LPT1:

Copies: 1 ❶

❸ OK

Cancel

Pages: ⦿ All
○ From: ☐ To: ☐

☐ Draft Quality ❷

Type the number of copies you want to print ❶.

If you want to print certain pages of the report, type the page range ❷.

Choose OK ❸.

Printing a Report

To print a report, choose File Print Report.

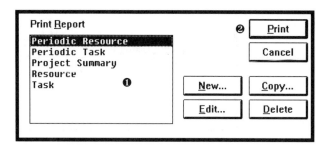

Select the report you want to print ❶.

Press Enter or click the Print button ❷.

To change the information in the report, choose the New, Copy, or Edit button. You can change the report name, the table and filter used for the report, sort the information, format the text, and specify that other types of information, such as totals or notes, be included.

For example, if you select Task in the Print Report box, and choose the Edit button, you see the following dialog box.

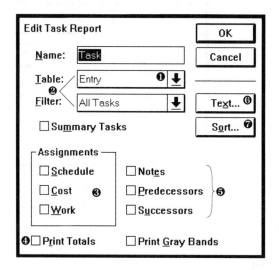

Type a name for the report ❶.

Select a different table or filter ❷.

For the resources assigned to the tasks, you can print the schedule, cost, or work information by turning on the appropriate check box ❸. This is the same information you see in the fields at the bottom of the Task Form.

Turn on this check box ❹ to print totals for the categories you selected under Assignments.

To print task notes, predecessors, or successors, turn on these check boxes ❺.

To change the way the text is formatted in the report, choose this button ❻.

To change the order of the tasks, choose this button ❼.

The names of the reports you create are added to the list in the Print Report box. The next time you want to use the same report, just select the report and choose the Print button.

When Do You Use New? When Copy? When Edit?

When you create a new report, you have three buttons to choose from. How do you decide which to use?

Use New to create a new report that is not based on an existing one.

Use Copy to create a new report that is similar to an existing one. The initial settings in the Edit Report dialog box will be those from the report you copied. The copied report remains unchanged.

Use Edit to change an existing report if you no longer want the original one.

Sample Reports

This section shows several printed views and reports with specific instructions for creating each one. Following each procedure is a list explaining how to customize the view or report to show exactly what you want and to look the way you prefer.

The reports in this section are the simplest reports, so that you can get an idea of the reporting capability available to you if you do practically nothing but print what is already available to you. In Chapter 16, "Using Microsoft Project Tools," are some customized reports to show you some of the variety available for your reports.

Hints when printing reports:

- If you are using outlining and the task names are cut off, consider turning off the Name Indentation check box in the Format Outline dialog box. All task names will then be aligned at the left margin.

- If you are using outlining and your outline is collapsed, you will see only those tasks visible on screen in your printed reports.

- If your columns are too wide to fit across one page, try printing in landscape mode. To change between portrait mode (page is printed vertically) and landscape mode (page is printed horizontally), choose File Printer Setup, choose the Setup button, and then select either the Landscape option or the Portrait option under Orientation.

Project Summary

The Project Summary report (see illustration on the following page) includes the total number of tasks, cost and work amounts, number of resources, start and finish dates, and project notes from the Options Project Info dialog box.

TO PRINT A PROJECT SUMMARY REPORT

1. Choose File Print Report.

2. In the Print Report box, select Project Summary.

3. Choose the Print button.

4. Type the number of copies to print.

5. Choose OK.

All you can change on this report is the type, color, and size.

New calculator
Compusystems
Marcia Cryer

Dates

Project Start:	9/17/90 8:00am
Project Finish:	8/29/91 9:00am
Current:	8/24/90 8:00am

Costs

Scheduled:	$84,345.05	Remaining:	$84,345.05
Planned:	$84,498.90	Actual:	$0.00
Variance:	($153.85)		

Work

Scheduled:	5382h	Remaining:	5382h
Planned:	5378h	Actual:	0h
Variance:	4h		

Task Status		Resource Status	
Tasks not yet started:	78	Resources:	24
Tasks in progress:	0	Overallocated Resources:	3
Tasks completed:	0		
Total Tasks:	78	Total Resources:	27

Notes

Goal: New, improved calculator ready for next back-to-school promotion.
Scope: Do add the most-requested features, fix bugs in existing code, and
           update manual to include new features.
           Do not redo all code, change packaging, or rewrite entire manual.
Assumptions: Technology is available to implement features; programmers will
           be available to do the work; existing packaging will work.

Summary of Tasks and Dates

If you have outlined your project, you can collapse the outline to show only the major phases and when they occur. If you print the Gantt Chart with the outline collapsed, you have a good presentation piece for a meeting or for an executive summary for management.

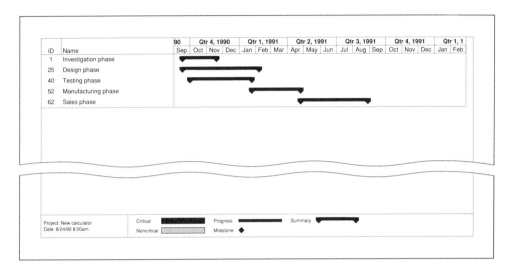

To make the Gantt Chart show just what you want, you can change the following:

You Can Change	Use This Command
Bars shown for each task, by either adding bars or removing bars	Format Palette
How the text looks	Format Text
What text appears on the chart	Format Palette
Order of the tasks	Format Sort
Color and pattern of the gridlines	Format Gridlines
Amount of time showing on the chart and the units for the major and minor timescales	Format Timescale
Information in the legend	File Page Setup
Columns of information	Table commands
Tasks included in the view	Filter commands

TO CREATE A SUMMARY GANTT CHART

1. Choose View Gantt Chart.
2. To select all the tasks, choose Edit Select All.
3. Collapse the outline by pressing Alt+Shift+ – (minus on the keypad) or clicking the collapse icon (⊟).
4. Choose Format Timescale.
5. In the Units boxes and Label boxes under Major Scale and Minor Scale, select the timescale units and labels you want, and choose OK.

   For example, to duplicate the example showing quarters and months: In the Units box under Major Scale, select Quarters; in the Label box select Qtr 1, 1987; in the Units box under Minor Scale, select Months.

6. Choose File Print.
7. In the Print Timescale dialog box, choose OK.
8. Type the number of copies and the page range you want to print.
9. Choose OK.

Tasks and the Critical Path

If you want a graphic representation of the project showing the tasks and the critical path, print the Gantt Chart. You can see the durations and start and finish dates of the tasks on the bar chart, plus the critical tasks.

TO PRINT A GANTT CHART

1. Choose View Gantt Chart.
2. Choose Format Timescale.
3. In the Units boxes under Major Scale and Minor Scale, select the timescale units you want, and choose OK.

   For example, to duplicate the example showing months and weeks: In the Units box under Major Scale, select Months; in the Units box under Minor Scale, select Weeks.

4. Choose File Print.
5. In the Print Timescale dialog box, choose OK.
6. Type the number of copies and the page range to print.
7. Choose OK.

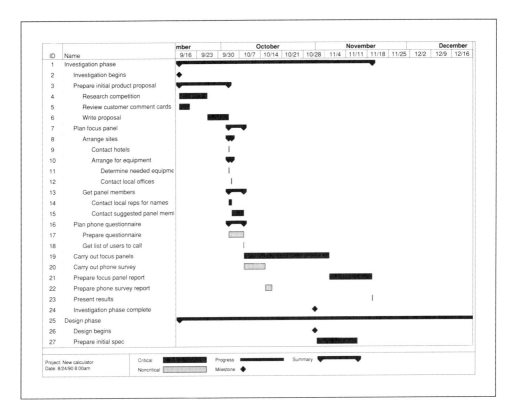

To print the Gantt Chart showing just what you want, you can change the following:

You Can Change	Use This Command
Bars shown for each task, by either adding bars or removing bars	Format Palette
How the text looks	Format Text
What text appears on the chart	Format Palette
Order of the tasks	Format Sort
Color and pattern of the gridlines	Format Gridlines
Amount of time showing on the chart and the units for the major and minor timescales	Format Timescale
Information in the legend	File Page Setup
Columns of information	Table commands
Tasks included in the view	Filter commands

All Tasks and Their Sequence

To show the tasks included in the plan and in what order they will be performed, print the PERT Chart—either with full-size nodes or with small nodes containing ID number only.

TO PRINT THE PERT CHART

1. Choose View PERT Chart.

2. To include a legend on every page, choose File Page Setup.

3. Choose the Legend button.

4. Select the Legend On Every Page option, and then choose OK twice.

5. Choose File Print.

6. Type the number of copies and the page range you want to print.

7. Choose OK.

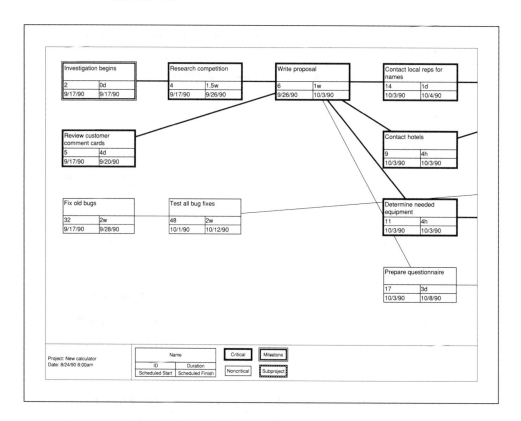

To print the PERT Chart with small nodes, choose Format Zoom before printing.

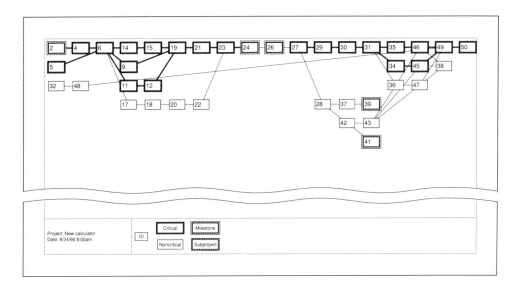

To make the PERT Chart show just what you want, you can change the following:

You Can Change	Use This Command
Information in each node	Format Palette
How the text looks	Format Text
How the borders look	Format Borders
Information in the legend	File Page Setup

List of Tasks, Dates, and Resources

You can print a list of the tasks, their start and finish dates, and the resources assigned to the tasks by printing the Task Sheet with the Entry table applied.

TO PRINT A TASK SHEET

1. Choose View Task Sheet.
2. If the Entry table is not applied, choose Table Entry.
3. Choose File Print.
4. Type the number of copies and the range of pages to print.
5. Choose OK.

CALCULAT.MPP

ID	Name	Duration	Scheduled Start	Scheduled Finish	Predecessors	Resource Names
1	Investigation phase	63.38ed	9/17/90 8:00am	11/19/90 5:00pm		
2	Investigation begins	0d	9/17/90 8:00am	9/17/90 8:00am		
3	Prepare initial product proposal	16.17ed	9/17/90 8:00am	10/3/90 12:00pm		
4	Research competition	1.5w	9/17/90 8:00am	9/26/90 12:00pm	2	Marcia,Marketing staff
5	Review customer comment cards	4d	9/17/90 8:00am	9/20/90 5:00pm		Marketing staff,Janet,F
6	Write proposal	1w	9/26/90 1:00pm	10/3/90 12:00pm	4,5	Marcia,Janet
7	Plan focus panel	4.96ed	10/3/90 1:00pm	10/8/90 12:00pm		
8	Arrange sites	0.96ed	10/3/90 1:00pm	10/4/90 12:00pm		
9	Contact hotels	4h	10/3/90 1:00pm	10/3/90 5:00pm	6	Cheryl
10	Arrange for equipment	0.96ed	10/3/90 1:00pm	10/4/90 12:00pm		
11	Determine needed equipme	4h	10/3/90 1:00pm	10/3/90 5:00pm	6	Cheryl
12	Contact local offices	4h	10/4/90 8:00am	10/4/90 12:00pm	11	
13	Get panel members	4.96ed	10/3/90 1:00pm	10/8/90 12:00pm		
14	Contact local reps for names	1d	10/3/90 1:00pm	10/4/90 12:00pm	6	Marketing staff
15	Contact suggested panel meml	2d	10/4/90 1:00pm	10/8/90 12:00pm	14	
16	Plan phone questionnaire	4.96ed	10/3/90 1:00pm	10/8/90 12:00pm		
17	Prepare questionnaire	3d	10/3/90 1:00pm	10/8/90 12:00pm	6	Roberto
18	Get list of users to call	2h	10/8/90 10:00am	10/8/90 12:00pm	17FF	
19	Carry out focus panels	4w	10/8/90 1:00pm	11/5/90 12:00pm	15,9,12	Marcia,Marketing staff
20	Carry out phone survey	1w	10/8/90 1:00pm	10/15/90 12:00pm	18	Research Inc.,Comput
21	Prepare focus panel report	2w	11/5/90 1:00pm	11/19/90 12:00pm	19	Marcia[0.1],Marketing
22	Prepare phone survey report	0.5w	10/15/90 1:00pm	10/17/90 5:00pm	20	Research Inc.
23	Present results	4h	11/19/90 1:00pm	11/19/90 5:00pm	21,22	Marcia
24	Investigation phase complete	0d	10/31/90 5:00pm	10/31/90 5:00pm	23	
25	Design phase	143.04ed	9/17/90 8:00am	2/7/91 9:00am		
26	Design begins	0d	10/31/90 5:00pm	10/31/90 5:00pm	24	
27	Prepare initial spec	2w	11/1/90 8:00am	11/14/90 5:00pm	26	Dave,Bill,Marcia[0.1],T
28	Distribute for review	1h	11/15/90 8:00am	11/15/90 9:00am	27	Terri
29	Meet with reviewers	4h	11/22/90 8:00am	11/22/90 12:00pm	27FS+1w	Dave,Bill
30	Incorporate comments/revise spec	1w	11/22/90 1:00pm	11/29/90 12:00pm	29	Dave,Bill,Terri[0.2]
31	Distribute final spec	1h	11/29/90 1:00pm	11/29/90 2:00pm	30	Terri
32	Fix old bugs	2w	9/17/90 8:00am	9/28/90 5:00pm		Bill[0.1],Design staff[2]
33	Code new features	28ed	11/29/90 2:00pm	12/27/90 2:00pm		

Page 1

If you have outlined the project, you can collapse and expand the project as appropriate for the level of detail in your report. For example, if you collapse the project to show summary tasks only, then expand one summary task at a time, you can create an individualized report for the manager of each major phase, showing the project as a whole, plus task details for each manager's phase.

TO PRINT A CUSTOMIZED TASK SHEET

1. Choose View Task Sheet.

2. To select all the tasks, choose Edit Select All.

3. Collapse the outline by pressing Alt + Shift + – (minus on the keypad) or clicking the collapse icon (⊟).

4. Select the summary task you want to expand, and then press Alt + Shift + + (plus on the keypad) or click the expand icon (⊞).

5. Choose File Print.

6. Type the number of copies and the page range to print.

7. Choose OK.

CALCULAT.MPP

ID	Name	Duration	Scheduled Start	Scheduled Finish	Predecessors	Resource Names
1	Investigation phase	63.38ed	9/17/90 8:00am	11/19/90 5:00pm		
2	Investigation begins	0d	9/17/90 8:00am	9/17/90 8:00am		
3	Prepare initial product proposal	16.17ed	9/17/90 8:00am	10/3/90 12:00pm		
7	Plan focus panel	4.96ed	10/3/90 1:00pm	10/8/90 12:00pm		
16	Plan phone questionnaire	4.96ed	10/3/90 1:00pm	10/8/90 12:00pm		
19	Carry out focus panels	4w	10/8/90 1:00pm	11/5/90 12:00pm	15,9,12	Marcia,Marketing staff
20	Carry out phone survey	1w	10/8/90 1:00pm	10/15/90 12:00pm	18	Research Inc.,Comput
21	Prepare focus panel report	2w	11/5/90 1:00pm	11/19/90 12:00pm	19	Marcia[0.1],Marketing
22	Prepare phone survey report	0.5w	10/15/90 1:00pm	10/17/90 5:00pm	20	Research Inc.
23	Present results	4h	11/19/90 1:00pm	11/19/90 5:00pm	21,22	Marcia
24	Investigation phase complete	0d	10/31/90 5:00pm	10/31/90 5:00pm	23	

40	Testing phase	115.25ed	10/1/90 8:00am	1/24/91 2:00pm		
52	Manufacturing phase	91ed	1/24/91 2:00pm	4/25/91 2:00pm		
62	Sales phase	125.79ed	4/25/91 2:00pm	8/29/91 9:00am		

Page 1

To make the Task Sheet show just what you want, you can change the following:

You Can Change	Use This Command
How the text looks	Format Text
Order of the tasks	Format Sort
Color and pattern of the gridlines	Format Gridlines
Columns of information	Table commands
Tasks included in the view	Filter commands

Tasks and Notes

To print a list of all the tasks, plus any notes you have entered about the tasks, print the Task report and turn on the Notes check box. You may want to print task notes if you have included information such as task scope or assumptions about duration in a note with each task. Choose Format Notes on the Task Form to see and enter notes.

TO PRINT A TASK REPORT SHOWING NOTES

1. Choose File Print Report.

2. In the Print Report box, select Task.

3. Choose the Copy button.

4. In the Name box, type "Tasks & Notes".

5. To print notes, turn on the Notes check box.

CALCULAT.MPP

ID	Name	Duration	Scheduled Start	Scheduled Finish	Predecessors	Resource Names
2	Investigation begins	0d	9/17/90 8:00am	9/17/90 8:00am		
4	Research competition	1.5w	9/17/90 8:00am	9/26/90 12:00pm	2	Marcia,Marketing staff

Notes
Assumptions: Competition reports from Research, Inc will be here by 9/17!

| 5 | Review customer comment cards | 4d | 9/17/90 8:00am | 9/20/90 5:00pm | | Marketing staff,Janet,F |

Notes
Make sure mail room has forwarded all comment cards to marketing by 9/17.

| 6 | Write proposal | 1w | 9/26/90 1:00pm | 10/3/90 12:00pm | 4,5 | Marcia,Janet |

Notes
Assumptions: Marcia and Janet will have finished marketing tour.

| 12 | Contact local offices | 4h | 10/4/90 8:00am | 10/4/90 12:00pm | 11 | |

Notes
Contingency plan: If offices don't have equipment, get name of local rental company.

14	Contact local reps for names	1d	10/3/90 1:00pm	10/4/90 12:00pm	6	Marketing staff
15	Contact suggested panel members	2d	10/4/90 1:00pm	10/8/90 12:00pm	14	
17	Prepare questionnaire	3d	10/3/90 1:00pm	10/8/90 12:00pm	6	Roberto

Page 1

6. Choose OK.

7. Choose the Print button.

8. Type the number of copies and the range of pages to print.

9. Choose OK.

To make the Task report show just what you want, you can change the following:

You Can Change	Use This Option in the Edit Task Report Dialog Box
Columns of information	Table box
Tasks that are printed	Filter box
Order of the tasks	Sort button
Whether schedule, cost, and work information are printed	Schedule, Cost, Work check boxes under Assignments
Whether totals, summary tasks, predecessors, and successors are printed	Print Totals, Summary Tasks, Predecessors, Successors check boxes
How the text looks	Text button

Task Work, Cost, and Totals

To see the work and cost for each task, print the Task Sheet with the Summary table applied.

CALCULAT.MPP

ID	Name	Duration	Scheduled Start	Scheduled Finish	% Comp	Cost	Work
1	Investigation phase	63.38ed	9/17/90 8:00am	11/19/90 5:00pm	0%	$25,508.46	1124h
2	Investigation begins	0d	9/17/90 8:00am	9/17/90 8:00am	0%	$0.00	0h
3	Prepare initial product proposa	16.17ed	9/17/90 8:00am	10/3/90 12:00pm	0%	$6,251.92	328h
4	Research competition	1.5w	9/17/90 8:00am	9/26/90 12:00pm	0%	$2,807.69	160h
5	Review customer comment ca	4d	9/17/90 8:00am	9/20/90 5:00pm	0%	$1,569.23	88h
6	Write proposal	1w	9/26/90 1:00pm	10/3/90 12:00pm	0%	$1,875.00	80h
7	Plan focus panel	4.96ed	10/3/90 1:00pm	10/8/90 12:00pm	0%	$184.62	16h
8	Arrange sites	0.96ed	10/3/90 1:00pm	10/4/90 12:00pm	0%	$61.54	8h
9	Contact hotels	4h	10/3/90 1:00pm	10/3/90 5:00pm	0%	$30.77	4h
10	Arrange for equipment	0.96ed	10/3/90 1:00pm	10/4/90 12:00pm	0%	$30.77	4h
11	Determine needed equipment	4h	10/3/90 1:00pm	10/3/90 5:00pm	0%	$30.77	4h
12	Contact local offices	4h	10/4/90 8:00am	10/4/90 12:00pm	0%	$0.00	0h
13	Get panel members	4.96ed	10/3/90 1:00pm	10/8/90 12:00pm	0%	$123.08	8h
32	Fix old bugs	2w	9/17/90 8:00am	9/28/90 5:00pm	0%	$2,019.23	168h
33	Code new features	28ed	11/29/90 2:00pm	12/27/90 2:00pm	0%	$7,211.54	600h

Page 1

TO PRINT A TASK SHEET SHOWING WORK AND COST

1. Choose View Task Sheet.
2. Choose Table Summary.
3. Choose File Print.
4. Type the number of copies and the range of pages to print.
5. Choose OK.

To make the Task Sheet show just what you want, you can change the following:

You Can Change	Use This Command
How the text looks	Format Text
Order of the tasks	Format Sort
Color and pattern of the gridlines	Format Gridlines
Columns of information	Table commands
Tasks included in the view	Filter commands

To see task work, cost, and totals, print the Task report with the Summary table applied.

CALCULAT.MPP

ID	Name	Duration	Scheduled Start	Scheduled Finish	% Comp	Cost	Work
50	Write testing report	1w	1/17/91 2:00pm	1/24/91 2:00pm	0%	$574.52	46h
51	Testing phase complete	0d	1/24/91 2:00pm	1/24/91 2:00pm	0%	$0.00	0h
53	Manufacturing begins	0d	1/24/91 2:00pm	1/24/91 2:00pm	0%	$0.00	0h
54	Review spec	1w	1/24/91 2:00pm	1/31/91 2:00pm	0%	$1,586.54	120h
55	Order parts	1w	1/31/91 2:00pm	2/7/91 2:00pm	0%	$557.69	40h
56	Plan production line changes	3w	2/7/91 2:00pm	2/28/91 2:00pm	0%	$0.00	0h
57	Set up production test	3w	2/28/91 2:00pm	3/21/91 2:00pm	0%	$1,442.31	180h
58	Test production	3w	3/21/91 2:00pm	4/11/91 2:00pm	0%	$4,326.92	360h
59	Begin production	0d	4/11/91 2:00pm	4/11/91 2:00pm	0%	$0.00	0h
60	Pass production function to Si	2w	4/11/91 2:00pm	4/25/91 2:00pm	0%	$1,250.00	80h
61	Manufacturing phase complet	0d	4/25/91 2:00pm	4/25/91 2:00pm	0%	$0.00	0h
63	Sales begins	0d	4/25/91 2:00pm	4/25/91 2:00pm	0%	$0.00	0h
64	Review spec	1w	4/25/91 2:00pm	5/2/91 2:00pm	0%	$1,298.08	80h
65	Prepare market plan	60h	5/2/91 2:00pm	5/14/91 9:00am	0%	$3,124.99	180h
66	Distribute plan for review	4h	5/14/91 9:00am	5/14/91 2:00pm	0%	$30.77	4h
67	Incorporate comments/revise	1w	5/14/91 2:00pm	5/21/91 2:00pm	0%	$788.45	54h
68	Distribute final market plan	4h	5/21/91 2:00pm	5/22/91 9:00am	0%	$30.77	4h
69	Contact sales force	3d	5/22/91 9:00am	5/27/91 9:00am	0%	$744.23	48h
70	Set up sales meetings	2d	5/27/91 9:00am	5/29/91 9:00am	0%	$742.31	48h
71	Contact major dealers	1w	5/29/91 9:00am	6/5/91 9:00am	0%	$1,230.77	80h
72	Prepare marketing materials	4w	6/5/91 9:00am	7/3/91 9:00am	0%	$3,230.77	192h
73	Prepare packaging	2w	7/3/91 9:00am	7/17/91 9:00am	0%	$0.00	0h
74	Prepare for major announcem	2w	7/17/91 9:00am	7/31/91 9:00am	0%	$0.00	0h
75	Make major announcement	1d	7/31/91 9:00am	8/1/91 9:00am	0%	$317.31	16h
76	Support sales force	4w	8/1/91 9:00am	8/29/91 9:00am	0%	$2,461.54	160h
77	Sales phase complete	0d	8/29/91 9:00am	8/29/91 9:00am	0%	$0.00	0h
78	Project complete	0d	8/29/91 9:00am	8/29/91 9:00am	0%	$0.00	0h
						$84,345.05	5382h

Page 2

TO PRINT A TASK REPORT SHOWING WORK, COST, AND TOTALS

1. Choose File Print Report.

2. In the Print Report box, select Task.

3. Choose the Copy button.

4. In the Name box, type "Task Work and Cost".

5. In the Table box, select Summary.

6. To print totals, turn on the Print Totals check box.

7. Choose OK.

8. Choose the Print button.

9. Type the number of copies and the range of pages to print.

10. Choose OK.

For information about making the Task report show just what you want, see the table in the "Tasks and Notes" section earlier in this chapter.

Task Schedule

To get started with the actual work on the project tasks, you'll want to print a list of tasks to be performed, when they have to be performed, and who will work on them. These are your actual working documents to let people know exactly what to do and when to do it, like a "to do" list.

To generate this schedule, print the Periodic Task report. You can print either the whole thing from project start to finish or just a portion. Periodically as you track the project, print a new list of tasks reflecting the latest status of the project, so everyone is always working with the latest schedule.

TO PRINT A TASK SCHEDULE

1. Choose File Print Report.

2. In the Print Report box, select Periodic Task.

3. Choose the Print button.

4. In the Start and Finish boxes, type the first date and last date for the period you want to print, and choose OK.

5. Type the number of copies and the range of pages to print.

6. Choose OK.

CALCULAT.MPP

ID	Name	Duration	Scheduled Start	Scheduled Finish	Predecessors
Week of September 16					
2	Investigation begins	0d	9/17/90 8:00am	9/17/90 8:00am	
4	Research competition	1.5w	9/17/90 8:00am	9/26/90 12:00pm	2
5	Review customer comment cards	4d	9/17/90 8:00am	9/20/90 5:00pm	
32	Fix old bugs	2w	9/17/90 8:00am	9/28/90 5:00pm	
Week of September 23					
4	Research competition	1.5w	9/17/90 8:00am	9/26/90 12:00pm	2
6	Write proposal	1w	9/26/90 1:00pm	10/3/90 12:00pm	4,5
32	Fix old bugs	2w	9/17/90 8:00am	9/28/90 5:00pm	
Week of September 30					
6	Write proposal	1w	9/26/90 1:00pm	10/3/90 12:00pm	4,5
9	Contact hotels	4h	10/3/90 1:00pm	10/3/90 5:00pm	6
11	Determine needed equipment	4h	10/3/90 1:00pm	10/3/90 5:00pm	6
12	Contact local offices	4h	10/4/90 8:00am	10/4/90 12:00pm	11
14	Contact local reps for names	1d	10/3/90 1:00pm	10/4/90 12:00pm	6
15	Contact suggested panel members	2d	10/4/90 1:00pm	10/8/90 12:00pm	14
17	Prepare questionnaire	3d	10/3/90 1:00pm	10/8/90 12:00pm	6
48	Test all bug fixes	2w	10/1/90 8:00am	10/12/90 5:00pm	32
Week of October 7					
15	Contact suggested panel members	2d	10/4/90 1:00pm	10/8/90 12:00pm	14
17	Prepare questionnaire	3d	10/3/90 1:00pm	10/8/90 12:00pm	6
18	Get list of users to call	2h	10/8/90 10:00am	10/8/90 12:00pm	17FF
19	Carry out focus panels	4w	10/8/90 1:00pm	11/5/90 12:00pm	15,9,12
20	Carry out phone survey	1w	10/8/90 1:00pm	10/15/90 12:00pm	18
48	Test all bug fixes	2w	10/1/90 8:00am	10/12/90 5:00pm	32
Week of October 14					
19	Carry out focus panels	4w	10/8/90 1:00pm	11/5/90 12:00pm	15,9,12
20	Carry out phone survey	1w	10/8/90 1:00pm	10/15/90 12:00pm	18
22	Prepare phone survey report	0.5w	10/15/90 1:00pm	10/17/90 5:00pm	20
Week of October 21					
19	Carry out focus panels	4w	10/8/90 1:00pm	11/5/90 12:00pm	15,9,12
Week of October 28					
19	Carry out focus panels	4w	10/8/90 1:00pm	11/5/90 12:00pm	15,9,12
24	Investigation phase complete	0d	10/31/90 5:00pm	10/31/90 5:00pm	23
26	Design begins	0d	10/31/90 5:00pm	10/31/90 5:00pm	24

Page 1

To make the Periodic Task report show just what you want, you can change the attributes and information in the table on the following page.

You Can Change	Use This Option in the Edit Periodic Report Dialog Box
Columns of information	Table box
Tasks that are printed	Filter box
Order of the tasks	Sort button
Period for which information is printed: days, weeks, months, quarters, or years	Period box
How many periods	Count box
Whether resource assignments are printed	Print Assignments check boxes
How the text looks	Text button

List of Resources

To print a list of all the resources working on the project, print the Resource report.

TO PRINT A RESOURCE REPORT

1. Choose File Print Report.

```
                                    CALCULAT.MPP
```

ID	Name	Initials	Group	Max. Units	Std. Rate	Ovt. Rate	Cost/Use	Accrue At	Code
1	Marcia	M	Marketing	1	$50,000.00/y	$0.00/h	$0.00	Prorated	
2	Marketing staff	M	Marketing	3	$32,000.00/y	$0.00/h	$0.00	Prorated	
3	Jim	J	Marketing	1	$32,500.00/y	$0.00/h	$0.00	Prorated	
4	Janet	J	Marketing	1	$47,500.00/y	$0.00/h	$0.00	Prorated	
5	Roberto	R	Marketing	1	$30,000.00/y	$0.00/h	$0.00	Prorated	
6	Carmen	C	Marketing	1	$60,000.00/y	$0.00/h	$0.00	Prorated	
7	Dave	D	Design	1	$30,000.00/y	$0.00/h	$0.00	Prorated	
8	Cheryl	C	Marketing	1	$16,000.00/y	$0.00/h	$0.00	Prorated	
9	Shop crew	S	Production	1	$15.00/h	$22.50/h	$0.00	Prorated	
10	Bill	B	Design	1	$25,000.00/y	$0.00/h	$0.00	Prorated	
11	Computer time	C	MIS	1	$60.00/h	$0.00/h	$50.00	End	
12	Research Inc.	R	Vendor	1	$500.00/d	$0.00/h	$0.00	Start	
13	Terri	T	Design	1	$6.50/h	$9.75/h	$0.00	Prorated	
14	Design staff	D	Design	4	$25,000.00/y	$0.00/h	$0.00	Prorated	
15	Documentation dept	D	Document	1	$20.00/h	$0.00/h	$0.00	Prorated	
16	Testing staff	T	Testing	3	$25,000.00/y	$0.00/h	$0.00	Prorated	
17	Marilynn	M	Testing	1	$32,500.00/y	$0.00/h	$0.00	Prorated	
18	Nancy	N	Production	1	$32,500.00/y	$0.00/h	$0.00	Prorated	
19	Production team	P	Production	3	$25,000.00/y	$0.00/h	$0.00	Prorated	
20	Jeff	J	Sales	1	$29,000.00/y	$0.00/h	$0.00	Prorated	
21	Karen	K	Sales	1	$35,000.00/y	$0.00/h	$0.00	Prorated	
22	Sales engineers	S	Sales	3	$32,000.00/y	$0.00/h	$0.00	Prorated	
23	Rick	R	Sales	1	$10.00/h	$15.00/h	$0.00	Prorated	
24	Bob	B	Production	1	$8.00/h	$12.00/h	$0.00	Prorated	
25	Mary	M	Sales	1	$20,000.00/y	$0.00/h	$0.00	Prorated	
26	Jane	J	Marketing	1	$40,000.00/h	$0.00/h	$0.00	Prorated	
27	Production team-swing	P	Production	1	$0.00/h	$0.00/h	$0.00	Prorated	

2. In the Print Report box, select Resource.

3. Choose the Print button.

4. Type the number of copies and the range of pages to print.

5. Choose OK.

To make the Resource report show just what you want, you can change the following:

You Can Change	Use This Option in the Edit Task Report Dialog Box
Columns of information	Table box
Tasks that are printed	Filter box
Order of the tasks	Sort button
Whether schedule, cost, and work information are printed	Schedule, Cost, Work check boxes under Assignments
Whether totals, notes, summary tasks, predecessors, and successors are printed	Print Totals, Notes, Summary Tasks, Predecessors, Successors check boxes
How the text looks	Text button

Resource Use During the Project

Print the Resource Usage view to show the percentage each resource is used during each period. To specify the period, use the Format Timescale command.

TO PRINT A LIST OF ALL RESOURCES AND THEIR USE DURING THE PROJECT

1. Choose View Resource Usage.

2. Choose Format Percent Allocation.

3. Choose Format Timescale.

4. In the Units boxes under Major Scale and Minor Scale, select the timescale units you want, and choose OK.

   For example, to duplicate the example showing months and weeks: In the Units box under Major Scale, select Months; in the Units box under Minor Scale, select Weeks.

5. Choose File Print.

6. In the Print Timescale dialog box, choose OK.

7. Type the number of copies and the page range to print.

8. Choose OK.

CALCULAT.MPP

ID	Name	mber		October					November				December		
		9/16	9/23	9/30	10/7	10/14	10/21	10/28	11/4	11/11	11/18	11/25	12/2	12/9	12/16
1	Marcia	100	50	50	90	100	100	64	19	16	11				
2	Marketing staff	93	33	6	60	6			30	33	3				
3	Jim														
4	Janet	80	50	50	90	100	100	100	10						
5	Roberto	60		50	100	100	100	100	10						
6	Carmen														
7	Dave							40	100	60	40	70			
8	**Cheryl**			20					22	25	2				
9	Shop crew														
10	Bill	10	10					40	100	60	40	70			
11	Computer time				9	1									
12	**Research Inc.**				112	85	25	25	2						
13	Terri							8	20	19	6	16			
14	**Design staff**	50	50									27	100	100	93
15	Documentation dept									37	100	100	100	100	100
16	Testing staff			66	66					25	54	33	33	30	42
17	Marilynn									28	50	10	10	6	
18	Nancy														
19	Production team														
20	Jeff														
21	Karen														
22	Sales engineers														
23	Rick														
24	Bob														
25	Mary														
26	Jane														
27	Production team-swing														

Page 1

To make the Resource Usage view show just what you want, you can change the following:

You Can Change	Use This Command
Information displayed in each usage box	Format Allocation, Format Overallocation
How the text looks	Format Text
Order of the tasks	Format Sort
Color and pattern of the gridlines	Format Gridlines
Amount of time covered by each usage box and the heading for the major and minor scales	Format Timescale
Columns of information	Table commands
Resources included in the view	Filter commands

Expected Resource Work and Cost

The Resource Sheet with the Summary table applied shows the total work and the cost of each resource assigned to work on the project; the Resource Usage view shows the cost by period so you can predict your expenditures. Resources that are overallocated are in bold or red, just as on your computer screen.

CALCULAT.MPP

ID	Name	Group	Max. Units	Peak	Std. Rate	Ovt. Rate	Cost	Work
1	Marcia	Marketing	1	1	$50,000.00/y	$0.00/h	$8,028.84	334h
2	Marketing staff	Marketing	3	3	$32,000.00/y	$0.00/h	$11,938.46	776h
3	Jim	Marketing	1	1	$32,500.00/y	$0.00/h	$1,375.00	88h
4	Janet	Marketing	1	1	$47,500.00/y	$0.00/h	$5,298.08	232h
5	Roberto	Marketing	1	1	$30,000.00/y	$0.00/h	$2,999.99	208h
6	Carmen	Marketing	1	0	$60,000.00/y	$0.00/h	$0.00	0h
7	Dave	Design	1	1	$30,000.00/y	$0.00/h	$1,788.46	124h
8	**Cheryl**	**Marketing**	**1**	**2**	**$16,000.00/y**	**$11.50/h**	**$430.77**	**56h**
9	Shop crew	Production	1	0	$15.00/h	$22.50/h	$0.00	0h
10	Bill	Design	1	1	$25,000.00/y	$0.00/h	$1,875.00	156h
11	Computer time	MIS	1	0.1	$60.00/h	$0.00/h	$245.00	4h
12	**Research Inc.**	**Vendor**	**1**	**1.25**	**$500.00/d**	**$0.00/h**	**$6,250.00**	**100h**
13	Terri	Design	1	1	$6.50/h	$9.75/h	$188.50	28h
14	**Design staff**	**Design**	**4**	**5**	**$25,000.00/y**	**$0.00/h**	**$12,019.24**	**1000h**
15	Documentation dept	Documentati	1	1	$20.00/h	$0.00/h	$9,600.00	480h
16	Testing staff	Testing	3	2	$25,000.00/y	$0.00/h	$9,134.63	760h
17	Marilynn	Testing	1	0.75	$32,500.00/y	$0.00/h	$875.00	56h
18	Nancy	Production	1	1	$32,500.00/y	$0.00/h	$1,875.00	120h
19	Production team	Production	3	3	$25,000.00/y	$0.00/h	$6,730.77	560h
20	Jeff	Sales	1	1	$29,000.00/y	$0.00/h	$557.69	40h
21	Karen	Sales	1	1	$35,000.00/y	$0.00/h	$673.08	40h
22	Sales engineers	Sales	3	1	$32,000.00/y	$0.00/h	$2,461.54	160h
23	Rick	Sales	1	0	$10.00/h	$15.00/h	$0.00	0h
24	Bob	Production	1	0	$8.00/h	$12.00/h	$0.00	0h
25	Mary	Sales	1	0	$20,000.00/y	$0.00/h	$0.00	0h
26	Jane	Marketing	1	0	$40,000.00/h	$0.00/h	$0.00	0h
27	Production team-swing	Production	1	1	$0.00/h	$0.00/h	$0.00	60h

Page 1

TO PRINT A RESOURCE SHEET SHOWING WORK AND COST INFORMATION

1. Choose View Resource Sheet.

2. Choose Table Summary.

3. Choose File Print.

4. Type the number of copies and the range of pages to print.

5. Choose OK.

To make the Resource Sheet show just what you want, you can change the following :

You Can Change	Use This Command
How the text looks	Format Text
Order of the tasks	Format Sort
Color and pattern of the gridlines	Format Gridlines
Columns of information	Table commands
Resources included in the view	Filter commands

On the Resource Usage view, you can show the cost of each resource during the period you select. For example, you can check weekly costs, or monthly costs, depending on how you change the timescale.

CALCULAT.MPP

ID	Name	Qtr 4, 1990				Qtr 1, 1991			Qtr 2, 1991	
		Sep	Oct	Nov	Dec	Jan	Feb	Mar	Apr	May
1	Marcia	$1,442.30	$3,846.15	$480.76						$1,298.07
2	Marketing staff	$2,338.46	$1,353.84	$1,230.76						$4,030.76
3	Jim								$421.87	$828.12
4	Janet	$1,187.50	$3,653.84	$456.73						
5	Roberto	$346.15	$2,365.38	$288.46						
6	Carmen									
7	Dave			$1,788.46						
8	**Cheryl**		$61.53	$153.84						$215.38
9	Shop crew									
10	Bill	$96.15		$1,490.38	$84.13	$204.32				
11	Computer time		$245.00							
12	**Research Inc.**		$6,250.00							
13	Terri			$188.50						
14	**Design staff**	$1,923.07		$528.84	$7,524.03	$2,043.26				
15	Documentation dept			$1,900.00	$3,360.00	$3,680.00	$660.00			
16	Testing staff		$1,923.07	$1,622.59	$2,680.28	$2,908.65				
17	Marilynn			$554.68	$101.56	$218.75				
18	Nancy					$625.00			$1,250.00	
19	Production team					$961.53	$36.05	$3,245.19	$2,487.98	
20	Jeff					$41.82	$515.86			
21	Karen								$454.32	$218.75
22	Sales engineers									
23	Rick									
24	Bob									
25	Mary									
26	Jane									
27	Production team-swing									

Page 1

**TO PRINT A LIST OF ALL RESOURCES AND THEIR COST
DURING THE PROJECT**

1. Choose View Resource Usage.

2. Choose Format Cost.

3. Choose Format Timescale.

4. In the Units boxes and Label boxes under Major Scale and Minor Scale, select the timescale units you want, and choose OK.

   For example, to duplicate the example showing quarters and months: In the Units box under Major Scale, select Quarters; in the Label box, select Qtr 1, 1987; in the Units box under Minor Scale, select Months.

   If the boxes in the Resource Usage view contain ### instead of a number, change the value in the Enlarge box until the numbers show. For example, for the illustration, the Enlarge box contained 200.

5. Choose File Print.

6. In the Print Timescale dialog box, choose OK.

7. Type the number of copies and the page range to print.

8. Choose OK.

To make the Resource Usage view show just what you want, you can change the following:

You Can Change	Use This Command
Information displayed in each usage box	Format Allocation; Format Overallocation; Format Percent Allocation
How the text looks	Format Text
Order of the tasks	Format Sort
Color and pattern of the gridlines	Format Gridlines
Amount of time covered by each usage box and the heading for the major and minor scales	Format Timescale
Columns of information	Table commands
Resources included in the view	Filter commands

Resource Schedule

The Periodic Resource report lists all resources scheduled to work on tasks during the time period you specify. You can print a report appropriate for each manager showing how that manager's resources will be used during each period.

```
                                          CALCULAT.MPP


   ID     Name                  Initials   Group    Max. Units   Std. Rate    Ovt. Rate   Cost/Use   Accrue At      Code
Week of September 16
   1      Marcia                M          Marketing      1    $50,000.00/y    $0.00/h      $0.00   Prorated
          ID    Task Name          Units    Work       Scheduled Start      Scheduled Finish
          4     Research competition   1      40h         9/17/90 8:00am       9/21/90 5:00pm
   2      Marketing staff       M          Marketing      3    $32,000.00/y    $0.00/h      $0.00   Prorated
          ID    Task Name          Units    Work       Scheduled Start      Scheduled Finish
          5     Review customer comme  1      32h         9/17/90 8:00am       9/20/90 5:00pm
          4     Research competition   2      120h        9/17/90 8:00am       9/26/90 12:00pm
   4      Janet                 J          Marketing      1    $47,500.00/y    $0.00/h      $0.00   Prorated
          ID    Task Name          Units    Work       Scheduled Start      Scheduled Finish
          5     Review customer comme  1      32h         9/17/90 8:00am       9/20/90 5:00pm
   5      Roberto               R          Marketing      1    $30,000.00/y    $0.00/h      $0.00   Prorated
          ID    Task Name          Units    Work       Scheduled Start      Scheduled Finish
          5     Review customer comme  1      24h         9/17/90 8:00am       9/19/90 5:00pm
   10     Bill                  B          Design         1    $25,000.00/y    $0.00/h      $0.00   Prorated
          ID    Task Name          Units    Work       Scheduled Start      Scheduled Finish
          32    Fix old bugs          0.1     8h          9/17/90 8:00am       9/28/90 5:00pm
   14     Design staff          D          Design         4    $25,000.00/y    $0.00/h      $0.00   Prorated
          ID    Task Name          Units    Work       Scheduled Start      Scheduled Finish
          32    Fix old bugs           2      160h        9/17/90 8:00am       9/28/90 5:00pm

Week of September 23
   1      Marcia                M          Marketing      1    $50,000.00/y    $0.00/h      $0.00   Prorated
          ID    Task Name          Units    Work       Scheduled Start      Scheduled Finish
          6     Write proposal         1      40h         9/26/90 1:00pm       10/3/90 12:00pm
   2      Marketing staff       M          Marketing      3    $32,000.00/y    $0.00/h      $0.00   Prorated
          ID    Task Name          Units    Work       Scheduled Start      Scheduled Finish
          4     Research competition   2      120h        9/17/90 8:00am       9/26/90 12:00pm


                                             Page 1
```

TO PRINT A RESOURCE SCHEDULE

1. Choose File Print Report.

2. In the Print Report box, select Periodic Resource.

3. Choose the Copy button.

4. In the Name box, type "Weekly Resources/Tasks".

5. Turn on the Print Assignments check box.

   When this check box is turned on, the tasks to which each resource is assigned during the period are printed.

6. Choose the Print button.

7. In the Start and Finish boxes, type the first date and last date for the period you want printed, and choose OK.

8. Type the number of copies and the range of pages to print.

9. Choose OK.

To make the Periodic Resource report show just what you want, you can change the following:

You Can Change	Use This Option in the Edit Periodic Report Dialog Box
Columns of information	Table box
Resources that are printed	Filter box
Order of the resources	Sort button
Period for which information is printed: days, weeks, months, quarters, or years	Period box
How many periods	Count box
Whether task assignments are printed	Print Assignments check box
How the text looks	Text button

PART 4

TRACKING PROGRESS AND MANAGING THE PROJECT

Managing a project is an ongoing process that begins once you create the project and ends when the project is complete. It's the continual process of adjusting task and resource information to reflect what has actually occurred, and monitoring the changes in the schedule so that you are aware of situations that could affect the outcome of your project.

Once the project gets going, your job changes from project planning to project tracking and managing. This involves the following steps:

- Collecting information about progress on the tasks (Chapter 11)
- Entering this "actual" data into Microsoft Project for Windows (Chapter 11)
- Comparing actual progress with the baseline schedule (Chapter 12)
- Analyzing the comparison to find problems areas, the causes of the problems, and solutions to these problems to get the project back on track (Chapter 12)
- Communicating progress, problems, and solutions to the project team and management (Chapter 13)

You repeat these steps over and over throughout the life of the project.

CHAPTER 11

Tracking Progress and Updating the Schedule

Your job, now that the project is under way, is to keep track of what is actually happening on the project. When are the tasks actually starting and finishing? At any point in time, how much work has been done on tasks in progress? How much remains to be done? What tasks are ahead of schedule? Behind schedule? What tasks are taking less or more time than planned? Just how much slack time is left in the schedule? And how are costs and work tracking with the baseline schedule?

To answer these questions, you periodically collect actual start and finish dates and other data about how tasks are progressing, such as what percentage of the work has been completed on a task, or how much longer a task will take.

After you collect this information, update the schedule and then compare the current schedule with your baseline schedule. This comparison shows where each task stands—whether it is on track, behind, or ahead of schedule—and helps you identify problem areas. You can then use this information to change the schedule as necessary to keep the project on track.

Tracking the progress of your tasks is the only way you can stay informed about project status and is the basis for controlling and reporting on the project. By tracking and updating, you get an up-to-date schedule that shows when the project will finish and what it will cost as currently scheduled. Tracking also tells you when you have reached milestones. Celebrating these milestones can boost team morale and give recognition to those working on the project.

By keeping track of progress on tasks, you also develop a history for use in future project planning. If you know how long tasks actually took, you can use this information the next time you have to schedule a similar project.

Collecting Project Data

When you collect project data, where do you start? What data do you want? How do you collect it? Who does it? How often? And then what do you do with it?

What Do You Collect?

When you collect data, you are, first of all, interested in the tasks on which there is or should be activity. Collect some combination of the following for each task.

For tasks that should have started or are in progress:

- Actual start date (or expected start date if the task still has not started)
- Percent complete
- Actual duration so far
- Remaining duration
- Actual work completed
- Expected finish date
- Expected duration, if progress to date indicates that scheduled duration is wrong

For tasks that have finished or should have finished:

- Actual finish date (or expected finish date if the task is not yet finished)
- Actual duration
- Actual work completed
- Actual cost after a task is complete if you are tracking actual cost

For tasks that have not started yet:

- Change in duration estimate
- Change in work estimate

You also want to collect other information, such as notes about deviation from the schedule on the tasks in progress, or information about tasks not yet in progress. For example, if resources were not available as expected, note this fact along with why; if some problem has occurred in executing a task, note any information you can gather about the problem. If you are now able to better define a task duration, note the new duration so you can update the schedule to see how the change will affect project completion. You will use this information in Chapter 12 when you are analyzing the updated schedule.

Where Do You Get the Data?

There are several ways you can collect data on task progress:

- You can collect all the data yourself. This might be feasible on a small project where you are keeping track of everything.
- Have the supervisor or manager report on the tasks in their area.
- Have the individual responsible for each task report on where they are.
- Verify progress through inspection, quality control, or test data.

The data collected should be based on some measurable physical progress, not just the time that has passed since that task started. Time from the start date to the present may not reflect the actual working time spent on the task nor progress made on the task because resources may not be actually working on the task as scheduled or actual progress may be faster or slower than planned. Measuring progress for physical tasks, such as laying pipe or erecting a building, is easy because you can measure the physical results; it is more difficult for "thinking" tasks, such as writing, designing, or computer programming. However, even in these areas, there is an end product that can be broken into measurable tasks.

Try to use objective data where possible. For what has happened, use sources such as time sheets, bills for materials and services from vendors, purchase orders, and other direct charges to projects. If a task involves using a certain quantity of a material, such as laying pipe or stringing wire, you can base progress on the quantity used to date versus expected total use, such as feet of pipe used versus the quantity needed for the completed task.

It is hard to be objective when estimating percent complete and remaining work or duration, but by using information from all your sources, you should be able to come up with data in which you have some confidence. Here, the judgment or experience of those in charge of the tasks will help when deciding just how far along a task is.

Agree on how you will measure progress, and how often, before you start the project. This should be discussed and settled in the planning stages. Those who will be collecting progress data should be involved in deciding how it will be measured.

How Often?

How frequently you collect data depends on the length of the project and on how closely you want to track progress. The shorter the project and the more closely you need to track, the more often you should collect data and update the schedule. The frequency also depends on the requirements of management or your client. When determining frequency, think about how critical it is that the schedule reflect reality at any point in time. For example, if you report biweekly, your schedule could be as much as two weeks off. This could be perfectly acceptable on some projects, but not on other projects.

You may decide to collect data and generate status reports at different frequencies. For example, you may want task supervisors to collect data frequently and track progress daily, while you want reports weekly; you may pass on summary information to management or a client monthly.

Decide the frequency before you start the project so everyone knows what is expected. If you later find you need to collect data more frequently, be sure you inform everyone so they can respond as requested.

USING MICROSOFT PROJECT FOR WINDOWS

When you saved your baseline schedule with the Options Set Plan command in Chapter 9, Microsoft Project saved the original schedule, costs, and work information in the Planned fields. The baseline schedule is kept separately from the current schedule so you can compare the two. Now you need to enter the information you have collected about task progress in the Actual fields. This information shows what has actually occurred on the project. You continually update the schedule with progress information so you always know the current status of the project. Microsoft Project replaces the dates in the current schedule so they match the actual dates you enter.

There are two ways you can enter actual information:

- For tasks whose actual start or finish date matches that in the current schedule, you can use the Options Set Actual command to have Microsoft Project copy the scheduled start or finish date into the Actual Start or Finish field.

- For tasks that have deviated from the schedule, you can type the actual values into Microsoft Project.

To show a task has started, you can enter any of the following:

- Actual start date
- Percent complete

- Actual duration
- Remaining duration

To show a task has finished, you can enter any of the following:

- Actual finish date
- Percent complete
- Actual duration greater than or equal to the scheduled duration
- Remaining duration of zero

To show progress on a task, you can enter any of the following:

- Percent complete
- Actual duration
- Remaining duration

To indicate the scheduled duration has changed:

- If the task uses resource-driven scheduling, do one of the following:

  Change the Work fields for the resources assigned to the task.

  Change the Duration field.

  Change the Remaining Duration field—if it is greater than that calculated by Microsoft Project, the duration is changed.

- If the task uses fixed-duration scheduling, change the Duration field.

The following table shows where you can enter progress information in Microsoft Project for Windows.

To Enter	You Can Use
Actual start and finish dates	Task Form; Task Sheet with Tracking table applied; Mouse on the Gantt Chart
Percent complete	Task Form; Task Sheet with Tracking table applied; Mouse on the Gantt Chart
Actual and remaining duration	Task Sheet with Tracking table applied
Scheduled duration	Task Form, Work fields or Duration box; Mouse on the Gantt Chart

You can also apply the Tracking table to the Gantt Chart, but you will have to scroll to see the columns in the table.

Choosing the Tracking Method

Before you start tracking, you need to make a decision about how Microsoft Project should track work. Initially, Microsoft Project automatically ties work to percent complete. When you update percent complete for tasks, Microsoft Project updates the actual work and cost fields accordingly. To calculate these values, Microsoft Project assumes work and cost to date are proportional to the percent complete for the task and multiplies the total work or cost by the percent complete.

If you want work tied to percent complete and do not want to track work yourself, you do not have to do anything.

If you do not want work tied to percent complete and want to track work yourself, you need to break this tie. To do so, choose Options Preferences and set the Auto Track Resources option to No. Do this only when you need to track work very closely and want to enter actual work information yourself to keep track of exactly how much work has been performed on each task.

Collecting the Data

Using Microsoft Project, you can generate a list of those tasks for which you need to collect data. Naturally, you do not need to collect data on all tasks if only a few are in progress. You can filter the Task Sheet to show only those tasks for which you want progress information; and create a new table to apply to the Task Sheet that includes blanks for writing information about progress.

For example, if you collect data on start and finish dates, percent complete, and remaining duration, you can create a new table containing columns for the scheduled information you want to track, plus blank columns where you write the corresponding actual information. Apply this table to the Task Sheet and print the Task Sheet.

CALCULAT.MPP

ID	Name	Duration	Sched. Start	Start Date	% Comp.	Rem. Dur.	Sched. Finish	Finish Date
2	Investigation begins	0d	9/17/90				9/17/90	
4	Research competition	1.5w	9/17/90				9/26/90	
5	Review customer comment ca	4d	9/17/90				9/20/90	
6	Write proposal	1w	9/26/90				10/3/90	
9	Contact hotels	4h	10/3/90				10/3/90	
11	Determine needed equipment	4h	10/3/90				10/3/90	
12	Contact local offices	4h	10/4/90				10/4/90	
14	Contact local reps for names	1d	10/3/90				10/4/90	
15	Contact suggested panel men	2d	10/4/90				10/8/90	
17	Prepare questionnaire	3d	10/3/90				10/8/90	
18	Get list of users to call	2h	10/8/90				10/8/90	
19	Carry out focus panels	4w	10/8/90				11/5/90	
20	Carry out phone survey	1w	10/8/90				10/15/90	
21	Prepare focus panel report	2w	11/5/90				11/19/90	
22	Prepare phone survey report	0.5w	10/15/90				10/17/90	
23	Present results	4h	11/19/90				11/19/90	
24	Investigation phase complete	0d	10/31/90				10/31/90	
26	Design begins	0d	10/31/90				10/31/90	
27	Prepare initial spec	2w	11/1/90				11/14/90	
28	Distribute for review	1h	11/15/90				11/15/90	
29	Meet with reviewers	4h	11/22/90				11/22/90	
30	Incorporate comments/revise	1w	11/22/90				11/29/90	
31	Distribute final spec	1h	11/29/90				11/29/90	
32	Fix old bugs	2w	9/17/90				9/28/90	
34	Code clock feature	4w	11/29/90				12/27/90	
35	Code notes feature	4w	11/29/90				12/27/90	
36	Code alarm feature	3w	11/29/90				12/20/90	
37	Revise manual	12w	11/15/90				2/7/91	
38	Fix bugs in new code	3w	12/25/90				1/15/91	
39	Design phase complete	0d	2/7/91				2/7/91	
41	Testing begins	0d	11/15/90				11/15/90	
42	Review spec	1w	11/15/90				11/22/90	
43	Create testing scripts	3w	11/22/90				12/13/90	

Page 1

Create a table with the columns you want for collecting data.

After you print the view, write the appropriate information in the blank fields as you collect the data.

TO CREATE A DATA COLLECTION VIEW

1. Choose Table Define Tables, and create a table containing the columns you want. For instructions on creating a table, see Chapter 16, "Using Microsoft Project Tools."

2. Choose View Task Sheet.

3. Apply the table you just created to the Task Sheet.

4. Choose Filter Date Range.

5. Type two dates and choose OK. The filter will find all tasks that have a scheduled start date between the two dates.

6. Choose File Print.

7. Choose OK.

By applying the Date Range filter, only tasks scheduled to start during the dates you specify are listed on the Task Sheet. As you collect the data, you write the information in the blanks. Then you enter the information into Microsoft Project.

You could also create a filter that looks for all tasks scheduled to start during a certain period and also all tasks that are in progress. Then you can create a custom view for collecting your data that includes the table and the filter you created. Each time you need to collect progress data, you display this view. Microsoft Project will ask you for the two dates, and then display all tasks that were scheduled to start during the period between the two dates and all tasks that are in progress.

For more information about creating a table, filter, and custom view, see Chapter 16, "Using Microsoft Project Tools."

Copying Scheduled Dates into Actual Fields

For tasks whose start or finish date matches the current schedule, use the Options Set Actual command to copy their scheduled dates into the Actual fields. If a task should have started, the scheduled start date is copied into the Actual Start field. If a task should have finished, the scheduled finish date is copied into the Actual Finish field, and the percent complete becomes 100 percent.

If you are using outlining in your project, you may want to hide the summary tasks when you are selecting the tasks to update. To hide the summary tasks, choose Format Outline and turn off the Summary Tasks check box.

Select the tasks that started or finished as scheduled ❶.

To select non-adjacent tasks, press F8, select the first group of tasks, press Shift+F8, move to the next group of tasks, and repeat the sequence. With the mouse, hold down Ctrl to select additional tasks.

Choose the Options Set Actual command.

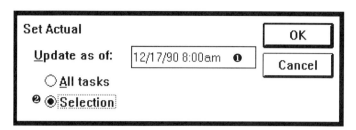

Type the date and time, if it is other than that shown in the box ❶. This is the data collection date.

Select the Selection option ❷ to indicate that you want to update only the selected tasks, not the whole schedule.

If all tasks are on schedule, you do not have to select all the tasks before you choose Options Set Actual. Just select the All Tasks option in the Options Set Actual dialog box.

Entering Percent Complete

To update percent complete for tasks in progress, you can use the Gantt Chart and the mouse. You also can enter percent complete on the Task Form or on the Task Sheet with the Tracking table applied.

When you enter percent complete, Microsoft Project assumes the task started on time and sets the actual start date. It also calculates the actual duration and remaining duration. If you enter 100 as the percent complete, Microsoft Project assumes the task finished on schedule, sets the actual finish date to match the scheduled finish date, and sets the actual duration to match the scheduled duration. If the task was critical, it becomes noncritical.

Changing Percent Complete with the Mouse

On the Gantt Chart, percent complete is shown as a narrow black progress bar superimposed on the task bar. If you are using a mouse, you can drag the percent complete bar to indicate progress.

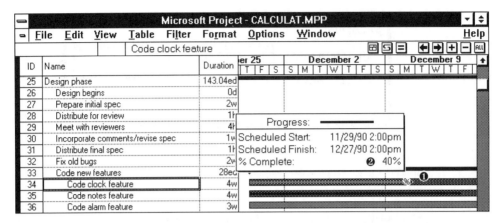

When you point to the progress bar (the thin black bar) with the mouse, the pointer changes (%▸) ❶.
Drag the bar until the correct percent complete is displayed in the box ❷.

ID	Name	Duration
25	Design phase	143.04ed
26	Design begins	0d
27	Prepare initial spec	2w
28	Distribute for review	1h
29	Meet with reviewers	4h
30	Incorporate comments/revise spec	1w
31	Distribute final spec	1h
32	Fix old bugs	2w
33	Code new features	28ed
34	Code clock feature	4w
35	Code notes feature	4w
36	Code alarm feature	3w
37	Revise manual	12w

If the percent complete bar is not yet visible because this is the first progress on the task, point to the left end of the bar ❶.
The pointer changes (%▸); drag it to indicate progress on the task.

Changing Percent Complete on the Task Form

On the Task Form, enter the percent complete in the Percent Complete box.

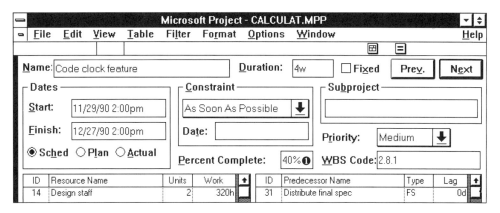

Type the percent complete here ❶.

Changing Percent Complete on the Task Sheet

On the Task Sheet, you can enter percent complete in the % Comp. column on the Tracking table. Choose View Task Sheet and then Table Tracking.

Microsoft Project - CALCULAT.MPP								
ID	Name	Actual Start	Actual Finish	% Comp.	Act. Dur.	Rem. Dur.	Act. Cost	Act. Work
25	Design phase	10/31/90 5:00pm	NA	22%	31.47ed	111.57ed	$6,198.12	495.2
26	Design begins	10/31/90 5:00pm	10/31/90 5:00pm	100%	0d	0d	$0.00	0
27	Prepare initial spec	11/1/90 8:00am	11/14/90 5:00pm	100%	2w	0w	$2,431.20	186
28	Distribute for review	11/15/90 8:00am	11/15/90 9:00am	100%	1h	0h	$6.50	1
29	Meet with reviewers	11/22/90 8:00am	11/22/90 12:00pm	100%	4h	0h	$105.77	8
30	Incorporate comments	11/22/90 1:00pm	11/29/90 12:00pm	100%	1w	0w	$1,109.69	88
31	Distribute final spec	11/29/90 1:00pm	11/29/90 2:00pm	100%	1h	0h	$6.50	1
32	Fix old bugs	NA	NA	0%	0w	2w	$0.00	0
33	Code new features	11/29/90 2:00pm	NA	33%	9.24ed	18.76ed	$2,538.46	211.2
34	Code clock feature	11/29/90 2:00pm	NA	40%	1.6w	2.4w	$1,538.46	128

Type the percent complete in this column ❶.

Entering Actual Start and Finish Dates

To enter actual start and finish dates, use either the Task Form, Edit Form dialog box for tasks, or Task Sheet with the Tracking table applied. You can also use the mouse on the Gantt Chart to indicate a start date if the task has a percent complete other than zero. When you enter an actual start or finish date, it replaces the date in the schedule.

You do not have to enter a start date if the task started as scheduled. When you enter a percent complete, Microsoft Project assumes the task started as scheduled and puts this date in the Actual Start field.

You do not have to enter a finish date if the task finished as scheduled. When you enter 100 as the percent complete, Microsoft Project assumes the task finished as scheduled and puts that date in the Actual Finish field. When you finish a critical task, it changes to noncritical.

Until you enter actual information, the Actual date fields contain NA.

When you enter actual start dates, you may get the message that the late finish is before the scheduled finish in this task or a successor task. You will see this message when the actual start date is later than the late start date and there is no longer time for the task to be completed in the time allowed by successor tasks. This is also called negative slack. Negative slack tells you there is a problem in the schedule—that you no longer have time to complete the task or a later task that depends on this task. In Chapter 12 is a discussion about corrective action for your schedule that will help you determine what to do about negative slack.

Entering Actual Dates on the Task Form

On the Task Form, enter date information in the Dates box.

Select Actual ❶.

Type the start date here ❷.

Type the finish date here ❸.

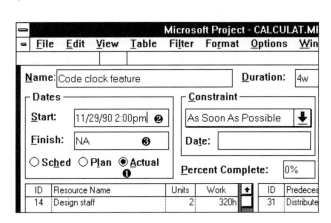

To use the Edit Form dialog box for tasks, first select the tasks on the Gantt Chart or Task Sheet. Then choose Edit Form or click the form icon ▤. You enter actual dates in the Edit Form dialog box for tasks in the same way as on the Task Form.

Entering Actual Dates on the Task Sheet

To enter actual dates on the Task Sheet, apply the Tracking table. The Tracking table includes columns for actual start and finish dates.

Choose View Task Sheet and then choose Table Tracking.

ID	Name	❶ Actual Start	❷ Actual Finish	% Comp.	Act. Dur.	Rem. Dur.	Act. Cost	Act. Worl
25	Design phase	10/31/90 5:00pm	NA	22%	31.47ed	111.57ed	$6,198.12	495.2
26	Design begins	10/31/90 5:00pm	10/31/90 5:00pm	100%	0d	0d	$0.00	0
27	Prepare initial spec	11/1/90 8:00am	11/14/90 5:00pm	100%	2w	0w	$2,431.20	186
28	Distribute for review	11/15/90 8:00am	11/15/90 9:00am	100%	1h	0h	$6.50	1
29	Meet with reviewers	11/22/90 8:00am	11/22/90 12:00pm	100%	4h	0h	$105.77	8
30	Incorporate comments	11/22/90 1:00pm	11/29/90 12:00pm	100%	1w	0w	$1,109.69	88
31	Distribute final spec	11/29/90 1:00pm	11/29/90 2:00pm	100%	1h	0h	$6.50	1
32	Fix old bugs	NA	NA	0%	0w	2w	$0.00	0
33	Code new features	11/29/90 2:00pm	NA	33%	9.24ed	18.76ed	$2,538.46	211.2
34	Code clock feature	11/29/90 2:00pm	NA	40%	1.6w	2.4w	$1,538.46	128

In the Actual Start field, type the start date for the task ❶.
In the Actual Finish field, type the finish date for the task ❷.

Setting Actual Start Dates with the Mouse

On the Gantt Chart, you can drag the left end of a task bar to set the
start date, if the task has a percent complete other than zero.

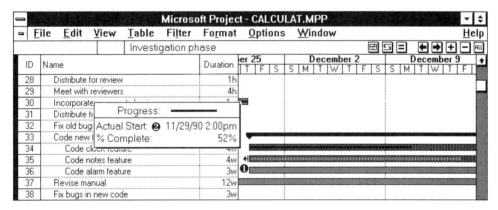

*When you point to the left end of the progress bar (the thin black bar), the mouse pointer changes
(↤) ❶.*
Drag the left end of the bar until the correct actual start date is displayed in the box ❷.

Entering Duration Information

There are three duration values you can enter: actual duration to date,
remaining duration on the task, and scheduled duration if this has
changed from your original estimate.

Entering Actual or Remaining Duration

When you enter the actual duration to date or the remaining duration, Microsoft Project calculates percent complete and the other duration value. If you enter a percent complete, both the actual duration and remaining duration are calculated. If you enter a remaining duration that is greater than that calculated by Microsoft Project, Microsoft Project recalculates the scheduled duration, as follows:

Scheduled duration = Actual duration + Remaining duration

To enter duration on the Task Sheet, apply the Tracking table. The Tracking table includes columns for actual duration and remaining duration.

Choose Task Sheet and then Table Tracking.

ID	Name	Actual Start	Actual Finish	% Comp.	Act. Dur.	Rem. Dur.	Act. Cost	Act. Work
25	Design phase	10/31/90 5:00pm	NA	22%	31.47ed	111.57ed	$6,198.12	495.2
26	Design begins	10/31/90 5:00pm	10/31/90 5:00pm	100%	0d	0d	$0.00	0
27	Prepare initial spec	11/1/90 8:00am	11/14/90 5:00pm	100%	2w	0w	$2,431.20	186
28	Distribute for review	11/15/90 8:00am	11/15/90 9:00am	100%	1h	0h	$6.50	1
29	Meet with reviewers	11/22/90 8:00am	11/22/90 12:00pm	100%	4h	0h	$105.77	8
30	Incorporate comments	11/22/90 1:00pm	11/29/90 12:00pm	100%	1w	0w	$1,109.69	88
31	Distribute final spec	11/29/90 1:00pm	11/29/90 2:00pm	100%	1h	0h	$6.50	1
32	Fix old bugs	NA	NA	0%	0w	2w	$0.00	0
33	Code new features	11/29/90 2:00pm	NA	33%	9.24ed	18.76ed	$2,538.46	211.2
34	Code clock feature	11/29/90 2:00pm	NA	40%	1.6w	2.4w	$1,538.46	128
35	Code notes feature	11/29/90 2:00pm	NA	52%	2.08w	1.92w	$1,000.00	83.2
36	Code alarm feature	11/29/90 2:00pm	NA	0%	0w	3w	$0.00	0

Type the actual duration in this column ❶.
Type the remaining duration in this column ❷.

Entering Scheduled Duration

There are two ways to change scheduled duration. One is to type a new value for duration anywhere you can enter a duration, such as the Duration field on the Entry table on the Task Sheet or Gantt Chart, or in the Duration box on the Task Form, just as you entered the original duration estimates.

The second way to change scheduled duration is to enter a value for remaining duration that is larger than that calculated by Microsoft Project. The scheduled duration is then recalculated by adding the actual duration and the remaining duration, as discussed in the previous section.

If you increase duration for a task using resource-driven scheduling, Microsoft Project assigns the additional work to the resource driving the task duration. If this is not appropriate, change the work scheduled for the resources on the Task Form, with the resource work fields at the bottom of the form (choose Format Resource Work).

You can also change the scheduled duration on the Gantt Chart with the mouse.

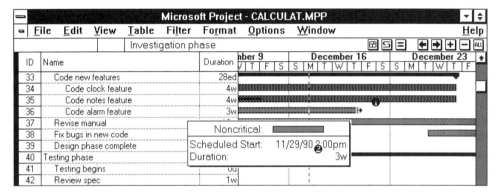

To change the scheduled duration, point to the right end of the task bar ❶.

When the pointer changes (↦), drag the bar until the duration indicated in the box is what you want ❷.

Entering Actual Work and Cost Information

If you left the Auto Track Resource option in the Options Preferences dialog box set to Yes and you are entering progress information for tasks, such as percent complete, duration information, and so on, you can enter actual work and cost only after a task is complete. If you enter an actual work amount while a task is in progress and have entered progress information for the task, Microsoft Project will replace the work you enter with the value it calculates based on percent complete.

If you are tracking work yourself, and you changed the Auto Track Resources option to No, enter the actual work information on the Task Form, with the resource work fields at the bottom. Enter the actual work for each resource assigned to the task, not for the task as a whole.

Choose View Task Form and then choose Format Resource Work.

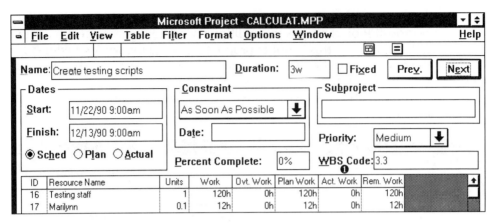

Type the actual work in the Act. Work field ❶ for each resource on the Task Form.

You can also enter work in the Actual Work field on the Task Sheet with the Work table applied. The actual work is divided among the resources assigned to the task.

After a task is complete, you can enter an actual work amount for each resource or for the task. Regardless of how you have set Auto Track Resources, Microsoft Project will not recalculate actual work or cost after remaining work is zero. You can also enter work information if you are not entering other progress information. Microsoft Project will not recalculate work if it has no other information about progress on the task.

Microsoft Project tracks costs automatically by calculating them based on the amount of actual work completed. When a task is complete, however, you can enter the actual cost if it is different from that calculated by Microsoft Project. Do not enter actual costs before a task is complete. If you do, Microsoft Project will recalculate the cost based on work progress.

To enter an actual cost after the task is complete, choose View Task Form, and then Format Resource Cost. If a task has resources assigned, you cannot enter a cost for the task as a whole, but must enter actual cost for each resource assigned to the task.

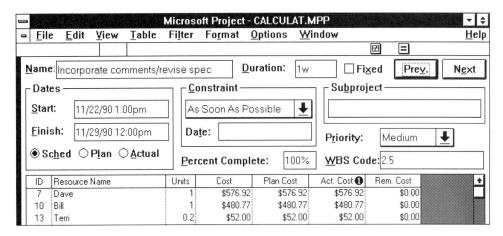

Type the actual cost here ❶ for each resource after the task is complete.

Your schedule now reflects the actual progress made on tasks in the project. In the next chapter, you will compare the actual information just entered with the baseline schedule saved in Chapter 9.

CHAPTER 12

Controlling the Project to Stay on Track

No matter how diligent you are with your planning, the implementation of the project probably will not match your baseline schedule. There are several reasons: your assumptions may be inaccurate, the scope of a task or the project may change, resources may not be available as scheduled, materials may be late, or tasks may simply require an amount of work different from your estimate. You prepared for this when you created the plan by thinking through and stating your plans as clearly as possible. Now you are ready to deal with the unexpected and recognize change and its causes when it occurs. The essential thing to remember is that things do change, and it is all right—as long as you are aware how the changes will affect your schedule, and take the appropriate action.

Controlling or managing a project involves not only spotting problem areas, but also finding solutions for these problems. That is what this chapter is about—seeing how progress on tasks compares with the baseline, understanding the differences, and then reaching the appropriate solution.

To control or manage a project, you follow these basic steps:

- Evaluate progress by comparing the current schedule, which reflects the actual information you entered in Chapter 11, to the baseline schedule you saved in Chapter 9.

- Analyze the differences between the two schedules and determine what is causing the variance.

- Based on your analysis, decide what to do about the variances. Change the schedule? Add resources? Decrease the project scope? Or perhaps do nothing because the projected dates and costs are acceptable.

EVALUATING PROGRESS TO DATE

To evaluate progress to date, compare the current schedule with the baseline schedule. The difference between the two is called variance.

First, check when the project will finish and what it will cost, now that you have updated the schedule with progress information. The finish date and costs indicate how the project will finish if you change nothing more.

Then check variance in each task. Check:

- Start and finish dates—did the task start or finish early, on time, or late?
- Percent complete—is the task ahead, on schedule, or behind?
- Scheduled finish date—is the task scheduled to finish early, on time, or late?
- Work—is work low, as scheduled, or high?
- Cost—is cost low, as scheduled, or high?

For finished tasks, check the variance between the actual duration, work, and cost, and the planned numbers. You may need to adjust the schedule to counteract numbers that are too high on completed tasks.

ANALYZING VARIANCE

The next step is to determine causes of a variance. Variances highlight those places in the schedule which need investigating. When you investigate a variance, decide if it was a one-time occurrence, such as a predecessor finishing late and forcing a late start on a successor task, or a continuing problem, such as work progressing more slowly than planned.

You may already know why progress on tasks does not match the baseline from information you gathered as you collected progress information. For example, you may know that a task start was delayed because materials needed for the task arrived late, or that a strike has halted work on some tasks.

But the answer may not be that straightforward. One tool to help you decide if tasks are progressing as planned is earned value. Earned value tells you if you are spending more or less than you planned to spend for the actual work that has been completed up to this point, and shows you how much tasks will cost at completion if the trend continues. For example, if you have completed 50 percent of work on a task, but have spent 75 percent of the planned budget, you know you need to find out what is costing more than expected.

The following table will help you analyze a variance in your schedule.

Problem	Investigate
Task started late	Predecessor tasks for late finish; resource availability
Resources not working hours as scheduled	Conflicting assignments; insufficient staff; absence or vacation; materials not available
Progress slower than planned	Start date; speed at which resources are working; materials not available

Collecting this information helps you decide what to do about the rest of the schedule. When you are deciding how to deal with tasks that are behind schedule, you need to make a prediction about the remaining duration on each task. If progress on a task continues at the same rate, and it is going more slowly than scheduled, how long will the task take if nothing is done to change the current rate of progress? For example, the resources may be working fewer hours than expected or they may be working slower than expected. How do you decide what applies for each task?

Remaining duration on a task can be predicted in one of three ways. You can:

- Decide, based on the data you collected, the problems that caused the past schedule delays, such as a late start, or slow work, are taken care of, and the remaining duration does not need to be adjusted for the task. For example, if the delay was caused by late arrival of material, but performance of the resource is on schedule, you do not want to assume that past slippage in a task will continue and so you leave the duration as scheduled.

- Assume that progress up to the present is representative of the future and adjust remaining duration as necessary to see when the task will finish and how it will affect the rest of the schedule.

- Ask those involved in the task how they expect the task to progress and to estimate remaining duration.

You also want to consider how progress will be on the rest of the project. Are past delays indicative of future delays? If the remainder of the project is unrelated to the part that was late, you may be more confident in the rest of the project proceeding as scheduled. If the remain-

der of the project includes work on tasks that are already behind schedule, you have to analyze why these tasks were delayed and whether the
delay is likely to continue. If the project is just proceeding more slowly
than planned in one area, or many areas, consider reanalyzing duration
estimates on future tasks to reflect the actual working speed on the current tasks.

For example, supposed productivity for a resource is lower than expected because the original estimates were overly optimistic. You not
only need to calculate new durations for the tasks in progress based on
observed performance, but to also look at other tasks to which this resource is assigned to decide if the durations on those tasks need to be revised. If you find that all your estimates were off by 50 percent after one
month of progress and the problem seems to be that estimates were
overly optimistic, you might want to consider revising all duration estimates to reflect progress so far.

DETERMINING CORRECTIVE ACTION

Once you have analyzed a variance in the schedule, you need to decide what to do about it. Do you reschedule the project? If you still want
to meet the original finish date, you need to decide how to change the
schedule to achieve that date. Whether you determine that a delay was a
one-time occurrence or a continuing problem, what do you do about it?

If a task in progress is behind schedule, or if the finish date for the
project is now too late, use the same basic methods discussed in Chapter 9 for refining the schedule to speed up ongoing or future tasks. The
following lists are not comprehensive—just a way to help you get
started.

Accelerate critical tasks by:

- Assigning overtime work
- Hiring additional staff
- Adding shifts
- Using subcontractors
- Training existing resources to do other tasks
- Shifting resources from other projects or from noncritical tasks

Reschedule tasks by:

- Making tasks concurrent if possible, instead of sequential
- Changing the project's scope by eliminating or simplifying tasks
- Changing scope of critical tasks to shorten them

If you find it necessary to make a change, or if change is being imposed by management or a client, be sure to think it through as thoroughly as you did the initial tasks in the plan. Use the original planning team to determine the best course of action so you have everyone's input about solutions. Reconsider the original assumptions. Do they still apply? If so, be sure to take them into account. If they have changed, be sure to consider your latest set of assumptions.

Once you determine the best solution, communicate changes in the schedule to all interested parties. And if you are adding new tasks, add them to your baseline schedule.

USING MICROSOFT PROJECT FOR WINDOWS

You have already entered all the progress information to date into Microsoft Project for Windows. Now you are ready to look at the updated schedule and compare it to the baseline schedule.

In this section, you will see how to:

- Evaluate progress to date by comparing the actual progress on tasks to the baseline schedule

- Analyze variances to focus on problem areas

- Use Microsoft Project to test proposed changes to the schedule and decide which alternatives are best

- Add new tasks to the baseline schedule

Evaluating Progress to Date

Use Microsoft Project views, tables, filters, and sorting to locate the variances between the baseline schedule and the current schedule. The following table (see the next page) shows where to go in Microsoft Project to find the information you want about the latest schedule and where the variances are.

To See	Use
Current project finish date and costs	Options Project Info
Summary of percent complete for major phases	Task Sheet with outline collapsed and Summary table applied
Graphically whether tasks are on schedule	Gantt Chart
Tasks that were supposed to start but have not	Task Sheet with Should Start filter applied
A comparison of planned and scheduled durations	Tracking Gantt
Variance in task start and finish dates, task work, or task cost	Task Sheet with Variance table, Work table, or Cost table applied and Overbudget filter applied
Amount of slack time remaining in the schedule	Task Sheet with Schedule table applied
Tasks that are behind schedule	Task Sheet with Slipping filter applied

Checking the Project Finish Date and Total Cost

Use the Options Project Info command to check the current finish date and what total work and cost will be if no additional changes are made to the schedule.

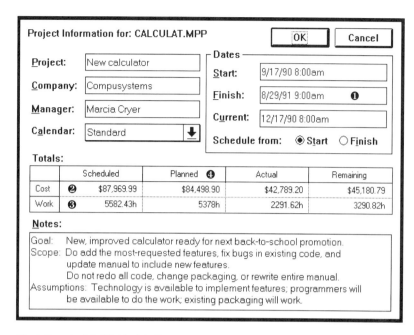

Check the scheduled finish date ❶.

Check the scheduled total cost for the project ❷.

Check the scheduled total work for the project ❸.

The planned cost and work were saved when you saved the baseline schedule ❹.

Reviewing Percent Complete of Major Phases

If you have outlined your project, you can collapse the outline to see the percent complete of the major phases. Percent complete for subordinate tasks is summarized by the summary tasks.

Choose View Task Sheet and then Table Summary. To collapse the outline, choose Edit Select All, and then press Alt+Shift+ – (minus on the keypad) or click the collapse icon (⊟).

ID	Name	Duration	Scheduled Start	Scheduled Finish	% Comp.	Cost	Work	
1	Investigation phase	63.38ed	9/17/90 8:00am	11/19/90 5:00pm	100%	$27,503.65	1193h	
25	Design phase	143.04ed	9/17/90 8:00am	2/7/91 9:00am	47%	$27,293.26	1927.43h	
40	Testing phase	115.25ed	10/1/90 8:00am	1/24/91 2:00pm	27%	$10,009.63	816h	
52	Manufacturing phase	91ed	1/24/91 2:00pm	4/25/91 2:00pm	0%	$9,163.46	780h	
62	Sales phase	125.79ed	4/25/91 2:00pm	8/29/91 9:00am	0%	$13,999.99	866h	
79								
80								

The percent complete ❶ reflects the percent complete of all tasks subordinate to this task.

Checking to See If Tasks Are on Schedule

Use the Gantt Chart for a quick visual check of whether tasks are on schedule. The Gantt Chart shows graphically which tasks are ahead of or behind schedule.

The current date line shows where you should be. Tasks to the left of the current date line should be finished; tasks to the right have not yet started. Tasks on the line should be in progress.

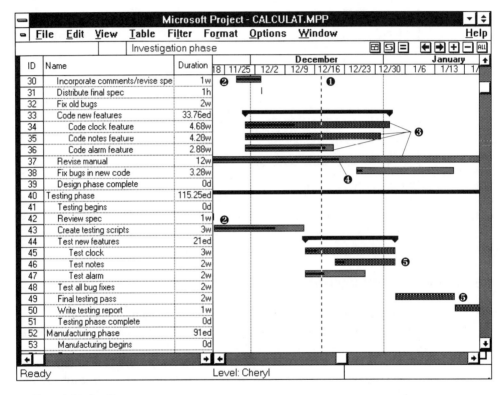

Current date line ❶.

These tasks ❷ should be finished.

These tasks ❸ should be in progress.

The narrow black progress bars ❹ show the actual percent complete on tasks in progress.

These tasks ❺ should not have yet started.

Changing the Current Date Line

The location of the current date line should match the date when data was collected rather than today's date. To change the current date line, choose Options Project Info. Type the appropriate date in the Current box, and then choose OK.

Listing Tasks That Should Have Started

By filtering the Task Sheet or Gantt Chart, you can list all tasks that should have started but have not. The Should Start filter finds tasks with a scheduled start date prior to the date you enter when you apply the filter, but that do not yet have an actual start date entered.

Choose View Task Sheet and then choose Filter Should Start. Type the data collection date in the dialog box. All tasks that do not have an actual start date but were scheduled to start before the date you typed are displayed on the Task Sheet.

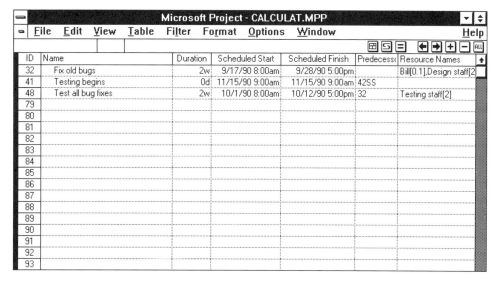

ID	Name	Duration	Scheduled Start	Scheduled Finish	Predecess(	Resource Names
32	Fix old bugs	2w	9/17/90 8:00am	9/28/90 5:00pm		Bill[0.1],Design staff[2
41	Testing begins	0d	11/15/90 9:00am	11/15/90 9:00am	42SS	
48	Test all bug fixes	2w	10/1/90 8:00am	10/12/90 5:00pm	32	Testing staff[2]
79						
80						
81						
82						
83						
84						
85						
86						
87						
88						
89						
90						
91						
92						
93						

All the tasks now showing on the Task Sheet should have started, but no actual start date has been entered for them.

Comparing Planned and Scheduled Duration

The Tracking Gantt is a special Gantt Chart that comes with Microsoft Project. It has one set of bars for planned duration and another for scheduled duration. Use the Tracking Gantt to check for changing task durations as well as to visually check and compare start and finish dates.

To display the Tracking Gantt (see illustration on next page), choose View Define Views. In the Views box, select Tracking Gantt, and press Enter or click the Set button.

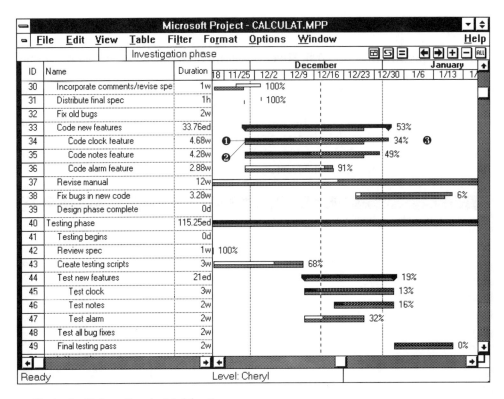

The top bar ❶ shows the scheduled duration.
The bottom bar ❷ shows the planned duration.
The number at the end of each bar indicates the percent complete on the task ❸.

On the Tracking Gantt chart, the top bars showing the scheduled duration are filled in as the percent complete changes.

Checking for Variance in Dates, Work, and Cost

Use the Task Sheet to check for variance in start and finish dates, task work, and task cost. Variance is the difference between the planned dates, work, or cost and the scheduled dates, work, or cost.

DATE VARIANCE

To check for variance in start and finish dates, apply the Variance table to the Task Sheet. Choose View Task Sheet and then choose Table Variance.

ID	Name	Sched. Start ❶	Sched. Finish	Planned Start ❷	Planned Finish	Start Var.	Finish Var. ❹
1	Investigation phase	9/17/90 8:00am	11/19/90 5:00pm	9/17/90 8:00am	11/14/90 10:00am ❸	0ed	5.29ed
2	Investigation beg	9/17/90 8:00am	9/17/90 8:00am	9/17/90 8:00am	9/17/90 8:00am	0ed	0ed
3	Prepare initial prc	9/17/90 8:00am	10/3/90 12:00pm	9/17/90 8:00am	9/27/90 3:00pm	0ed	5.88ed
4	Research cor	9/17/90 8:00am	9/26/90 12:00pm	9/17/90 8:00am	9/21/90 5:00pm	0ed	4.79ed
5	Review custo	9/17/90 8:00am	9/20/90 5:00pm	9/17/90 8:00am	9/19/90 5:00pm	0ed	1ed
6	Write propose	9/26/90 1:00pm	10/3/90 12:00pm	9/20/90 3:00pm	9/27/90 3:00pm	5.92ed	5.88ed

Scheduled dates ❶.

Planned dates ❷.

Variance in the start dates ❸.

Variance in the finish dates ❹ (scroll to the right to see this column).

To limit the tasks displayed, apply a filter such as In Progress. The In Progress filter displays only those tasks for which there is an actual start date, but no actual finish date exists. Use the In Progress filter to review date variance for tasks in progress. To apply the In Progress filter, choose Filter In Progress.

To review the start and finish variance for completed tasks, apply the Completed filter. Only those tasks that have a finish date are displayed. Use the Completed filter to review completed tasks whose variance from the schedule may be causing problems now. To apply the Completed filter, choose Filter Completed.

WORK VARIANCE

To check for variance in task work, apply the Work table to the Task Sheet.

Choose View Task Sheet and then Table Work.

ID	Name	Work	Planned Work	Variance	Actual Work	Rem. Work
25	Design phase	1927.43h	1772h	155.43h	870.47h	1056.97h
26	Design begins	0h	0h	0h	0h	0h
27	Prepare initial spec	232h	186h ❶	46h	232h	0h
28	Distribute for review	1h	1h	0h	1h	0h
29	Meet with reviewers	8h	8h	0h	8h	0h
30	Incorporate comments/revi	88h	88h	0h	88h	0h
31	Distribute final spec	1h	1h	0h	1h	0h
32	Fix old bugs	168h	168h	0h	0h	168h
33	Code new features	660.8h	600h	60.8h	315.6h	345.2h
34	Code clock feature	374.4h	320h	54.4h	128h	246.4h
35	Code notes feature	171.2h	160h	11.2h	83.2h	88h
36	Code alarm feature	115.2h	120h ❷	-4.8h	104.4h	10.8h
37	Revise manual	480h	480h	0h	206.4h	273.6h

The actual work for this task was higher than the planned work ❶.

The actual work so far for this task is lower than planned ❷.

Again, use the In Progress filter or Completed filter to limit the list of tasks displayed. Use the In Progress filter to check for variance in work on tasks in progress; if you find a task that is out of line, check the resources assigned to the task to determine the cause. Use the Completed filter to check for completed tasks that may have caused the schedule of current or future tasks to slip.

COST VARIANCE

To check for variance in task cost, apply the Cost table to the Task Sheet.

ID	Name	Cost	Planned Cost	Variance	Actual Cost	Rem. Cost
25	Design phase	$27,293.26	$25,375.05	$1,918.21	$12,405.80	$14,887.46
26	Design begins	$0.00	$0.00	$0.00	$0.00	$0.00
27	Prepare initial spec	$3,034.12	$2,431.20	❶ $602.92	$3,034.12	$0.00
28	Distribute for review	$6.50	$6.50	$0.00	$6.50	$0.00
29	Meet with reviewers	$105.77	$105.77	$0.00	$105.77	$0.00
30	Incorporate comments/revise spec	$1,109.69	$1,109.69	$0.00	$1,109.69	$0.00
31	Distribute final spec	$6.50	$6.50	$0.00	$6.50	$0.00
32	Fix old bugs	$2,019.23	$2,019.23	$0.00	$0.00	$2,019.23
33	Code new features	$7,942.31	$7,211.54	$730.77	$3,793.27	$4,149.04
34	Code clock feature	$4,500.00	$3,846.15	$653.85	$1,538.46	$2,961.54
35	Code notes feature	$2,057.69	$1,923.08	$134.61	$1,000.00	$1,057.69
36	Code alarm feature	$1,384.62	$1,442.31	❷ ($57.69)	$1,254.81	$129.81
37	Revise manual	$9,600.00	$9,600.00	$0.00	$4,128.00	$5,472.00

Microsoft Project - CALCULAT.MPP

File Edit View Table Filter Format Options Window   Help

Investigation phase

Because the actual work for this task was higher than the planned work, the cost is also higher ❶.
Because the actual work so far for this task is lower than planned, the cost is also lower ❷.

Apply the Overbudget filter to display only those tasks whose actual cost is greater than planned cost. To apply the Overbudget filter, choose Filter Overbudget. Again, use the In Progress filter or Completed filter to look at current and past tasks.

Checking for Slack in the Schedule

Slack tells you how much flexibility you have in your schedule. If you find a negative value in the total slack column, it means that, as currently scheduled, you do not have sufficient time in the schedule to complete that task.

To check slack, apply the Schedule table to the Task Sheet. The Task Sheet has been scrolled so you can see the slack fields in the following art.

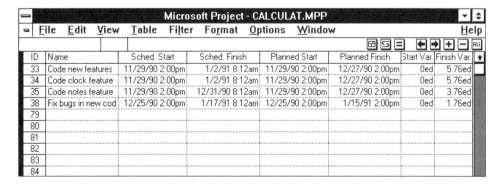

ID	Scheduled Start	Scheduled Finish	Late Start	Late Finish	Free Slack❶	Total Slack
25	9/17/90 8:00am	2/7/91 9:00am	10/31/90 5:00pm	8/29/91 9:00am	0ed	44.38ed
26	10/31/90 5:00pm	10/31/90 5:00pm	10/31/90 5:00pm	10/31/90 5:00pm	0ed	0ed
27	11/1/90 8:00am	11/14/90 5:00pm	11/1/90 8:00am	11/14/90 5:00pm	0ed	0ed
28	11/15/90 8:00am	11/15/90 9:00am	11/15/90 8:00am	11/15/90 9:00am	0ed	0ed
29	11/27/90 8:00am	11/27/90 1:00pm	11/27/90 8:00am	11/27/90 1:00pm	0ed	0ed
30	11/27/90 1:00pm	12/3/90 12:00pm	11/27/90 1:00pm	12/3/90 12:00pm	0ed	0ed
31	12/3/90 1:00pm	12/3/90 2:00pm	12/3/90 1:00pm	12/3/90 2:00pm	0ed	0ed
32	9/17/90 8:00am	9/28/90 5:00pm	12/6/90 2:00pm	12/20/90 2:00pm	2.63ed	80.25ed
33	11/29/90 2:00pm	1/2/91 8:12am	11/29/90 2:00pm	12/27/90 2:00pm	0ed ❷	-5.76ed
34	11/29/90 2:00pm	1/2/91 8:12am	11/29/90 2:00pm	12/27/90 2:00pm	0ed	-5.76ed
35	11/29/90 2:00pm	12/31/90 8:12am	11/29/90 2:00pm	12/27/90 2:00pm	0ed	-3.76ed
36	11/29/90 2:00pm	12/20/90 8:12am	11/29/90 2:00pm	12/27/90 2:00pm	0ed	7.24ed
37	11/15/90 9:00am	2/7/91 9:00am	11/15/90 9:00am	8/29/91 9:00am	0ed	203ed
38	12/25/90 2:00pm	1/17/91 8:12am	12/25/90 2:00pm	8/29/91 9:00am	224.03ed	224.03ed
39	2/7/91 9:00am	2/7/91 9:00am	8/29/91 9:00am	8/29/91 9:00am	203ed	203ed
40	10/1/90 8:00am	1/24/91 2:00pm	11/15/90 9:00am	8/29/91 9:00am	0ed	45.04ed
41	11/15/90 9:00am	11/15/90 9:00am	8/29/91 9:00am	8/29/91 9:00am	287ed	287ed

The Free Slack and Total Slack columns ❶ tell you how much slack time remains in your schedule.

A negative value ❷ tells you that, as currently scheduled, you do not have enough time to complete the task.

Listing Tasks That Are Behind Schedule

To see all the tasks that are behind schedule, you can apply the Slipping filter to the Task Sheet. Microsoft Project displays only those tasks scheduled to finish later than planned. This helps you focus on problem areas in your project.

Choose View Task Sheet and then choose Filter Slipping.

ID	Name	Sched. Start	Sched. Finish	Planned Start	Planned Finish	Start Var.	Finish Var.
33	Code new features	11/29/90 2:00pm	1/2/91 8:12am	11/29/90 2:00pm	12/27/90 2:00pm	0ed	5.76ed
34	Code clock feature	11/29/90 2:00pm	1/2/91 8:12am	11/29/90 2:00pm	12/27/90 2:00pm	0ed	5.76ed
35	Code notes feature	11/29/90 2:00pm	12/31/90 8:12am	11/29/90 2:00pm	12/27/90 2:00pm	0ed	3.76ed
38	Fix bugs in new cod	12/25/90 2:00pm	1/17/91 8:12am	12/25/90 2:00pm	1/15/91 2:00pm	0ed	1.76ed
79							
80							
81							
82							
83							
84							

All the tasks now showing on the Task Sheet are scheduled to finish later than planned.

To see all tasks again, choose Filter All Tasks.

Analyzing Variance

Now that you have located the variances in the schedule, analyze the variances to determine the causes. To do this, you may need to collect more data. Talk to those involved in any task not on schedule. Find answers to all the questions suggested earlier in this chapter.

Use the following Microsoft Project tools to help in this analysis:

To See	Use
Tasks that caused the project cost or work to increase	Task Sheet, with Cost or Work table applied, and Overbudget filter applied
Resources that caused project cost or work to increase	Resource Sheet, with Cost or Work table applied and Cost Overbudget or Work Overbudget filter applied
A list of tasks in progress, to check if any of these are interfering with other tasks	Task Sheet with In Progress filter applied
Variance between planned duration to date and actual duration to date, expressed as costs	Task Sheet with Earned Value table applied

Task Cost or Work Variance

Identifying tasks costing more than planned can help you decide how to control costs on the rest of the schedule. For example, if the resources on a task are costing more per hour than originally budgeted, you may want to check for those resources in later tasks to decide how to handle the potential cost overrun on those tasks. By placing the Task Form below the Task Sheet, you can compare the actual cost of each resource on an over budget task with the planned cost.

The Task Sheet in the top view has the Cost table applied so you can see the cost information for each task. With the Overbudget filter applied, the Task Sheet shows only those tasks that are over budget.

Choose Format Resource Cost on the Task Form to display the list of resources working on the task and their costs.

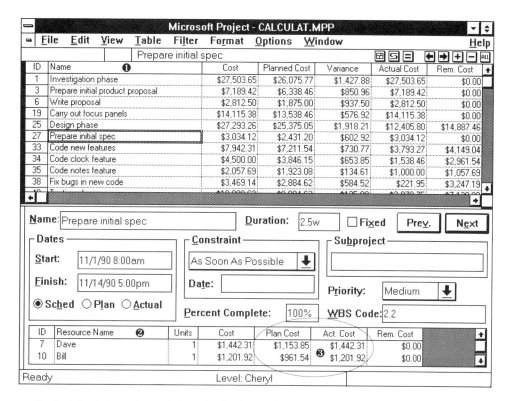

The Task Sheet shows the cost information for those tasks that are over budget ❶. The amounts in the Variance fields are all positive.

The Task Form lists the resources assigned to the task, along with their cost information ❷.

In this example, both resources contributed to the variance in costs since the actual cost for both resources was higher than the planned cost ❸.

To see all tasks again, choose Filter All Tasks.

To see if the same resource or subcontractor is always over budget, put the Resource Sheet under the Task Sheet. Check the list of resources on the Resource Sheet assigned to each task on the Task Sheet. Apply the Cost table to the Resource Sheet to see cost information, including variance, for each resource.

ID	Name	Cost	Planned Cost	Variance	Actual Cost	Rem. Cost
	Carry out focus panels					
1	Investigation phase	$27,503.65	$26,075.77	$1,427.88	$27,503.65	$0.00
3	Prepare initial product proposal	$7,189.42	$6,338.46	$850.96	$7,189.42	$0.00
6	Write proposal	$2,812.50	$1,875.00	$937.50	$2,812.50	$0.00
19	Carry out focus panels ❶	$14,115.38	$13,538.46	$576.92	$14,115.38	$0.00
25	Design phase	$27,293.26	$25,375.05	$1,918.21	$12,405.80	$14,887.46
27	Prepare initial spec	$3,034.12	$2,431.20	$602.92	$3,034.12	$0.00
33	Code new features	$7,942.31	$7,211.54	$730.77	$3,793.27	$4,149.04
34	Code clock feature	$4,500.00	$3,846.15	$653.85	$1,538.46	$2,961.54
35	Code notes feature	$2,057.69	$1,923.08	$134.61	$1,000.00	$1,057.69
38	Fix bugs in new code	$3,469.14	$2,884.62	$584.52	$221.95	$3,247.19

ID	Name ❷	Cost	Planned Cost	Variance	Actual Cost	Rem. Cost
1	Marcia	$8,557.69	$8,509.61	$48.08	$6,298.08	$2,259.61
2	Marketing staff	$11,938.46	$12,553.84	❸ ($615.38)	$4,923.08	$7,015.38
4	Janet	$6,211.54	$5,115.39	$1,096.15	$6,211.54	$0.00
5	Roberto	$3,288.45	$2,653.84	$634.61	$3,288.45	$0.00
12	**Research Inc.**	**$6,562.50**	**$6,250.00**	**$312.50**	**$6,562.50**	**$0.00**

Ready   Level: Cheryl

This task is overallocated ❶.
These are the resources ❷ assigned to the task.
The Marketing staff is under budget on the task ❸, but the other resources are all over budget.

You can get similar information for work variance. Apply the Work table and Overbudget filter to the Task Sheet, and choose Format Resource Work on the Task Form. To see if the same resource or subcontractor is always working more than planned, put the Resource Sheet under the Task Sheet. Select all the tasks on the Task Sheet, and check the list of resources on the Resource Sheet. Apply the Work table to the Resource Sheet to see work information, including variance, for each resource.

Resource Cost or Work Variance

By checking for resources that worked more or less than planned on completed tasks, you get information on what might be causing a task now in progress to be behind schedule. This will tell you specifically where you need more data about what is causing the variance.

Choose View Resource Sheet, choose Table Work, and then choose Filter Work Overbudget.

```
┌─────────────────────────────────────────────────────────────────────────────────┐
│ ▭              Microsoft Project - CALCULAT.MPP                          ▼ ◆       │
│ ▭  File   Edit   View   Table   Filter   Format   Options   Window          Help  │
│                                         ❷                    ⊞  ⊟                 │
│   ID  Name              Work ❶  Planned Work  Variance ❸  Ovt. Work  Actual Work  Rem. Work │
│    8  Cheryl                58h          56h          2h        0h         30h        28h  │
│   12  Research Inc.        105h         100h          5h        0h        105h         0h  │
│   14  Design staff       1083.2h       1000h       83.2h        0h       332.4h     750.8h │
│   28                                                                                      │
│   29                                                                                      │
└─────────────────────────────────────────────────────────────────────────────────┘
```

All the resources now showing on the Resource Sheet have scheduled work ❶ greater than planned work ❷.

Check the Variance column ❸ for the difference between scheduled work and planned work.

To see all resources again, choose Filter All Resources.

You can see similar information for cost variance. On the Resource Sheet, apply the Cost table and the Cost Overbudget filter.

Earned Value

The Earned Value table compares where you expect to be (the planned percent complete) with where you are (the actual percent complete). The Earned Value table does not show percent complete, however; instead, it shows everything in terms of costs. It shows the dollars you planned to spend (planned percent complete * planned cost) compared to the dollars you have actually spent (actual percent complete * planned cost).

The column titles on the Earned Value table (continued on next page) have the following meanings:

Title	Means	Description
BCWS	Budgeted Cost of Work Scheduled	Planned percent complete times the planned cost
BCWP	Budgeted Cost of Work Performed	Actual percent complete times the planned cost to date
ACWP	Actual Cost of Work Performed	Actual cost to date
SV	Earned Value Schedule Variance	BCWP minus BCWS
CV	Earned Value Cost Variance	BCWP minus ACWP

Title	Means	Description
BAC	Budgeted At Completion	Planned cost
FAC	Forecast At Completion	Scheduled cost
Variance	Variance	BAC minus FAC

Determining Corrective Action

You should now have enough information to have formed some ideas about how to correct tasks with problems. You could consider adding new resources. Or would shifting resources from another task be better? Or maybe you are considering changing the scope of the project by deleting some tasks or changing the scope of future tasks.

List possible solutions and then use Microsoft Project to try the solutions and see the effect on the schedule, resources, and project cost. Repeat the steps in Chapters 8 and 9 to refine the schedule. For example, try shifting resources from one task to another, and see how it affects the future tasks and the finish date of the project. Or if you add resources, check the project finish date and project cost to see how they changed. Use the Gantt Chart, Task Sheet, and Task Form to change durations, change resources, and add or delete tasks.

Remember also to consider changes you need to make in future tasks. For example, you may want to review all future tasks using a resource that is behind schedule on task now in progress. Apply the Using Resource filter to the Task Sheet to display all tasks using the resource of interest. Then decide what to do about the task durations. Get the project team together to decide. For example, you may want to increase all durations. Or add resources to all the tasks using this resource to maintain the original duration estimates. Or cut scope on this set of tasks.

Another thing to check as you look for solutions is tasks that are now near critical. Knowing that a task is almost critical may help you determine how to handle another problem. For example, suppose you need to shift resources from one task to another. If a task will become critical if you remove its resources, you may not want to borrow these resources for another task.

To see tasks that are near critical, you can do one of two things:

- Create a filter that displays all tasks with slack less than an amount you specify.

- Change the Show As Critical If Slack <= option in the Options Preferences dialog box to a value other than zero. For example, if you change it to 3, all tasks with less than three days of slack time are displayed when you apply the Critical filter to the Task Sheet. To distinguish critical tasks with zero slack from those with a little slack, apply the Schedule table to the Task Sheet. Check the Total Slack field for how much slack time is available for the task.

You may also want to check for overallocated resources as you work on solutions. If a resource is already overallocated during a certain period, you know that it is part of your problem, and not part of your solution. To view overallocated resources, apply the Overallocated filter to the Resource Sheet. Place the Resource Sheet over the Resource Usage view to see when each resource is overallocated. This will help you decide how to move tasks around to take advantage of open times for resources, and eliminate those times when resources are overallocated.

Use the Gantt Chart to see how the changes affect the project as a whole; use the Options Project Info dialog box to check the new finish date and total work and cost for the project. Repeat the steps in Chapter 9, as needed, to optimize the schedule again.

Adding New Tasks to the Baseline Schedule

If it is necessary to add tasks to the schedule, either because you needed to break up tasks so resources would be available or because changes imposed by a client or management require new tasks, add these new tasks to the baseline schedule so you can track their progress.

To do this, you select the new tasks, and then choose Options Set Plan.

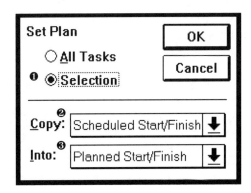

Select the Selection option ❶.
Copy the scheduled information ❷ into the Planned fields ❸.

When you are ready to track progress on these new tasks, their plan values will be available along with all the other plan values.

The next chapter has more information about communicating with those on the project team, management, or a client. More sample reports are included to help you convey the appropriate information at this stage in the project.

CHAPTER 13

Communicating
Progress

Keeping everyone informed about an ongoing project is an important part of your job. Once a project is underway, you periodically share information about progress on the project. Management or a client will want to know how things are progressing and project team members need to have the latest schedule information.

You communicate four types of information:

- Summary reports show information about progress on tasks.
- "Exception" reports show schedule variance.
- "Solution" reports show possible resolutions to problems and how the schedule looks with each possible solution. These reports give management the data to make decisions about the exceptions.
- "Direction" reports for task supervisors let them know the tasks to be performed and the resources needed during the next period.

When preparing a report for management or a client, include a summary report plus reports showing problem areas—exception reports—and either the solution or proposals for solutions—solution reports—for which you may need support, such as money or resources. The purpose of this set of reports is to show how the project is progressing and to show a list of "exceptions" so management can see what to concentrate on. If tasks are proceeding as planned, you have nothing to report other than a general status, with a note that all is progressing as planned. If there is variance in the actual progress, show these areas, along with a summary of the information you gathered as to the causes and solutions.

To control a project effectively, management needs to get reports showing exactly what they need, no more—they don't need reams of paper about every detail—and no less—they do need sufficient detail to make an informed decision. This information should be distributed quickly so that decisions can be made about how to get the project back on track as soon as possible.

Just as in the reports you created earlier, you might want to create several reports, each appropriate for the recipient, either summary or detail. Don't try to generate one huge report that fits everyone.

If possible, generate reports showing the problems and solutions graphically. Those receiving the reports can get the information they need much more quickly from a chart or graph than from words. If you make the information easily accessible, you are more likely to get a timely response when you need a decision quickly.

How frequently you generate progress reports depends on the requirements of management, a client, or contract. It also depends on the recipient. You may, for example, print direction reports frequently for work supervisors, giving them the detailed task and resource lists for the next period, but not so frequently for management who may just want periodic reassurance that progress is being made. You know best the reporting requirements of your organization. Set up a reporting cycle that satisfies these requirements.

USING MICROSOFT PROJECT FOR WINDOWS

When you generate reports to communicate progress information, you use the same set of tools used to print the original schedule reports. You can print views and reports, using any combination of a table and filter that shows what you want and is appropriate for the view or report.

When preparing exception reports, filter the tasks or resources to pinpoint the area of concern and avoid excessive detail. For example, you could filter the resource pool such that only those resources whose scheduled work is greater than planned appear in the report. The recipient of the report does not have to look through all the resources in the resource pool to find those few resources with problems, because only the resources with problems appear in the report.

You can also use sorting to highlight problem areas. For example, you could sort the resource pool such that those with the greatest variance in work are at the top of the list. These are the resources that require your readers' attention.

Another way to highlight tasks of interest is to mark the tasks and then change the font, style, or color of the text for the marked tasks. You mark tasks by selecting those tasks you want to mark, and then turning on the Marked check box in the Edit Form dialog box for tasks. In the Format Text dialog box, one of your options in the Item To Change box is Marked Tasks. Select this option, and then select the font, style, and color (if you have a color printer) to make the marked tasks stand out from the rest of the tasks.

If you used a certain combination of view, table, and filter in Chapter 12 to locate variance, and then find a solution to the variance, you might want to print that view, or use that table and filter in a report.

Before you print, be sure the settings in the File Printer Setup dialog box are appropriate for your printer, and the page is set up as you want in the File Page Setup dialog box. For more information, see Chapter 10, "Communicating the Plan."

Printing Summary Reports

To show a summary of progress on tasks and to show generally where the project stands, you can print any of the following views or the Project Summary report.

To Show	Print
Progress on tasks	Gantt Chart; PERT Chart; Task Sheet with the Tracking table applied
Percent complete and planned vs. actual duration	Tracking Gantt Chart
Summary of progress	Project Summary report
Summary of progress on major phases	Task Sheet with outline collapsed and Summary table applied
Summary of costs	Task report with Cost table applied
Completed tasks	Task Sheet or Task report with Completed filter applied

Showing Task Progress

There are several ways you can show progress on tasks. To show progress graphically, print the Gantt Chart or the PERT Chart.

Since the Gantt Chart includes progress bars and shows the date on which you collected the data, print the Gantt Chart to show the amount of progress on tasks and how progress compares to where you expected to be by the data collection date.

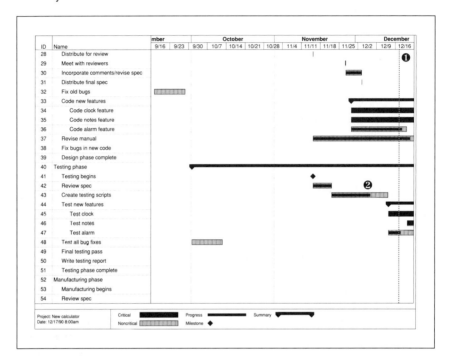

The current date line ❶ should match the date on which you collected data. You change this date in the Project Info dialog box.

The progress bars ❷ reflect the progress information entered about each task. Just as on screen, by comparing progress to the current date line, you see at a glance which tasks are on schedule, and which are ahead or behind.

TO PRINT THE GANTT CHART

1. Choose View Gantt Chart.

2. Choose Format Timescale.

3. In the Units boxes under Major Scale and Minor Scale, select the timescale units you want, and choose OK.

   For example, to duplicate the example showing months and weeks: In the Units box under Major Scale, select Months; in the Units box under Minor Scale, select Weeks.

4. To change the current date line so it matches the data collection date, choose Options Project Info.

5. In the Current box, type the data collection date, and choose OK.

6. To have the data collection date printed in the legend, instead of today's date, choose File Page Setup.

7. Choose the Legend button. In the Legend Text box, change the line "Date: &D" to "Date: &d" and choose OK twice.

A list of all codes used in the Legend Text box is included in Chapter 10, "Communicating the Plan," and is also included in Microsoft Project's Help. To see Help, press F1.

8. Choose File Print.

9. In the Print Timescale dialog box, choose OK.

10. Type the number of copies and the page range to print.

11. Choose OK.

Print the PERT Chart to show graphically tasks that have not started, tasks that are in progress (percent complete greater than 0 but less than 100), and tasks that are finished. For tasks that have started but not finished, the PERT node has one diagonal line. For tasks that are finished, the PERT node has two diagonal lines. In the next illustration, the finish date in each PERT node has been replaced with the percent complete.

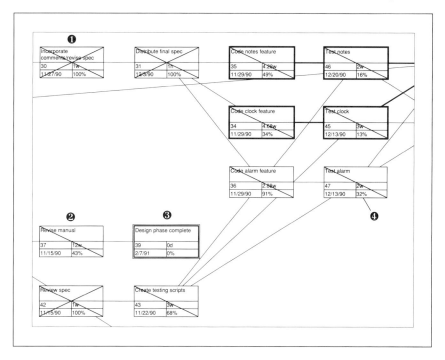

Tasks with two diagonal lines—an X—are finished ❶.

Tasks with one diagonal line have started but are not finished ❷.

Tasks with no lines have not started ❸.

Each node now shows the percent complete of the task ❹.

TO PRINT A PERT CHART

1. Choose View PERT Chart.

2. To replace the scheduled finish date with the percent complete in each node, choose Format Palette.

3. In the 5 box containing Scheduled Finish, select % Complete, and choose OK.

4. Choose File Print.

5. Type the number of copies and the page range you want to print.

6. Choose OK.

You can also print a list of tasks showing information about progress. For example, you can print the Task Sheet with the Tracking table applied to show the actual start and finish dates for tasks, the percent complete, and actual and remaining duration. If an actual start or finish date has not been entered, the field contains NA.

CALCULAT.MPP

ID	Name	Actual Start	Actual Finish	% Comp	Act. Dur.	Rem. Dur	Act. Cost	Act. Work
34	Code clock feat	11/29/90 2:00pm	NA	34%	1.6w	3.08w	$1,538.46	128h
35	Code notes feat	11/29/90 2:00pm	NA	49%	2.08w	2.2w	$1,000.00	83.2h
36	Code alarm fea	11/29/90 2:00pm	NA	91%	2.61w	0.27w	$1,254.81	104.4h
37	Revise manual	11/15/90 9:00am	NA	43%	5.16w	6.84w	$4,128.00	206.4h
38	Fix bugs in new co	12/25/90 2:00pm	NA	6%	0.21w	3.07w	$221.95	18.47h
39	Design phase com	NA	NA	0%	0d	0d	$0.00	0h
40	Testing phase	11/15/90 9:00am	NA	27%	31.12ed	84.13ed	$2,879.75	228.15h
41	Testing begins	NA	NA	0%	0d	0d	$0.00	0h
42	Review spec	11/15/90 9:00am	11/22/90 9:00am	100%	1w	0w	$1,430.29	110h
43	Create testing scrip	11/22/90 9:00am	NA	68%	2.04w	0.96w	$1,108.11	89.75h
44	Test new features	12/13/90 2:00pm	NA	19%	3.99ed	17.01ed	$341.35	28.4h
45	Test clock	12/13/90 2:00pm	NA	13%	0.39w	2.61w	$187.50	15.6h
46	Test notes	12/20/90 2:00pm	NA	16%	0.32w	1.68w	$153.85	12.8h
47	Test alarm	12/13/90 2:00pm	NA	32%	0.64w	1.36w	$0.00	0h
48	Test all bug fixes	NA	NA	0%	0w	2w	$0.00	0h
49	Final testing pass	NA	NA	0%	0w	2w	$0.00	0h
50	Write testing report	NA	NA	0%	0w	1w	$0.00	0h
51	Testing phase com	NA	NA	0%	0d	0d	$0.00	0h
52	Manufacturing phase	NA	NA	0%	0ed	91ed	$0.00	0h
53	Manufacturing begi	NA	NA	0%	0d	0d	$0.00	0h
54	Review spec	NA	NA	0%	0w	1w	$0.00	0h
55	Order parts	NA	NA	0%	0w	1w	$0.00	0h
56	Plan production line	NA	NA	0%	0w	3w	$0.00	0h
57	Set up production t	NA	NA	0%	0w	3w	$0.00	0h
58	Test production	NA	NA	0%	0w	3w	$0.00	0h
59	Begin production	NA	NA	0%	0d	0d	$0.00	0h
60	Pass production fu	NA	NA	0%	0w	2w	$0.00	0h
61	Manufacturing pha:	NA	NA	0%	0d	0d	$0.00	0h
62	Sales phase	NA	NA	0%	0ed	125.79ed	$0.00	0h
63	Sales begins	NA	NA	0%	0d	0d	$0.00	0h
64	Review spec	NA	NA	0%	0w	1w	$0.00	0h
65	Prepare market pla	NA	NA	0%	0h	60h	$0.00	0h
66	Distribute plan for r	NA	NA	0%	0h	4h	$0.00	0h

Page 2

TO PRINT A TASK SHEET SHOWING PROGRESS

1. Choose View Task Sheet.
2. Choose Table Tracking.
3. Choose File Print.
4. Type the number of copies and the page range you want to print.
5. Choose OK.

Showing Percent Complete and Changing Durations

Print the Tracking Gantt Chart to show how schedules are changing as tasks progress, and also to show the percent complete for each task.

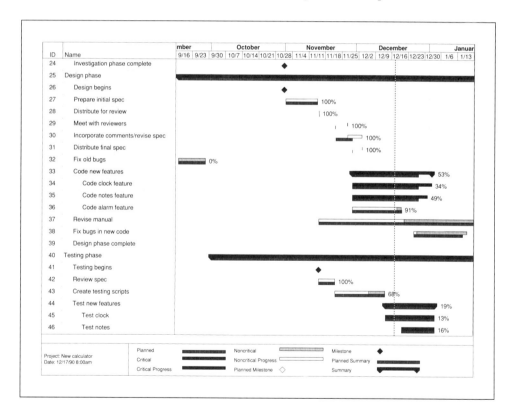

TO PRINT THE TRACKING GANTT CHART

1. Choose View Define Views.
2. In the Views box, select Tracking Gantt.
3. Choose the Set button.

4. Choose Format Timescale.

5. In the Units boxes under Major Scale and Minor Scale, select the timescale units you want, and choose OK.

For example, to duplicate the example showing months and weeks: In the Units box under Major Scale, select Months; in the Units box under Minor Scale, select Weeks.

6. Choose File Print.

7. In the Print Timescale dialog box, specify the time period you want to print and choose OK.

8. Type the number of copies and the page range to print.

9. Choose OK.

You specify legend information in the File Page Setup dialog box.

Printing a Summary Report

To give management or a client a quick review of where the project stands, print the Project Summary report. This report includes information about task costs, work, and progress for the project as a whole, including statistics on the number of tasks in progress and completed.

New calculator
Compusystems
Marcia Cryer

Dates

Project Start:	9/17/90 8:00am
Project Finish:	8/29/91 9:00am
Current:	12/17/90 8:00am

Costs

Scheduled:	$87,969.99	Remaining:	$45,180.79
Planned:	$84,498.90	Actual:	$42,789.20
Variance:	$3,471.09		

Work

Scheduled:	5582.43h	Remaining:	3290.82h
Planned:	5378h	Actual:	2291.62h
Variance:	204.43h		

Task Status

		Resource Status	
Tasks not yet started:	34	Resources:	24
Tasks in progress:	13	Overallocated Resources:	3
Tasks completed:	31		
Total Tasks:	78	Total Resources:	27

TO PRINT THE PROJECT SUMMARY REPORT

1. Choose View Print Report.
2. In the Print Report box, select Project Summary.
3. Choose the Print button.
4. Type the number of copies to print.
5. Choose OK.

Printing a Summary of Progress on Major Phases

If you included an outline in your project, you can collapse the outline to show progress information on major phases of the project. The percent complete is a summary of progress on the tasks subordinate to each summary task.

CALCULAT.MPP

ID	Name	Duration	Scheduled Start	Scheduled Finish	% Comp	Cost	Work
1	Investigation phase	63.38ed	9/17/90 8:00am	11/19/90 5:00pm	100%	$27,503.65	1193h
25	Design phase	143.04ed	9/17/90 8:00am	2/7/91 9:00am	47%	$27,293.26	1927.43h
40	Testing phase	115.25ed	10/1/90 8:00am	1/24/91 2:00pm	27%	$10,009.63	816h
52	Manufacturing phase	91ed	1/24/91 2:00pm	4/25/91 2:00pm	0%	$9,163.46	780h
62	Sales phase	125.79ed	4/25/91 2:00pm	8/29/91 9:00am	0%	$13,999.99	866h

Page 1

TO PRINT THE PERCENT COMPLETE OF MAJOR PHASES

1. Choose View Task Sheet.
2. To select all the tasks, choose Edit Select All.
3. Collapse the outline by pressing Alt + Shift + – (minus on the keypad) or clicking the collapse icon (⊟).
4. Choose Table Summary.
5. Choose File Print.
6. Type the number of copies and the page range you want to print.
7. Choose OK.

Printing a Summary of Costs

To print a summary of costs to date, print the Task report with the Cost table applied. If you have included an outline in your project, turn on the Summary Tasks check box to include costs to date for each major phase of the project. The costs printed for each summary task recap the costs for its subordinate tasks.

CALCULAT.MPP

ID	Name	Cost	Planned Cost	Variance	Actual Cost	Rem. Cost
1	Investigation phase	$27,503.65	$26,075.77	$1,427.88	$27,503.65	$0.00
2	Investigation begins	$0.00	$0.00	$0.00	$0.00	$0.00
3	Prepare initial product proposal	$7,189.42	$6,338.46	$850.96	$7,189.42	$0.00
4	Research competition	$2,807.69	$2,807.69	$0.00	$2,807.69	$0.00
5	Review customer comment cards	$1,569.23	$1,655.77	($86.54)	$1,569.23	$0.00
6	Write proposal	$2,812.50	$1,875.00	$937.50	$2,812.50	$0.00
7	Plan focus panel	$184.62	$184.62	$0.00	$184.62	$0.00
8	Arrange sites	$61.54	$61.54	$0.00	$61.54	$0.00
9	Contact hotels	$30.77	$61.54	($30.77)	$30.77	$0.00
10	Arrange for equipment	$30.77	$0.00	$30.77	$30.77	$0.00
11	Determine needed equipment	$30.77	$0.00	$30.77	$30.77	$0.00
12	Contact local offices	$0.00	$0.00	$0.00	$0.00	$0.00
13	Get panel members	$123.08	$123.08	$0.00	$123.08	$0.00
14	Contact local reps for names	$123.08	$123.08	$0.00	$123.08	$0.00
	Collect suggested panel members	$0.00	$0.00		$0.00	
77	Sales phase complete	$0.00	$0.00	$0.00	$0.00	$0.00
78	Project complete	$0.00	$0.00	$0.00	$0.00	$0.00
		$87,969.99	$84,498.90	$3,471.09	$42,789.20	$45,180.79

Page 3

TO PRINT A COST SUMMARY REPORT

1. Choose File Print Report.

2. In the Print Report box, select Task.

3. Choose the Copy button.

4. In the Name box, type "Cost Summary".

5. In the Table box, select Cost.

6. Turn on the Summary Tasks check box.

7. Turn on the Print Totals check box.

8. Choose OK.

9. Choose the Print button.

10. Type the number of copies and the range of pages to print.

11. Choose OK.

To show only a summary of the costs on major phases of the project, print the Task Sheet with the outline collapsed and the Cost table applied. The costs for the subordinate tasks will be summarized in each summary task.

Printing a List of Completed Tasks

To show all the tasks that have been completed, print the Task Sheet or Task report with the Completed filter applied. To print the Task Sheet with the Completed filter applied, just choose View Task Sheet, Filter Completed, and then File Print. To print a Task report showing completed tasks, use the File Print Report command.

CALCULAT.MPP

ID	Name	Actual Start	Actual Finish	% Comp	Act. Dur.	Rem. Dur	Act. Cost	Act. Work
2	Investigation begins	9/17/90 8:00am	9/17/90 8:00am	100%	0d	0d	$0.00	0h
4	Research competition	9/17/90 8:00am	9/26/90 12:00pm	100%	1.3w	0w	$2,807.69	144h
5	Review customer com	9/17/90 8:00am	9/20/90 5:00pm	100%	4d	0d	$1,569.23	88h
6	Write proposal	9/26/90 1:00pm	10/3/90 12:00pm	100%	1.5w	0w	$2,812.50	120h
9	Contact hotels	10/3/90 1:00pm	10/3/90 5:00pm	100%	4h	0h	$30.77	4h
11	Determine needed equ	10/3/90 1:00pm	10/3/90 5:00pm	100%	4h	0h	$30.77	4h
12	Contact local offices	10/4/90 8:00am	10/4/90 12:00pm	100%	4h	0h	$0.00	0h
14	Contact local reps for i	10/3/90 1:00pm	10/4/90 12:00pm	100%	1d	0d	$123.08	8h
15	Contact suggested par	10/4/90 1:00pm	10/8/90 12:00pm	100%	2d	0d	$0.00	0h
17	Prepare questionnaire	10/3/90 1:00pm	10/8/90 12:00pm	100%	3d	0d	$346.15	24h
18	Get list of users to call	10/8/90 10:00am	10/8/90 12:00pm	100%	2h	0h	$0.00	0h
19	Carry out focus panels	10/8/90 1:00pm	11/5/90 12:00pm	100%	4.5w	0w	$14,115.38	625h
20	Carry out phone surve	10/8/90 1:00pm	10/15/90 12:00pm	100%	1w	0w	$2,745.00	44h
21	Prepare focus panel re	11/5/90 1:00pm	11/19/90 12:00pm	100%	2w	0w	$1,576.93	108h
22	Prepare phone survey	10/15/90 1:00pm	10/17/90 5:00pm	100%	0.5w	0w	$1,250.00	20h
23	Present results	11/19/90 1:00pm	11/19/90 5:00pm	100%	4h	0h	$96.15	4h
24	Investigation phase co	10/31/90 5:00pm	10/31/90 5:00pm	100%	0d	0d	$0.00	0h
26	Design begins	10/31/90 5:00pm	10/31/90 5:00pm	100%	0d	0d	$0.00	0h
27	Prepare initial spec	11/1/90 8:00am	11/14/90 5:00pm	100%	2.5w	0w	$3,034.12	232h
28	Distribute for review	11/15/90 8:00am	11/15/90 9:00am	100%	1h	0h	$6.50	1h
29	Meet with reviewers	11/27/90 8:00am	11/27/90 1:00pm	100%	4h	0h	$105.77	8h
30	Incorporate comments	11/27/90 1:00pm	12/3/90 12:00pm	100%	1w	0w	$1,109.69	88h
31	Distribute final spec	12/3/90 1:00pm	12/3/90 2:00pm	100%	1h	0h	$6.50	1h
42	Review spec	11/15/90 9:00am	11/22/90 9:00am	100%	1w	0w	$1,430.29	110h

Page 1

TO PRINT A REPORT OF COMPLETED TASKS

1. Choose File Print Report.
2. In the Print Report box, select Task.
3. Choose the Copy button.
4. In the Name box, type "Completed Tasks".
5. In the Table box, select Tracking.
6. In the Filter box, select Completed.
7. Choose OK.
8. Choose the Print button.
9. Type the number of copies and the range of pages to print.
10. Choose OK.

Printing Exception Reports

There are many ways you can generate a report showing exceptions to the scheduled project.

To Show	Print
Tasks starting late	Task Sheet or Task report with Variance table applied and Should Start filter applied
Tasks scheduled to finish late	Task Sheet or Task report with Variance table applied and Slipping filter applied
Tasks that have a work amount different from planned	Task Sheet or Task report with Work table applied and Overbudget filter applied
Tasks costing more than planned	Task Sheet or Task report with Cost table applied and Overbudget filter applied
Resources working more than planned	Resource Sheet or Resource report with Work table applied and Work Overbudget filter applied
Resources costing more than planned	Resource Sheet or Resource report with Cost table applied and Cost Overbudget filter applied
Resources which are now overallocated due to changes in the schedule	Resource Sheet with the Overallocated filter applied
Earned value	Task Sheet or Task report with the Earned Value table applied

Showing Tasks That Have Started Late

When looking at late-starting tasks, you may be interested in two things: completed tasks or tasks now in progress that started late; and tasks that were scheduled to have started but have not yet started.

To see all tasks that started late, apply to the Task Sheet the Variance table and a filter that looks for tasks with a positive number in the Start Variance field. (The filter criterion would be Start Variance >0.) For more information about creating this filter, see Chapter 16, "Using Microsoft Project Tools." Of course, you could also use this filter in a Task report to show all tasks that started late.

CALCULAT.MPP

ID	Name	Sched. Start	Sched. Finish	Planned Start	Planned Finish	Start Var	Finish Var
6	Write proposal	9/26/90 1:00pm	10/3/90 12:00pm	9/20/90 3:00pm	9/27/90 3:00pm	5.92ed	5.88ed
7	Plan focus panel	10/3/90 1:00pm	10/8/90 12:00pm	9/27/90 3:00pm	10/2/90 3:00pm	5.92ed	5.88ed
8	Arrange sites	10/3/90 1:00pm	10/4/90 12:00pm	9/27/90 3:00pm	9/28/90 3:00pm	5.92ed	5.88ed
9	Contact hotels	10/3/90 1:00pm	10/3/90 5:00pm	9/27/90 3:00pm	9/28/90 3:00pm	5.92ed	5.08ed
10	Arrange for equipme	10/3/90 1:00pm	10/4/90 12:00pm	9/27/90 3:00pm	9/28/90 3:00pm	5.92ed	5.88ed
11	Determine needed e	10/3/90 1:00pm	10/3/90 5:00pm	9/27/90 3:00pm	9/28/90 10:00am	5.92ed	5.29ed
12	Contact local offices	10/4/90 8:00am	10/4/90 12:00pm	9/28/90 10:00am	9/28/90 3:00pm	5.92ed	5.88ed
13	Get panel members	10/3/90 1:00pm	10/8/90 12:00pm	9/27/90 3:00pm	10/2/90 3:00pm	5.92ed	5.88ed
14	Contact local reps fc	10/3/90 1:00pm	10/4/90 12:00pm	9/27/90 3:00pm	9/28/90 3:00pm	5.92ed	5.88ed
15	Contact suggested p	10/4/90 1:00pm	10/8/90 12:00pm	9/28/90 3:00pm	10/2/90 3:00pm	5.92ed	5.88ed
16	Plan phone questior	10/3/90 1:00pm	10/8/90 12:00pm	9/27/90 3:00pm	10/2/90 3:00pm	5.92ed	5.88ed
17	Prepare questionnai	10/3/90 1:00pm	10/8/90 12:00pm	9/27/90 3:00pm	10/2/90 3:00pm	5.92ed	5.88ed
18	Get list of users to c	10/8/90 10:00am	10/8/90 12:00pm	10/2/90 1:00pm	10/2/90 3:00pm	5.88ed	5.88ed
19	Carry out focus pan	10/8/90 1:00pm	11/5/90 12:00pm	10/2/90 3:00pm	10/30/90 3:00pm	5.92ed	5.88ed
20	Carry out phone sur	10/8/90 1:00pm	10/15/90 12:00pm	10/2/90 3:00pm	10/9/90 3:00pm	5.92ed	5.88ed
21	Prepare focus panel	11/5/90 1:00pm	11/19/90 12:00pm	10/30/90 3:00pm	11/13/90 3:00pm	5.92ed	5.88ed
22	Prepare phone surv	10/15/90 1:00pm	10/17/90 5:00pm	10/9/90 3:00pm	10/12/90 10:00am	5.92ed	5.29ed
23	Present results	11/19/90 1:00pm	11/19/90 5:00pm	11/13/90 3:00pm	11/14/90 10:00am	5.92ed	5.29ed
29	Meet with reviewers	11/27/90 8:00am	11/27/90 1:00pm	11/22/90 8:00am	11/22/90 12:00pm	5ed	5.04ed
30	Incorporate commer	11/27/90 1:00pm	12/3/90 12:00pm	11/22/90 1:00pm	11/29/90 12:00pm	5ed	4ed
31	Distribute final spec	12/3/90 1:00pm	12/3/90 2:00pm	11/29/90 1:00pm	11/29/90 2:00pm	4ed	4ed

Page 1

TO PRINT TASKS WITH A LATE START DATE

1. Choose View Task Sheet.

2. Choose Table Variance.

3. Apply a filter that finds all tasks with a positive number in the Start Variance field.

4. Choose File Print.

5. Type the number of copies and the page range you want to print.

6. Choose OK.

To see a list of all tasks that were scheduled to start, but for which you have not entered a start date, apply the Should Start filter to the Task Sheet.

CALCULAT.MPP

ID	Name	Duration	Scheduled Start	Scheduled Finish	Predecessors	Resource Names
32	Fix old bugs	2w	9/17/90 8:00am	9/28/90 5:00pm		Bill[0.1],Design staff[2]
41	Testing begins	0d	11/15/90 9:00am	11/15/90 9:00am	42SS	
48	Test all bug fixes	2w	10/1/90 8:00am	10/12/90 5:00pm	32	Testing staff[2]

TO PRINT TASKS THAT SHOULD HAVE STARTED BUT HAVE NOT

1. Choose View Task Sheet.

2. Choose Filter Should Start.

3. In the Date box, type the data collection date.

4. Choose File Print.

5. Type the number of copies and the page range you want to print.

6. Choose OK.

7. Type the data collection date and choose OK.

You can, of course, print the Task report instead of the Task Sheet, using the same tables and filters. One advantage of printing the Task report is that you can include notes in the report. If you have included notes with your tasks about the causes of late starts, print the notes to share this information with those receiving the report. To enter notes, choose Format Notes on the Task Form. Type the notes in the box at the bottom of the form.

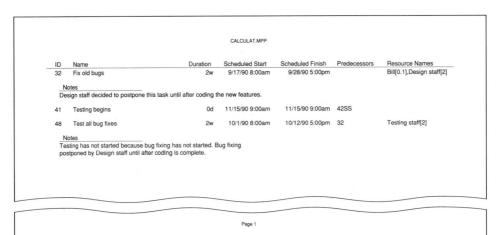

CALCULAT.MPP

ID	Name	Duration	Scheduled Start	Scheduled Finish	Predecessors	Resource Names
32	Fix old bugs	2w	9/17/90 8:00am	9/28/90 5:00pm		Bill[0.1],Design staff[2]

Notes
Design staff decided to postpone this task until after coding the new features.

| 41 | Testing begins | 0d | 11/15/90 9:00am | 11/15/90 9:00am | 42SS | |
| 48 | Test all bug fixes | 2w | 10/1/90 8:00am | 10/12/90 5:00pm | 32 | Testing staff[2] |

Notes
Testing has not started because bug fixing has not started. Bug fixing
postponed by Design staff until after coding is complete.

TO PRINT LATE-STARTING TASKS AND NOTES

1. Choose File Print Report.
2. In the Print Report box, select Task.
3. Choose the Copy button.
4. In the Name box, type "Late Tasks with Notes".
5. In the Table box, select Entry.
6. In the Filter box, select Should Start.
7. Turn on the Notes check box.
8. Choose OK.
9. Choose the Print button.
10. Type the number of copies and the range of pages to print.
11. Choose OK.
12. Type the data collection date and choose OK.

Showing Tasks That Have Finished or Will Finish Late

When looking at late-finishing tasks, you may be interested in two things: tasks scheduled to finish late, and tasks that have actually finished late.

To see all tasks now in progress that are schedule to finish late, apply the Variance table and Slipping filter to the Task Sheet. The Slipping filter shows all tasks in progress whose scheduled finish date is later than the planned finish date.

CALCULAT.MPP

ID	Name	Sched. Start	Sched. Finish	Planned Start	Planned Finish	Start Var	Finish Var
33	Code new features	11/29/90 2:00pm	1/2/91 8:12am	11/29/90 2:00pm	12/27/90 2:00pm	0ed	5.76ed
34	Code clock feature	11/29/90 2:00pm	1/2/91 8:12am	11/29/90 2:00pm	12/27/90 2:00pm	0ed	5.76ed
35	Code notes feature	11/29/90 2:00pm	12/31/90 8:12am	11/29/90 2:00pm	12/27/90 2:00pm	0ed	3.76ed
38	Fix bugs in new cod	12/25/90 2:00pm	1/17/91 8:12am	12/25/90 2:00pm	1/15/91 2:00pm	0ed	1.76ed

Page 1

TO PRINT TASKS SCHEDULED TO FINISH LATE

1. Choose View Task Sheet.

2. Choose Table Variance.

3. Choose Filter Slipping.

4. Choose File Print.

5. Type the number of copies and the page range you want to print.

6. Choose OK.

To see a list of all tasks that actually finished late, apply to the Task Sheet the Variance table and a filter that looks for tasks with a positive number in the Finish Variance field. For more information about creating this filter, see Chapter 16, "Using Microsoft Project Tools."

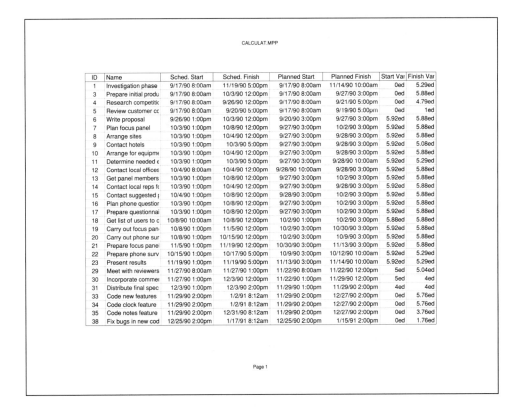

CALCULAT.MPP

ID	Name	Sched. Start	Sched. Finish	Planned Start	Planned Finish	Start Var	Finish Var
1	Investigation phase	9/17/90 8:00am	11/19/90 5:00pm	9/17/90 8:00am	11/14/90 10:00am	0ed	5.29ed
3	Prepare initial produ	9/17/90 8:00am	10/3/90 12:00pm	9/17/90 8:00am	9/27/90 3:00pm	0ed	5.88ed
4	Research competitic	9/17/90 8:00am	9/26/90 12:00pm	9/17/90 8:00am	9/21/90 5:00pm	0ed	4.79ed
5	Review customer cc	9/17/90 8:00am	9/20/90 5:00pm	9/17/90 8:00am	9/19/90 5:00pm	0ed	1ed
6	Write proposal	9/26/90 1:00pm	10/3/90 12:00pm	9/20/90 3:00pm	9/27/90 3:00pm	5.92ed	5.88ed
7	Plan focus panel	10/3/90 1:00pm	10/8/90 12:00pm	9/27/90 3:00pm	10/2/90 3:00pm	5.92ed	5.88ed
8	Arrange sites	10/3/90 1:00pm	10/4/90 12:00pm	9/27/90 3:00pm	9/28/90 3:00pm	5.92ed	5.88ed
9	Contact hotels	10/3/90 1:00pm	10/3/90 5:00pm	9/27/90 3:00pm	9/28/90 3:00pm	5.92ed	5.08ed
10	Arrange for equipme	10/3/90 1:00pm	10/4/90 12:00pm	9/27/90 3:00pm	9/28/90 3:00pm	5.92ed	5.88ed
11	Determine needed e	10/3/90 1:00pm	10/3/90 5:00pm	9/27/90 3:00pm	9/28/90 10:00am	5.92ed	5.29ed
12	Contact local offices	10/4/90 8:00am	10/8/90 12:00pm	9/28/90 10:00am	9/28/90 3:00pm	5.92ed	5.88ed
13	Get panel members	10/3/90 1:00pm	10/8/90 12:00pm	9/27/90 3:00pm	10/2/90 3:00pm	5.92ed	5.88ed
14	Contact local reps fo	10/3/90 1:00pm	10/4/90 12:00pm	9/27/90 3:00pm	9/28/90 3:00pm	5.92ed	5.88ed
15	Contact suggested p	10/4/90 1:00pm	10/8/90 12:00pm	9/28/90 3:00pm	10/2/90 3:00pm	5.92ed	5.88ed
16	Plan phone questior	10/3/90 1:00pm	10/8/90 12:00pm	9/27/90 3:00pm	10/2/90 3:00pm	5.92ed	5.88ed
17	Prepare questionnai	10/3/90 1:00pm	10/8/90 12:00pm	9/27/90 3:00pm	10/2/90 3:00pm	5.92ed	5.88ed
18	Get list of users to c	10/8/90 10:00am	10/8/90 12:00pm	10/2/90 1:00pm	10/2/90 3:00pm	5.88ed	5.88ed
19	Carry out focus pan	10/8/90 1:00pm	11/5/90 12:00pm	10/2/90 3:00pm	10/30/90 3:00pm	5.92ed	5.88ed
20	Carry out phone sur	10/8/90 1:00pm	10/15/90 12:00pm	10/2/90 3:00pm	10/9/90 3:00pm	5.92ed	5.88ed
21	Prepare focus panel	11/5/90 1:00pm	11/19/90 12:00pm	10/30/90 3:00pm	11/13/90 3:00pm	5.92ed	5.88ed
22	Prepare phone surv	10/15/90 1:00pm	10/17/90 12:00pm	10/9/90 3:00pm	10/12/90 10:00am	5.92ed	5.29ed
23	Present results	11/19/90 1:00pm	11/19/90 5:00pm	11/13/90 3:00pm	11/14/90 10:00am	5.92ed	5.29ed
29	Meet with reviewers	11/27/90 8:00am	11/27/90 1:00pm	11/22/90 8:00am	11/22/90 12:00pm	5ed	5.04ed
30	Incorporate commer	11/27/90 1:00pm	12/3/90 12:00pm	11/22/90 1:00pm	11/29/90 12:00pm	5ed	4ed
31	Distribute final spec	12/3/90 1:00pm	12/3/90 2:00pm	11/29/90 1:00pm	11/29/90 2:00pm	4ed	4ed
33	Code new features	11/29/90 2:00pm	1/2/91 8:12am	11/29/90 2:00pm	12/27/90 2:00pm	0ed	5.76ed
34	Code clock feature	11/29/90 2:00pm	1/2/91 8:12am	11/29/90 2:00pm	12/27/90 2:00pm	0ed	5.76ed
35	Code notes feature	11/29/90 2:00pm	12/31/90 8:12am	11/29/90 2:00pm	12/27/90 2:00pm	0ed	3.76ed
38	Fix bugs in new cod	12/25/90 2:00pm	1/17/91 8:12am	12/25/90 2:00pm	1/15/91 2:00pm	0ed	1.76ed

Page 1

TO PRINT TASKS THAT FINISHED LATE

1. Choose View Task Sheet.

2. Apply a filter that finds all tasks with a positive number in the Finish Variance field.

3. Choose File Print.

4. Type the number of copies and the page range you want to print.

5. Choose OK.

You can, of course, print the Task report instead of the Task Sheet, using the same tables and filters. One advantage of printing the Task report is that you can include notes in the report. If you have included notes with your tasks about the causes of late finishes, print the notes to share this information with those receiving the report. To print notes, turn on the Notes check box in the Edit Task Report dialog box. To enter notes, choose Format Notes on the Task Form. Type the notes in the box at the bottom of the form.

Showing Tasks That Have a Different Work Amount

Print the Task Sheet or Task report with the Work table and the Overbudget filter applied to show the work for all tasks that are over budget. The Overbudget filter looks for all tasks whose costs are over budget, but because costs are directly proportional to work, the list of tasks with cost over budget will be the same as those tasks with work greater than scheduled.

CALCULAT.MPP

ID	Name	Work	Planned Work	Variance	Actual Work	Rem. Work
1	Investigation phase	1193h	1152h	41h	1193h	0h
3	Prepare initial product proposal	352h	336h	16h	352h	0h
6	Write proposal	120h	80h	40h	120h	0h
19	Carry out focus panels	625h	600h	25h	625h	0h
25	Design phase	1927.43h	1772h	155.43h	870.47h	1056.97h
27	Prepare initial spec	232h	186h	46h	232h	0h
33	Code new features	660.8h	600h	60.8h	315.6h	345.2h
34	Code clock feature	374.4h	320h	54.4h	128h	246.4h
35	Code notes feature	171.2h	160h	11.2h	83.2h	88h
38	Fix bugs in new code	288.63h	240h	48.63h	18.47h	270.17h
40	Testing phase	816h	808h	8h	228.15h	587.85h
49	Final testing pass	168h	160h	8h	0h	168h

Page 1

TO PRINT TASKS WITH WORK GREATER THAN SCHEDULED

1. Choose View Task Sheet.

2. Choose Table Work.

3. Choose Filter Overbudget.

4. Choose File Print.

5. Type the number of copies and the page range you want to print.

6. Choose OK.

Again, you can print the Task report instead of the Task Sheet and include notes about the causes of work variances in the report.

Showing Tasks That Have a Different Cost Amount

Print the Task Sheet or Task report with the Cost table and the Overbudget filter applied to show the cost for all tasks that are over budget. If you include notes in the Notes box on the Task Form (choose Format Notes) about the cause of the variance, you can print these notes when you print the Task report.

CALCULAT.MPP

ID	Name	Cost	Planned Cost	Variance	Actual Cost	Rem. Cost
6	Write proposal	$2,812.50	$1,875.00	$937.50	$2,812.50	$0.00

Notes
Because Marcia and Janet didn't have all the information they were promised, they had to do additional research to complete the proposal. This additional work resulted in the proposal being released 3 days late, and caused costs to go up.

| 19 | Carry out focus panels | $14,115.38 | $13,538.46 | $576.92 | $14,115.38 | $0.00 |

Notes
These ended up taking 4 1/2 weeks instead of the 4 weeks originally planned because we couldn't arrange the New York and Boston focus panels until one week later, throwing off the rest of the schedule.

| 27 | Prepare initial spec | $3,034.12 | $2,431.20 | $602.92 | $3,034.12 | $0.00 |

Notes
Because of the tight schedule, we had to cut features in the initial spec before sending it out for review. This added 1/2 week to the process because we had to decide what to cut.

| 34 | Code clock feature | $4,500.00 | $3,846.15 | $653.85 | $1,538.46 | $2,961.54 |

Notes
The original method of implementing this feature didn't work, so we had to rethink our plan. This put us behind schedule, and over budget, but we hope to make up this time.

| 35 | Code notes feature | $2,057.69 | $1,923.08 | $134.61 | $1,000.00 | $1,057.69 |

Notes
Continued discussion on how to implement the alphabet has caused delays in this task.

| 38 | Fix bugs in new code | $3,469.14 | $2,884.62 | $584.52 | $221.95 | $3,247.19 |
| 49 | Final testing pass | $2,048.08 | $1,923.08 | $125.00 | $0.00 | $2,048.08 |

Page 1

TO PRINT TASKS WITH COST GREATER THAN SCHEDULED

1. Choose File Print Report.
2. In the Print Report box, select Task.
3. Choose the Copy button.
4. In the Name box, type "Tasks Overbudget".
5. In the Table box, select Cost.

6. In the Filter box, select Overbudget.

7. Turn on the Print Totals check box.

8. Turn on the Notes check box.

9. Choose OK.

10. Choose the Print button.

11. Type the number of copies and the range of pages to print.

12. Choose OK.

You can print the Task Sheet instead of the Task report, although any notes you have entered about the causes of the variances won't be printed.

Showing Resources That Have a Different Work Amount

Print the Resource Sheet or Resource report with the Work table and the Work Overbudget filter applied to show the work for all resources that are over budget.

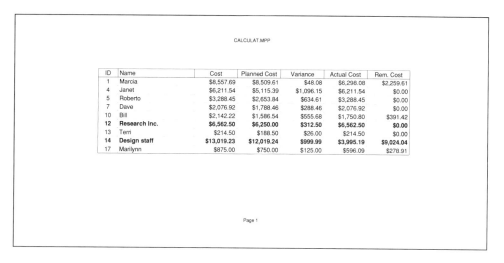

CALCULAT.MPP

ID	Name	Cost	Planned Cost	Variance	Actual Cost	Rem. Cost
1	Marcia	$8,557.69	$8,509.61	$48.08	$6,298.08	$2,259.61
4	Janet	$6,211.54	$5,115.39	$1,096.15	$6,211.54	$0.00
5	Roberto	$3,288.45	$2,653.84	$634.61	$3,288.45	$0.00
7	Dave	$2,076.92	$1,788.46	$288.46	$2,076.92	$0.00
10	Bill	$2,142.22	$1,586.54	$555.68	$1,750.80	$391.42
12	**Research Inc.**	**$6,562.50**	**$6,250.00**	**$312.50**	**$6,562.50**	**$0.00**
13	Terri	$214.50	$188.50	$26.00	$214.50	$0.00
14	**Design staff**	**$13,019.23**	**$12,019.24**	**$999.99**	**$3,995.19**	**$9,024.04**
17	Marilynn	$875.00	$750.00	$125.00	$596.09	$278.91

Page 1

TO PRINT RESOURCES WITH WORK GREATER THAN SCHEDULED

1. Choose View Resource Sheet.

2. Choose Table Work.

3. Choose Filter Work Overbudget.

4. Choose File Print.

5. Type the number of copies and the page range you want to print.

6. Choose OK.

You can also print a Resource report using the same table and filter and include notes about the causes of work variances. To print Notes, turn on the Notes check box in the Edit Resource Report dialog box. To enter notes about resources, choose Format Notes on the Resource Form. Type the notes in the box at the bottom of the form.

Showing Resources That Have a Different Cost Amount

Print the Resource Sheet or Resource report with the Cost table and the Cost Overbudget filter applied to show the cost for all overbudget resources.

CALCULAT.MPP

ID	Name	Cost	Planned Cost	Variance	Actual Cost	Rem. Cost
1	Marcia	$8,557.69	$8,509.61	$48.08	$6,298.08	$2,259.61

Notes

Marcia had to spend extra time on writing the proposal because information was not available as planned and on helping with the spec, which took longer than planned because decisions had to be made about cutting features.

| 4 | Janet | $6,211.54 | $5,115.39 | $1,096.15 | $6,211.54 | $0.00 |

Notes

Janet was assigned to reviewing the customer comment cards, writing the proposal, and working the focus panels. See the Tasks Overbudget report for a description of the problems on these tasks.

| 5 | Roberto | $3,288.45 | $2,653.84 | $634.61 | $3,288.45 | $0.00 |

Notes

Roberto helped out on reviewing the customer comment cards, although he was not originally assigned to the task. He was also involved with the focus panels, which took longer than expected because of delays in two of the panels.

| 7 | Dave | $2,076.92 | $1,788.46 | $288.46 | $2,076.92 | $0.00 |

Notes

Preparing the initial spec took longer than expected because of the discussions on cutting features, which Dave was involved in.

| 10 | Bill | $2,142.22 | $1,586.54 | $555.68 | $1,750.80 | $391.42 |

Notes

Bill was also involved in the spec feature discussions and has also worked on bug fixes, to which he was not originally assigned.

| 12 | Research Inc. | $6,562.50 | $6,250.00 | $312.50 | $6,562.50 | $0.00 |

Notes

Additional time on the focus panel caused our bill from Research, Inc.

Page 1

TO PRINT RESOURCES WITH COST GREATER THAN SCHEDULED

1. Choose File Print Report.
2. In the Print Report box, select Resource.
3. Choose the Copy button.
4. In the Name box, type "Resources Overbudget".

5. In the Table box, select Cost.

6. In the Filter box, select Cost Overbudget.

7. Turn on the Print Totals check box.

8. Turn on the Notes check box.

9. Choose OK.

10. Choose the Print button.

11. Type the number of copies and the range of pages to print.

12. Choose OK.

You can also print the Resource Sheet using the same table and filter although any notes you have entered about the causes of cost variances won't be printed.

Showing Resources That Are Overallocated

To print a list of all resources that are currently assigned more work than you have units available, apply the Overallocated filter to the Resource Sheet or Resource report.

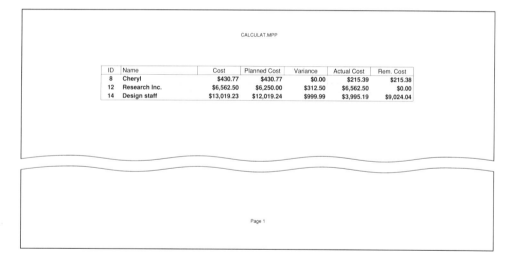

TO PRINT OVERALLOCATED RESOURCES

1. Choose View Resource Sheet.

2. Choose Filter Overallocated.

3. Choose File Print.

4. Type the number of copies and the page range you want to print.

5. Choose OK.

Earned Value Report

There are two ways you can generate an earned value report. You can print the Task Sheet with the Earned Value table applied or you can print a Task report with the Earned Value table applied. Both include the same information, but the Task report can also includes totals. Because of the space required for the columns across the page, the Indentation check box in the Format Outline dialog box was turned off, allowing more space for the names. To make the summary tasks stand out without the indentation, the summary tasks were changed to bold text.

CALCULAT.MPP

Name	BCWS	BCWP	ACWP	SV	CV	BAC	FAC	Variance
Investigation phase	$26,075.77	$26,075.77	$27,503.65	$0.00	($1,427.88)	$26,075.77	$27,503.65	$1,427.88
Investigation begins	$0.00	$0.00	$0.00	$0.00	$0.00	$0.00	$0.00	$0.00
Prepare initial produc	$6,338.46	$6,338.46	$7,189.42	$0.00	($850.96)	$6,338.46	$7,189.42	$850.96
Research competition	$2,807.69	$2,807.69	$2,807.69	$0.00	$0.00	$2,807.69	$2,807.69	$0.00
Review customer comm	$1,655.77	$1,655.77	$1,569.23	$0.00	$86.54	$1,655.77	$1,569.23	($86.54)
Write proposal	$1,875.00	$1,875.00	$2,812.50	$0.00	($937.50)	$1,875.00	$2,812.50	$937.50
Plan focus panel	$184.62	$184.62	$184.62	$0.00	$0.00	$184.62	$184.62	$0.00
Arrange sites	$61.54	$61.54	$61.54	$0.00	$0.00	$61.54	$61.54	$0.00
Contact hotels	$61.54	$61.54	$30.77	$0.00	$30.77	$61.54	$30.77	($30.77)
Arrange for equipmen	$0.00	$0.00	$30.77	$0.00	($30.77)	$0.00	$30.77	$30.77
Determine needed equi	$0.00	$0.00	$30.77	$0.00	($30.77)	$0.00	$30.77	$30.77
Contact local offices	$0.00	$0.00	$0.00	$0.00	$0.00	$0.00	$0.00	$0.00
Get panel members	$123.08	$123.08	$123.08	$0.00	$0.00	$123.08	$123.08	$0.00
Contact local reps for n	$123.08	$123.08	$123.08	$0.00	$0.00	$123.08	$123.08	$0.00
Contact suggested pan	$0.00	$0.00	$0.00	$0.00	$0.00	$0.00	$0.00	$0.00
Plan phone questionn	$346.15	$346.15	$346.15	$0.00	$0.00	$346.15	$346.15	$0.00
Prepare questionnaire	$346.15	$346.15	$346.15	$0.00	$0.00	$346.15	$346.15	$0.00
Get list of users to call	$0.00	$0.00	$0.00	$0.00	$0.00	$0.00	$0.00	$0.00
Carry out focus panels	$13,538.46	$13,538.46	$14,115.38	$0.00	($576.92)	$13,538.46	$14,115.38	$576.92
Carry out phone survey	$2,745.00	$2,745.00	$2,745.00	$0.00	$0.00	$2,745.00	$2,745.00	$0.00
Prepare focus panel rep	$1,576.93	$1,576.93	$1,576.93	$0.00	$0.00	$1,576.93	$1,576.93	$0.00
Prepare phone survey r	$1,250.00	$1,250.00	$1,250.00	$0.00	$0.00	$1,250.00	$1,250.00	$0.00
Present results	$96.15	$96.15	$96.15	$0.00	$0.00	$96.15	$96.15	$0.00
Investigation phase con	$0.00	$0.00	$0.00	$0.00	$0.00	$0.00	$0.00	$0.00
Design phase	$15,986.28	$11,926.27	$12,405.80	($4,060.01)	($479.53)	$25,375.05	$27,293.26	$1,918.21
Design begins	$0.00	$0.00	$0.00	$0.00	$0.00	$0.00	$0.00	$0.00
Prepare initial spec	$2,431.20	$2,431.20	$3,034.12	$0.00	($602.92)	$2,431.20	$3,034.12	$602.92
Distribute for review	$6.50	$6.50	$6.50	$0.00	$0.00	$6.50	$6.50	$0.00
Meet with reviewers	$105.77	$105.77	$105.77	$0.00	$0.00	$105.77	$105.77	$0.00
Incorporate comments/r	$1,109.69	$1,109.69	$1,109.69	$0.00	$0.00	$1,109.69	$1,109.69	$0.00
Distribute final spec	$0.00	$6.50	$6.50	$6.50	$0.00	$6.50	$6.50	$0.00
Fix old bugs	$2,019.23	$0.00	$0.00	($2,019.23)	$0.00	$2,019.23	$2,019.23	$0.00
Code new features	$4,543.27	$3,822.11	$3,793.27	($721.16)	$28.84	$7,211.54	$7,942.31	$730.77

Page 1

TO PRINT THE TASK SHEET SHOWING EARNED VALUE

1. Choose View Task Sheet.
2. Choose Table Define Tables.
3. In the Tables box, select Earned Value.
4. Choose the Set button.
5. Choose Format Outline, turn off the Name Indentation check box, and then choose OK.

6. Choose Format Text.

7. In the Item To Change box, select Summary Tasks.

8. Turn on the Bold check box and choose OK.

9. Choose File Print.

10. Type the number of copies and the range of pages to print.

11. Choose OK.

CALCULAT.MPP

Name	BCWS	BCWP	ACWP	SV	CV	BAC	FAC
Investigation phase	**$26,075.77**	**$26,075.77**	**$27,503.65**	**$0.00**	**($1,427.88)**	**$26,075.77**	**$27,503.65**
Investigation begins	$0.00	$0.00	$0.00	$0.00	$0.00	$0.00	$0.00
Prepare initial produc	**$6,338.46**	**$6,338.46**	**$7,189.42**	**$0.00**	**($850.96)**	**$6,338.46**	**$7,189.42**
Research competition	$2,807.69	$2,807.69	$2,807.69	$0.00	$0.00	$2,807.69	$2,807.69
Review customer comm	$1,655.77	$1,655.77	$1,569.23	$0.00	$86.54	$1,655.77	$1,569.23
Write proposal	$1,875.00	$1,875.00	$2,812.50	$0.00	($937.50)	$1,875.00	$2,812.50
Plan focus panel	**$184.62**	**$184.62**	**$184.62**	**$0.00**	**$0.00**	**$184.62**	**$184.62**
Arrange sites	**$61.54**	**$61.54**	**$61.54**	**$0.00**	**$0.00**	**$61.54**	**$61.54**
Contact hotels	$61.54	$61.54	$30.77	$0.00	$30.77	$61.54	$30.77
Arrange for equipmen	**$0.00**	**$0.00**	**$30.77**	**$0.00**	**($30.77)**	**$0.00**	**$30.77**
Determine needed equij	$0.00	$0.00	$30.77	$0.00	($30.77)	$0.00	$30.77
Contact local offices	$0.00	$0.00	$0.00	$0.00	$0.00	$0.00	$0.00
Get panel members	**$123.08**	**$123.08**	**$123.08**	**$0.00**	**$0.00**	**$123.08**	**$123.08**
Sales phase complete	$0.00	$0.00	$0.00	$0.00	$0.00	$0.00	$0.00
Project complete	$0.00	$0.00	$0.00	$0.00	$0.00	$0.00	$0.00
	$45,470.68	$40,478.89	$42,789.20	($4,991.79)	($2,310.31)	$84,498.90	$87,969.99

Page 3

TO PRINT A TASK REPORT SHOWING EARNED VALUE

1. Choose File Print Report.

2. In the Print Report box, select Task.

3. Choose the Copy button.

4. In the Name box, type "Earned Value".

5. In the Table box, select Earned Value.

6. Choose the Text button.

7. In the Item To Change box, select Summary Tasks.

8. Turn on the Bold check box and choose OK.

9. Turn on the Summary Tasks check box.

10. Turn on the Print Totals check box.

11. Choose OK.

12. Choose the Print button.

13. Type the number of copies and the range of pages to print.

14. Choose OK.

Showing Possible Solutions

When you find a problem and then use "what-if" analysis to come up with a solution or proposed solutions, share these solutions with management, a client, or the project team. Print the same views and reports to permit the recipients to compare the schedule now with how it will be if you change it as proposed. For example, if you move tasks to ease resource overallocation, change task dependencies to shorten the critical path, and add resources to a group of tasks to accelerate them, you will want to show how the schedule, work, and cost will change for the project.

To Show	Print
New schedule	Gantt Chart; Tracking Gantt Chart
New project finish date, cost, and work	Project Summary report
Change in costs for individual tasks	Task Sheet or Task report with the Cost table applied
Change in costs for individual resources	Resource Sheet or Resource report with Cost table applied
Change in earned value	Task Sheet or Task report with the Earned Value table applied

You print these reports as described earlier in this chapter, and then highlight those sections you want the recipient to concentrate on. One way to highlight the information is to mark the tasks of interest, and then change the font, style, and color of the text for the marked tasks, as described earlier in this chapter. For example, to show how adding resources to certain tasks will change the schedule, mark these tasks and make the text bold. Point out the change in the critical path on the Gantt Chart and the finish date on the Project Summary report.

Printing Direction Reports

Just as you printed periodic task and resource reports for the work supervisors before the project started, continue to print these reports as needed throughout the project. It is especially important to print these reports any time you make a change to the schedule that will affect the way or time a task is carried out.

To Show	Print
Tasks to be performed during the next period	Periodic Task report
Resources used during the next period	Periodic Resource report

Print these reports as often as necessary. For more information about printing these reports, see Chapter 10, "Communicating the Plan."

MULTIPLE PROJECTS, SHARING INFORMATION, AND USING THE TOOLS

Part 5 describes several features included in Microsoft Project for Windows that will make your project management job easier. While these tools are not directly related to the project management process, they are related to the every day mechanics of getting your job done.

- Chapter 14 shows you how to use subprojects and work with multiple projects, a very real occurrence in today's busy world.

- Chapter 15 shows you how you can share information between Microsoft Project for Windows and Microsoft Excel, Lotus 1-2-3, or Microsoft Word for Windows. Using Microsoft Excel, you can create graphs of your cost information, and share resource information that might already be in a Microsoft Excel file. Using Word for Windows, you can write a report, and then place selected information from Microsoft Project directly into the report.

- Chapter 16 gives you explicit procedures for using Microsoft Project's tables, filters, views, and reports. Procedures to create a new table, filter, view, and report are included in this chapter, as well as some general instructions on creating your own tables, filters, views, calendars, and reports.

CHAPTER 14

Managing Multiple Projects

For many project managers, the biggest challenge is managing several projects, all starting and finishing at different times, and using the same set of resources. Microsoft Project for Windows can help you keep track of all your projects and avoid resource conflicts, making sure resources are not needed at the same time on different projects.

You can work with multiple projects in many ways. For example, you can:

- Create projects for groups of tasks you do over and over, and then use these projects as subprojects within other projects. For example, if one part of every new product is creating the documentation, you might have a project containing all the steps necessary to produce the manual, from the manual design document to printing. You would use this project as a subproject in each new project for a product that required a manual.

- If many of your projects are similar—for example, creating and producing marketing brochures, or designing buildings, create a project template to use as the basis for future projects. This template project contains a list of all tasks normally done in such a project. Each time you get a new project, rename the template, and then customize it to match the current project.

- Store all resource information in one project, and then link all other projects to the project containing the resources.

- Open the projects of interest and view resource use for all open projects.

- Combine all projects in one window to see how the schedules overlap, check resource use, or create one report showing a summary of all projects.

Using Subprojects

A subproject is a group of tasks which has its own project file, but is represented as a single task in another project, called a master project. Use subprojects:

- To keep the most detailed tasks in a project separate from the master project. This makes it easy for each subproject manager to keep track of their tasks, and the manager of the whole project can see a project summary without dealing with the detail tasks included in the subprojects.
- When you have similar sets of tasks to perform in many projects. Rather than reentering same set of tasks each time they occur in a project, you can specify sets of tasks as subprojects. From then on you enter and manage the subproject as one task.
- To conserve memory in your computer. If you don't open subprojects, the amount of computer memory needed to calculate project information is reduced.

Work with the master project when you are interested in the broadest level of detail; work with individual subprojects when you want to concentrate on more detailed tasks.
Subprojects have the following advantages:

- You avoid entering the same set of tasks over and over, for each new project.
- If some step changes in the subproject, you change it once—in the subproject—instead of over and over in each project that contains the subproject.
- If you are working with very large projects, using subprojects can help you conserve memory. You can leave the subprojects closed except when you need to work with the tasks in the subproject.

You may think of your projects modularly, with each module being a separate subproject. These subprojects are then combined to make your master project. You can use a subproject over and over in one project or in many projects. It is similar to outlining in that it is another way to organize your tasks into a hierarchy—instead of subordinate tasks, however, the detail tasks are in a subproject. Use subprojects when you want to use a set of tasks over and over; use an outline when you don't.

Each subproject is summarized by a subproject task instead of a summary task. A subproject task summarizes the tasks in the subproject, just as a summary task does. The duration for a subproject task is the elapsed duration for the tasks in the subproject and the costs and work are the totals for the tasks in the subproject. Subproject tasks don't indicate percent complete for the subproject the way summary tasks do for their subordinate tasks, however.

For example, if you are scheduling all new products for the next two years, you could have a subproject for a new business calculator, one for a new high-end scientific calculator, and another for a calculator upgrade. These subprojects would be included in a master project, and each subproject could contain additional subprojects for the planning, design, manual, and so on.

Master Project: Two-year Product Plan

- New business calculator (subproject)
- New scientific calculator (subproject)
- Calculator upgrade (subproject)
- and so on

The individual calculator projects would each contain the following tasks:

- Planning (subproject)
- Design (subproject)
- Manual (subproject)
- and so on

If the subproject is always the same—same resources, same duration for all tasks within the subproject, and so on—you can use the same subproject name over and over, as needed in any master projects. If you use this method, however, you can't track resource usage across projects, nor can you track progress. A better way is to rename the file each time you use it so you can track resource usage across projects and track progress. Choose File Save As to duplicate the file and save it with a new name, and then change any details within the subproject as appropriate. For example, you may have a subproject called Manual that includes all the basic steps for creating a manual; each time you use the subproject, rename it and change the duration for tasks in the subproject depending on the manual size and style.

Creating a Subproject

What makes a project a subproject is not how you create it, but how you later use it. When you create a project that you plan to use as a subproject, follow the same steps as creating any project.

CREATING A SUBPROJECT

1. Choose File New.
2. Type the tasks in this project.
3. Enter durations and dependencies.
4. Assign resources. If you want to use the resources that are in another project, choose File Resources, and select the project containing the resources you want to share.
5. To save the project, use the File Save As command.

If you want to track resource usage across projects, do use resource pools with subprojects because you can manage your resources better. Since a subproject is used in another project, either use the resources in the master project, or in the project in which all the resource information is stored. For more information, see "Sharing Resources Among Projects" later in this chapter.

You can also change a group of tasks in an existing project into a subproject.

CREATING A SUBPROJECT FROM EXISTING TASKS

1. Open the project containing the tasks you want in a subproject.
2. Select the tasks.
3. Choose Edit Cut if you want to remove the tasks from the project or Edit Copy if you want to copy the tasks.
4. To create a new project, choose File New.
5. To insert the tasks into the new project, choose Edit Paste.
6. To save the project, use the File Save As command.

Using a Subproject

To use a subproject, enter one task in the master project to represent the subproject. For example, one of the tasks in the new calculator project is "Revise manual." This task can be a subproject task that represents the Manual subproject.

The new calculator project contains the following tasks:

36. Code alarm feature

37. Revise manual

38. Fix bugs in new code

and so on

The subproject task, "Revise manual," represents all the tasks in the Manual subproject.

The Manual subproject contains the following tasks:

1. Write manual design document

2. Distribute design document for review

3. Revise design document

4. Write manual

and so on

To enter a subproject task, use the Task Entry view or Edit Form dialog box for tasks.

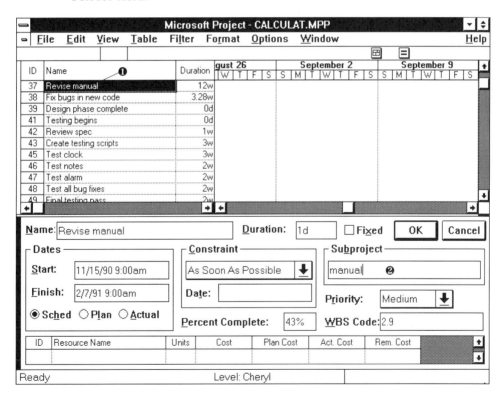

Type a task ❶ that represents the tasks in the subproject.
In the Subproject box on the Task Form ❷, type the name of the subproject file.

After you choose OK, Microsoft Project for Windows changes the duration and the information in the Subproject box.

The duration for the subproject task is the total elapsed duration of all the tasks in the subproject. Microsoft Project calculates this value; you can't type a duration for a subproject task.

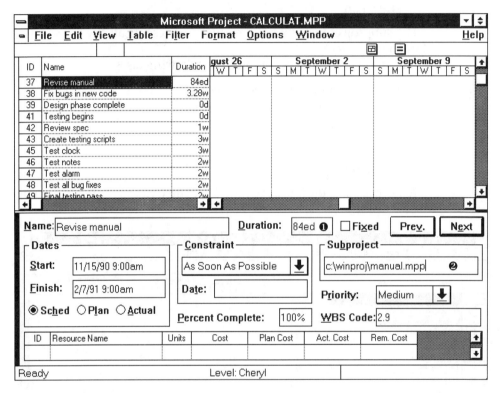

Microsoft Project calculates the duration of the subproject and enters it as the duration for the subproject task ❶.

Microsoft Project replaces the name you typed with the full to the subproject ❷.

When you type the name of the subproject file, you don't have to include the path or the MPP extension unless the file uses a different extension. Microsoft Project searches for a file by that name and replaces what you typed with the full path to the subproject file. If it can't find the subproject, Microsoft Project displays a dialog box similar to the File Open dialog box in which you specify the drive and directory containing the file.

You cannot assign resources to the subproject task—resources can be assigned only to the tasks within the subproject.

> **Update Links to Unopened Subprojects?**
>
> You will see this message if the subprojects are not open when you open a project containing subprojects. Choose Yes if you want Microsoft Project to get the latest information from the subproject file; choose No if you don't want to change the subproject information in the project file you are opening. Because you can use subprojects over and over, the start and finish dates in the subproject file reflect the most recent use of the subproject.

Reporting Project Information Using Subprojects

Just as with an outline, you can use subprojects to control the amount of detail included in a report. By including the detail tasks in subprojects instead of in the master project, you can create reports to the level of detail you want. For example, if you just print the master project, you'll see all the tasks that represent the subprojects, but none of the detail tasks in the subprojects. For those who need the details, create reports by opening the subprojects and printing them. For more information about viewing information for both the master project and subprojects, see "Viewing Multiple Projects" later in this chapter.

USING A PROJECT TEMPLATE

A project template is a good shortcut for quickly creating projects having the same basic tasks. First, create the project template—it contains the basic tasks. Then, each time you have a new project, open the project template, copy the template by saving it with a new name (use the File Save As command), and change the copy of the template to match your current project.

For example, if you manage a documentation group, your projects often may be preparing manuals for your products. All manuals require the same basic phases: Plan, Write, Edit, Format, QA, Print; within these phases, the tasks are similar for each manual. What may change from project to project is the duration of each task, depending on the size of the piece you are preparing, and the resources involved. Each time you are faced with a new project, customize the project template to match the specifics of the new project.

SHARING RESOURCES AMONG PROJECTS

If your resources work on more than one project at the same time, using one shared resource pool—all resources in one project—is a powerful way to manage resource use across all of your projects. In Microsoft Project for Windows, you can open all the projects using the resources, and then use the Resource Usage view and Resource Histogram to see how resources are allocated. You also can use the fields at the bottom of the Resource Form to check the tasks in the open projects to which a resource is assigned. For more information about checking resource usage, see "Viewing Multiple Projects" next in this chapter.

To share resources, open the project containing the resources and then open the project that will use the resources. You tell Microsoft Project that you want to share a resource pool by using the File Resources command.

Choose File Resources.

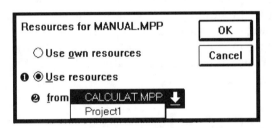

Select Use Resources ❶.
In the From box, select the project containing the resources you want to use ❷.

All resources in the resource pool are now available for you to use in your project. If you add resources to the project containing the resources or to any project sharing the resources, these new resources are added to the resource pool and are available to all projects sharing this resource pool.

If you later want to disconnect a project from a resource pool—for example, if you are finished with the project—use the File Resources command and select Use Own Resources. The resource information for the project you disconnect is removed from the resource pool and placed in the project you disconnected.

You can create a "resource" project containing only resources and no tasks. This is a good approach when you have one set of resources and many projects. When you update the information for a resource, such as changing the resource's standard rate, the cost and schedule automatically change as appropriate in each project. When you finish a project, you can unlink it from the resource pool and delete the project file, leaving the resource pool intact.

If you already have resources as part of your projects and you decide a separate resource pool would be better, you can create a resource project from existing projects. All resource information in each project is moved to the resource pool.

CREATING A RESOURCE PROJECT FROM EXISTING PROJECTS

1. Choose File New.
2. Choose File Save As.
3. Type a name for the resource project.
4. Choose OK.
5. From each project that is to use the resource pool, choose File Resources. Select Use Resources; in the From box, select the name of the resource project you created with the File Save As command.

You can also create a resource project from scratch. Just create a new project and enter all the resources, either by typing them or importing a list from another application. For example, if you have a list of resources in another application, such as Microsoft Excel or Lotus 1-2-3, you can import this information into an existing project or a new resource project. For more information about importing information from another application, see Chapter 15, "Sharing Information".

CREATING A RESOURCE PROJECT

1. Choose File New.
2. Choose View Resource Sheet.
3. Enter all resource information.
4. Choose File Save All.

Use File Resources to attach all existing projects to this resource project.

VIEWING MULTIPLE PROJECTS

If you are managing multiple projects, there are probably times when you want to create one big report summarizing all the projects. Or perhaps, if your projects share a resource pool, you want to look at resource usage across all projects. To view multiple project information, you must open all the projects. Then you can either look at a resource view, such as the Resource Form, that shows all tasks a resource is assigned in all open projects, or you can combine all the open projects in one window to create one report showing information about all projects.

To open all projects using a resource pool, or to open all subprojects used in a project, use the File Links command. To open all projects using a resource pool, choose the File Links command from the project containing the resource pool. To open all subprojects used by a project, choose File Links from the master project.

The list of projects you see in the File Links dialog box depends on the project that is active when you choose the command. It shows all the projects that are linked to the active project, either sharing its resources or used as subprojects. If you see a project name listed twice, it tells you that the project is both a subproject of the active project and shares the resources in the active project. If the project is a subproject, the Change button will be available when you select it; if the project is sharing resources, the Change button will not be available.

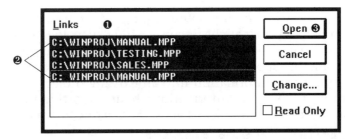

To open one or more of the projects linked to the active project, select the filenames in this box ❶. *To select more than one project, hold down Shift as you select the names.*

The Manual project ❷ *is listed twice because it both shares resources with the active project and is a subproject of the active project.*

Select all the projects you want to open and then choose the Open button ❸.

Want to Change a Subproject Link?

The Change button in the File Links dialog box lets you do that. For example, suppose you have three manual subprojects, one for each of three types of manual projects. You now have to change from writing a new manual to revising an existing manual and want to change the subproject to match. In the File Links dialog box, select the manual subproject currently used, choose the Change button, and then select the manual subproject you want to use instead.

When you look at resource usage across multiple projects, the resource views show information for all projects. For example, use the Resource Form over the Task Form to see all the tasks a resource is assigned to, plus details about each task. By checking the task details, including the other resources assigned to the task, you can make decisions about how to change resource assignments if necessary.

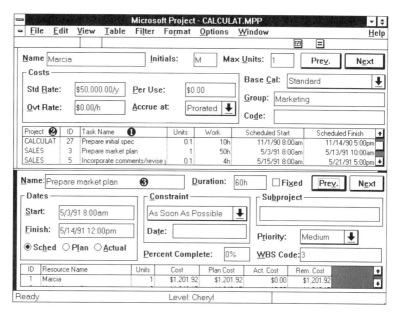

The Resource Form shows all the tasks this resource is assigned to in all open projects ❶.

The project name ❷ is listed so you can identify each task.

The Task Form ❸ show the details about each task the resource is assigned to.

Use the Resource Form over the Resource Histogram to see the details about this resource's assignments, plus a graphical view of the resource's allocation.

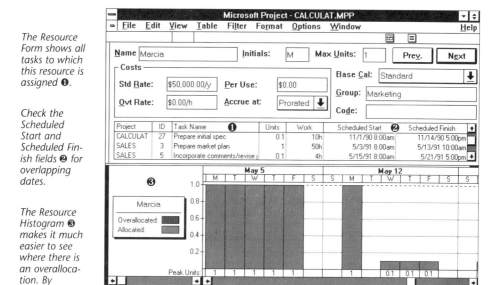

The Resource Form shows all tasks to which this resource is assigned ❶.

Check the Scheduled Start and Scheduled Finish fields ❷ for overlapping dates.

The Resource Histogram ❸ makes it much easier to see where there is an overallocation. By checking the Resource Histogram first for overallocations, you can then refer to the Resource Form for the tasks that overlap during the periods found on the histogram.

Two other useful views are the Resource Histogram over the Gantt Chart and the Resource Usage view over the Gantt Chart. Use these combination views to locate overallocated resources in the top view, and then check the tasks causing the overallocation on the Gantt Chart.

The Resource Usage view shows all resources and the percent they are used on all open projects ❶.

The Design staff is overallocated during the week of 12/23 ❷.

The Gantt Chart shows the tasks to which the Design staff is assigned ❸. You can see the tasks causing the overallocation ❹.

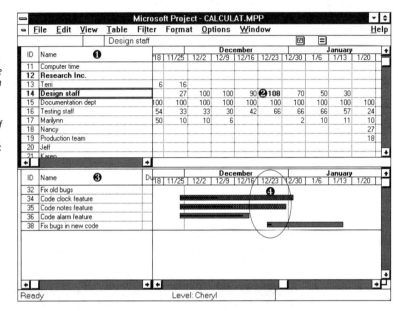

Another combination view you can use is the Resource Usage view, showing percentages of maximum capacity (choose Format Percent Allocation) to check for overallocations for all resources, over the Resource Form to check the tasks that are causing the overallocations.

When you want to see all the projects in one window—for example, to create a summary report of all the projects you are managing—use the Window New Window command.

Choose Window New Window.

In the Projects box ❶, select the projects you want in one window. To select more than one project, hold down Shift as you select the projects.

In the View box ❷, select the view for the new window.

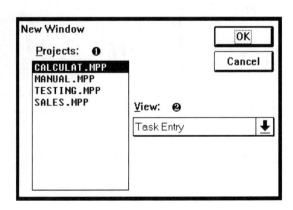

The new window will contain all the tasks in the projects you selected. Each project will retain its task ID numbers, so task ID numbers will be repeated. Initially, the tasks will be grouped by project, but you can organize the information in any way that suits the type of report you need to generate. For example, you can sort the tasks by department to show all the tasks in all the projects assigned to each department. You may want to add the Project field to the Task Sheet so that the project for each task can be identified after you sort the projects.

SAVING A WORKSPACE

When you often work with multiple projects and especially subprojects and a resource project, you may want these projects open so that the information in the subprojects and resource pool is available. If there is a certain set of projects you often use together, such as a master project, its subprojects, and the resource project, you can open these projects, and then save them as a workspace. A list of the open files is saved in the workspace file; the project information remains in the project files. When you open a workspace file, all files that were open when you saved a workspace file are opened at once.

To save a workspace file, choose File Save Workspace. Workspace files are saved with the extension. MPW so you can identify them when you are opening files. Use the File Open command to open a workspace.

Hiding a Window

Sometimes, you might want a project open so its information is available to the project on which you are working—such as the project containing the resources—but you don't want to actually work with the project. You can hide a project by choosing the Window Hide command. The information in the project is available but you don't see the project on the screen. If you later want to use the project, you choose Window Unhide to show the project again.

CHAPTER 15

Sharing Information

Departments in an organization don't operate in a vacuum, although many often act as if they did. The information used or created by one department would often be useful to another if it was easy to share the information. With Microsoft Project for Windows, it is easy.

There are many kinds of information you can share. For example, you can share:

- View files so everyone in the company has the same set of reports, views, tables, and filters at their fingertips.

- Calendar files so everyone has the latest information about working days and hours for the resources.

- Resource pool file containing all resources available for projects, plus their individual calendars and other resource information. For more information about creating a resource project containing only resources, see Chapter 14, "Managing Multiple Projects."

You can also exchange information with other applications to do things that Microsoft Project for Windows doesn't do. For example, with a spreadsheet application, such as Microsoft Excel or Lotus 1-2-3, you can:

- Move resource cost information from the spreadsheet application to Microsoft Project to calculate task and project costs, and then move task costs back to the spreadsheet application to draw cost curves. Since many companies already have a database containing resources or cost information, you can move this information between the spreadsheet or database application and Microsoft Project instead of entering the information again.

- If you are using the PERT method of determining durations, as discussed in Chapter 5, "Estimating Time to Perform Tasks," use a spreadsheet application to calculate the duration estimates, and then move these estimates to Microsoft Project.

Microsoft Project for Windows can read files created by other software applications, including Microsoft Excel, Lotus 1-2-3, dBase II, III, and III Plus, CSV files, and other text files, so that if you have information in another application, you will not need to retype the information in Microsoft Project for Windows.

With a word processing application, such as Microsoft Word for Windows, you can share project information, such as a Gantt Chart or Task Sheet, to illustrate a report or other document about the project.

SHARING VIEW AND CALENDAR FILES

In Microsoft Project for Windows, a view file contains all the views, tables, filters, and reports; a calendar file contains all the base calendars.

The view file VIEW.MPV contains the views, tables, filters, and reports that come with Microsoft Project, plus any views, tables, filters, or reports you have created or changed. When you exit Microsoft Project, this information is automatically saved in the view file.

The calendar file CALENDAR.MPC contains the Standard calendar that comes with Microsoft Project, plus all additional base calendars you create. When you exit Microsoft Project, this information is automatically saved in the calendar file.

You can create as many view files and calendar files as you want, named whatever you want. Perhaps you will want to create a view file and calendar file for each project. Or maybe create just one of each, to be used by everyone in the company for all projects, so that all reports will look alike, no matter who creates them, and working hours will be consistent for all projects.

Because you can add or delete commands on the View, Table, and Filter menus, you can create a totally customized version of Microsoft Project that includes only those views, tables, and filters used in your company or for a specific project. For example, the following illustrations shows customized View, Table, and Filter menus.

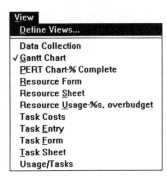

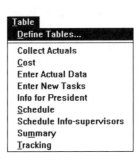

Any view, table, or filter that you remove from the menu is still available in the View Define Views, Table Define Tables, or Filter Define Filters dialog box, unless you actually delete it. For more information about customizing the menus, see Chapter 16, "Using Microsoft Project Tools."

Although the reports do not appear on a menu, the File Print Report dialog box contains all reports you have created. These reports are also saved in the view file. The following illustration shows the list of reports in the File Print Report dialog box.

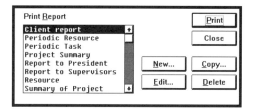

Neither do the calendars appear on a menu, but rather in the Options Base Calendars dialog box. The following illustration shows all the base calendars in the current calendar file.

By creating all the views, tables, filters, reports, and calendars for your company, then sharing the view and calendar files, it is easy to standardize everything for all users.

Saving and Opening a View File

To create a view file, first make sure all the views, tables, filters, and reports are as you want them and that the View, Table, and Filter menus include the appropriate items. Check the views in the View Define Views dialog box, the tables in the Table Define Tables dialog box, the filters in the Filter Define Filters dialog box, and the reports in the File Print Reports dialog box. If anything is missing, create it; if anything is extra, delete it. For more information about creating tables, filters, and views, and changing the menus, see Chapter 16, "Using Microsoft Project Tools." For more information about creating reports, see Chapters 10, "Communicating the Plan," and Chapter 13, "Communicating Progress."

Once you have all the views, tables, filters, and reports as you want them, choose View Define Views.

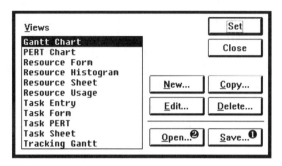

Choose the Save button ❶.

When you want to open a view file, choose the Open button ❷.

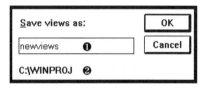

Type a name for the view file ❶.

Include a path name if you want to save it in a directory other than the directory shown here ❷.

When you type a name, you do not have to include an extension. Microsoft Project automatically adds the extension .MPV. It is most convenient to use this extension because, when you want to open a view file, only those files with the extension .MPV initially appear in the dialog box.

To open a view file, choose View Define Views, and then choose the Open button.

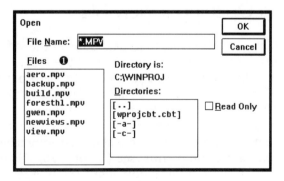

Initially, all files with the extension .MPV in the indicated directory are displayed ❶. *Select the view file you want to open.*

Saving and Opening a Calendar File

Make sure all calendars are just as you want them for the company or project. For more information about creating calendars, see Chapter 16, "Using Microsoft Project Tools." Then, to create a calendar file, choose Options Base Calendars.

Choose the Save button ❶.

When you want to open a calendar file, choose the Open button ❷.

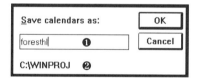

Type a name for the calendar file ❶.

Include a path name if you want to save it in a directory other than the directory shown here ❷.

When you type a name in a calendar file, Microsoft Project automatically adds the extension .MPC. It is again convenient to use this extension because when you want to open a calendar file, only those files with the extension .MPC initially appear in the dialog box.

To open a calendar file, choose Options Base Calendars, and then choose the Open button.

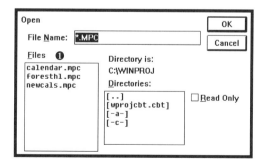

Initially, all files with the extension .MPC in the indicated directory are displayed ❶. Select the calendar file you want to open.

Want to Control What Is Saved to the View or Calendar File?

If you have created a standard view or calendar file, you may not want view or calendar changes to be saved automatically in the view or calendar file. You can control this by using the Calendar File and View File options in the Options Preferences dialog box. The settings for these options include Don't Save, Auto Save, and Prompt For Save. Initially, both are set to Auto Save—every time you exit Microsoft Project, any changes made to views, tables, filters, reports, and calendars are automatically saved. If you do not want these files to be changed, select Don't Save for both options. Or if you want to be prompted so that you can choose whether or not to save the changes, select the Prompt For Save option. Every time you exit Microsoft Project, you will be given the choice of saving or not saving the changes.

EXCHANGING INFORMATION WITH A SPREADSHEET OR DATABASE APPLICATION

To exchange information with a spreadsheet or database application, you follow two basic steps:

- Create a table, if one doesn't already exist, containing the fields you want to import (bring into Microsoft Project) or export (take out of Microsoft Project)
- Choose File Save or File Copy to export the information; choose File Open or File Paste to import the information.

When you are exporting information, the table tells Microsoft Project which fields of information to export. For example, if you want to export task names and durations, you'd create a table with the Name and Duration fields. When you are importing information, the table tells Microsoft Project where to put the information. For example, if you are importing resource names and standard rates from Microsoft Excel, you'd create a table containing those two fields (Resource Name and Standard Rate).

If there is a column of information in another application that you want to import into Microsoft Project, but for which Microsoft Project doesn't have a matching field—such as manager or skill level—you can use a custom field. Custom fields in Microsoft Project can be used for anything you want. There are six custom text fields for tasks and two custom text fields for resources.

After you have the table, there are two ways to import information and two ways to export information.

TO IMPORT INFORMATION

- Use the File Open command and select the file created in the other application. Microsoft Project will detect that this file is not in Microsoft Project format, and ask for the name of the table you want to use. The table tells Microsoft Project what the information is—resource names and costs, for example—so it is entered into the project in the correct fields.

- Use the Edit Paste command to import information cut or copied from another Windows application. Before choosing the Edit Paste command, you must first apply the table to the view as Microsoft Project does not prompt you for a table as it does when you use File Open. Information is pasted into the table starting from the leftmost column.

TO EXPORT INFORMATION

- Use the File Save command to save the information in a format the other application recognizes. Microsoft Project will ask you for the name of the table you want to use. The fields in the table tell Microsoft Project which information to copy to the file.

- Use the Edit Copy command to export information to another Windows application. Before choosing the Edit Copy command, you must apply the table to the view, and select the information you want to copy.

The following two examples—"Importing Resources and Costs from Microsoft Excel" and "Calculating Durations in Microsoft Excel"—can be used as examples for exchanging information with any application, not just Microsoft Excel. The first example explains how to import information; the second covers both exporting and importing.

Follow the steps in "Importing Resources and Costs from Microsoft Excel" to import from any spreadsheet or database application; follow the steps in "Calculating Durations in Microsoft Excel" for both exporting information from Microsoft Project to another application and also for importing information back into Microsoft Project. The only difference when using an application other than Microsoft Excel is that, when exporting from Microsoft Project, you select a different file format—the one that matches the application to which you are exporting the information. For either example, if you are importing or exporting different fields, be sure the fields in the table match the information you want to import or export.

Importing Resources and Costs from Microsoft Excel

Both ways of importing are included in this section. First, the example explains how to import using the File Open command. Importing using Edit Copy in Microsoft Excel and Edit Paste in Microsoft Project follows.

Importing Using the File Open Command

Suppose you have the following information in Microsoft Excel and you want to import into Microsoft Project for Windows the information in the first three columns—the resource name, salary, and overtime rate.

	Microsoft Excel - RESOURCE.XLS				
▢	File Edit Formula Format Data Options Macro Window				Help
A24					
	A	**B**	**C**	**D**	**E**
1	Name	Salary	Overtime Rate	Start Date	Adddress
2	Jim Anderson	300/w	11.25/h	7/17/89	9280 17th St. #407
3	Carmen Bizet	57,500/y		11/2/82	4713 N. View Drive
4	Cheryl Bowers	5.25/h	7.87/h	2/4/90	417 S. Spiers Road
5	Terri Conklin	50,000/y		5/15/73	930 Windham Way
6	Marcia Cryer	$32,500/y		6/2/79	12919 4th N
7	Bill Davenport	$30,000/y		1/3/82	17 Avon Avenue
8	Roberto Gomez	$60,000/y		5/4/78	3840 Canfield Road
9	Bob Hayward	$30,000/y		4/22/86	1722 Jamaica Court
10	Bob Johnson	$25,000/y		9/15/82	3797 Peachtree Circle
11	Nancy Jones	$6.50/h	$9.75/h	10/15/89	201 Galer #303
12	Marilynn Kelly	$32,500/y		7/17/87	3331 Calaveras
13	Karen Kennedy	$32,500/y		3/29/87	201 Hermosa Drive
14	Rick Klein	$29,000/y		1/4/86	20132 Peninsula Road
15	Jane Olsen	$35,000/y		2/5/79	1980 Thomas Drive
16	Jeff Owen	$10/h	$15.00/h	5/4/88	504 SuriEllen Lane
17	Janet Paxton	$8/h	$12.00/h	12/2/87	305 N Michillinda
18	Mary Stanwell	$20,000/y		8/28/88	9813 10th Ave #75
19	Dave Thompson	$40,000/h		11/4/82	4217 Forest Hills Drive
20	Jennifer Torrey	25,000/y		7/18/82	417 E. Jean
21	Lila Beth Williams	10.75/h	16.12/h	9/17/87	4722 E. Hills Drive
22	Jody Young	8/h	12/h	3/5/90	433 N. Stewart
Ready					

You want to import the information in columns A, B, and C.

In Microsoft Excel: Save the worksheet as you normally do.

In Microsoft Project: Create a resource table with the three columns—Name, Standard Rate, and Overtime Rate—if one doesn't already exist. While these fields are included in the Entry table for resources, the order is not the same as for the information you are importing, so you must create a separate table. Choose Table Define Tables, select the Resource option, and then choose the New button.

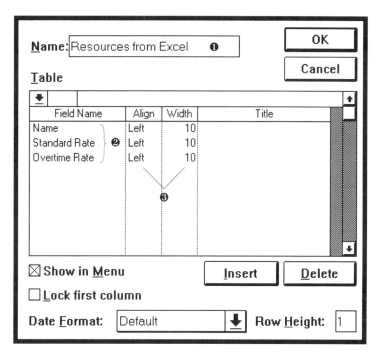

Name the table such that it identifies the purpose of the table ❶.

Include the fields you plan to import, in the order that matches their order in the other application ❷.

Use the default values in the Align and Width fields ❸.

The values in the Align and Width columns do not matter. All information will be imported regardless of the settings so just use the default settings Microsoft Project enters after you select the field names.

For more information about creating a table, see Chapter 16, "Using Microsoft Project Tools."

When applied to the Resource Sheet, the table looks like this:

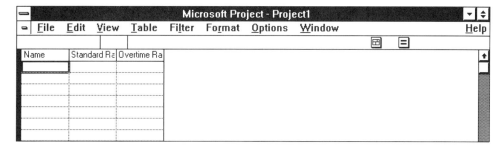

To import the information from Microsoft Excel, choose File Open.

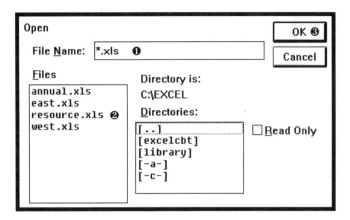

Type the extension of the file you want to open ❶. Change directories if necessary.
Select the name of the file you want to open ❷.
Choose OK ❸.

Microsoft Project will detect that this is not a Microsoft Project file, and display the Opening dialog box, where you specify whether tasks or resources are being imported, and the table to use to import the information.

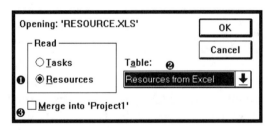

Select the Resources option ❶ to indicate you are importing resources.
Select the table containing the columns for the information you are importing from Microsoft Excel ❷.
The Merge Into check box ❸ controls where the information is placed—in the current project or in a new file.

When you import information, it can either replace information already in the project or be placed in a new project. This is controlled with the Merge Into check box. If you don't want to replace the existing information, turn off this check box; the information is placed in its own file and temporarily named the same as the file you imported. Copy the new information into the current project, as appropriate.

If the Merge Into check box is turned on, the information replaces existing information in the project. For example, if you already have a list of resources in your project, and you import information that includes a list of resources, these resources will replace the existing resources. This may be what you want—for example, if this is the full list of resources in your company, and you periodically get a file from personnel containing an updated list of all resources and salaries.

> **Import Errors**
>
> If you put titles on your columns in Microsoft Excel, you may get error messages when you import the information into Microsoft Project for Windows. For example, the Salary and Overtime Rate titles in cells B1 and C1 will cause error messages because Microsoft Project is expecting a number in the Rate fields, not text. The error message identifies the location (row and column) of the field causing the error and tells you what's wrong (for example, "Rate not valid"). The messages warn you of problems, but don't prevent Microsoft Project from importing the information in the file. If you want to keep the titles in Microsoft Excel because the database is used for other purposes and needs the headings, just ignore the messages when you import the information. In Microsoft Project, delete the row containing the headings.
>
> You will also get error messages if the columns do not match the kind of information you are importing, such as if you select the wrong table. In this case, you will get lots of error messages, one for every field you import; you'll probably want to stop importing and check your table.

Importing Using the Edit Copy and Edit Paste Commands

Suppose you already have all your resource information in your project, but you want to add a handful of new resources. Rather than importing all the resources again, you can use Edit Copy in Microsoft Excel to copy the new resources, and then use Edit Paste in Microsoft Project to paste the information. Remember, you can use this procedure only if the other application can save information to the Windows Clipboard.

In Microsoft Project: You must have a table that matches the columns and order of the information you are importing. Apply the table containing the appropriate columns to the Task Sheet, if you are importing tasks, or the Resource Sheet if you are importing resources. For example, to copy resource names, salaries, and overtime rates, apply the Resources From Excel table used in the previous example to the Resource Sheet.

In Microsoft Excel: Select the information you want to copy, and then choose Edit Copy.

In Microsoft Project: Select the field after the last resource. Choose Edit Paste. The information will be pasted into Microsoft Project, starting at the left-most field.

Calculating Durations in Microsoft Excel

This section includes an example using the File Open and File Save commands, and then a description of how to do the same thing using Edit Copy and Edit Paste.

Exchanging Using the File Save and File Open Commands

If you are using the PERT method to determine task duration, you can use Microsoft Excel to calculate the durations for you.

In Microsoft Project: Export your list of tasks to Microsoft Excel.

Create a table containing the task name, and, if you want to use the same table when you import the information back into Microsoft Excel, durations.

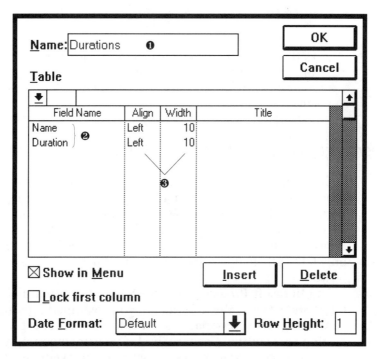

Name the table such that it identifies the purpose of the table ❶.
Include the fields that you plan to export ❷.
Use the default values in the Align and Width fields ❸.

For more information about creating a table, see Chapter 16, "Using Microsoft Project Tools."

Choose File Save As.

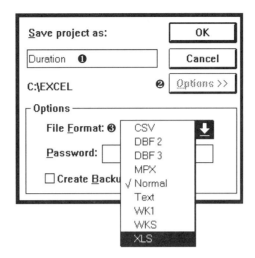

Type a name for the file ❶.
Choose the Options button ❷.
Select the file format that matches the application into which you are importing the information ❸. *For example, select XLS to export to Microsoft Excel.*

Microsoft Project displays the Saving dialog box where you specify what information to save in the file and the table to use.

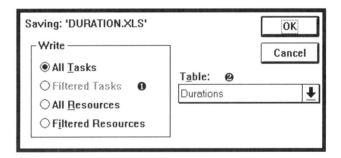

Select the appropriate task or resource option ❶, *depending on what you want to export.*
Select the table containing the columns you want to export ❷.

You could also filter the list of tasks or resources before you export so only those that meet the requirements in the filter are exported. For example, if you want to use the PERT method to determine durations for the tasks performed by the Design group only, and you have a column in which you enter the department, you could filter the tasks such that only those tasks assigned to Design will appear in the view. Then in the Saving dialog box, select the Filtered Tasks option. The partial list of tasks is exported instead of the complete list.

If you are using outlining, you might want to hide the summary tasks before saving the file. Choose Format Outline, and then turn off the Summary Tasks check box. In the Saving dialog box, select the option Filtered Tasks.

In Microsoft Excel: Open the file you just created. Choose File Open.

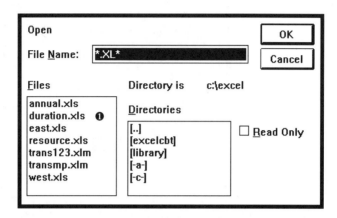

Select the file you want to open ❶ and choose OK.

The file contains all tasks you exported and their initial durations.

	A	B	C	D	E	F	G
1	Investigation begins	1					
2	Research competition	1					
3	Review customer comment cards	1					
4	Write proposal	1					
5	Contact hotels	1					
6	Determine needed equipment	1					
7	Contact local offices	1					
8	Contact local reps for names	1					
9	Contact suggested panel members	1					
10	Prepare questionnaire	1					
11	Get list of users to call	1					
12	Carry out focus panels	1					
13	Carry out phone survey	1					
14	Prepare focus panel report	1					
15	Prepare phone survey report	1					
16	Present results	1					
17	Investigation phase complete	1					
18	Design begins	1					
19	Prepare initial spec	1					
20	Distribute for review	1					
21	Meet with reviewers	1					
22	Incorporate comments/revise spec	1					
23	Distribute final spec	1					

The task names are in column A; the durations are in column B.

Add the columns for the three duration estimates and one for the standard deviation.

	A	B	C ❶	D ❷	E ❸	F❹
		Microsoft Excel - DURATION.XLS				
	File Edit Formula Format Data Options Macro Window					**Help**
	D22					
1	**Name**	**Duration**	**Optimistic**	**Pessimistic**	**Most Likely**	**Std. Dev.**
2	Investigation begins	1				
3	Research competition	1				
4	Review customer comment cards	1				
5	Write proposal	1				
6	Contact hotels	1				

Add a column for the optimistic duration ❶, pessimistic duration ❷, most likely duration ❸, and the standard deviation ❹.

To have Microsoft Excel calculate the value in the Duration column for each task, you need to enter the equation. The duration is the weighted average of the three duration estimates. Type "=(c2+d2+4*e2)/ 6" in B2. Select B2 and the cells below B2 and then choose the Edit Fill Down command.

To calculate the standard deviation, type "=stdev(c2:e2)" in cell F2. Select F2 and the cells below F2 and then choose the Edit Fill Down command.

Gather your duration estimates and enter them for each task. Microsoft Excel will calculate the duration and standard deviation for you.

	A	B	C	D	E	F
		Microsoft Excel - DURATION.XLS				
	File Edit Formula Format Data Options Macro Window					**Help**
	C17					
1	**Name**	**Duration**	**Optimistic**	**Pessimistic**	**Most Likely**	**Std. De**
2	Investigation begins	0				#DIV/0
3	Research competition	5.5 ❶	3	10	5 ❷	3.605551
4	Review customer comment cards	3.083333	1.5	5	3	1.7559422
5	Write proposal	5	3	7	5	2
6	Contact hotels	0.533333	0.2	1	0.5	0.4041451
7	Determine needed equipment	0.625	0.25	1.5	0.5	0.6614376
8	Contact local offices	0.708333	0.25	2	0.5	0.946484
9	Contact local reps for names	1.25	0.5	3	1	1.322875
10	Contact suggested panel members	2.833333	1	8	2	3.785938
11	Prepare questionnaire	3.166667	2	5	3	1.527525

Gather the three duration estimates from those involved in the tasks.

Type the values in columns C, D, and E.

Microsoft Excel calculates the duration ❶ and standard deviation ❷ based on the three estimates.

Until you enter data in columns C, D, and E, the Std. Dev. column will show the #DIV/0 error. As soon as you enter the duration estimates, the error will be replaced by the standard deviation.

Save the file as a normal Microsoft Excel file.

In Microsoft Project: Open the file you just created in Microsoft Excel. Choose File Open. Select the filename. Microsoft Project detects it is not a Microsoft Project file and displays the Opening dialog box.

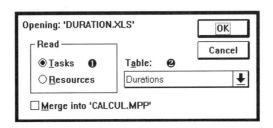

Select the Tasks option ❶.
Select the Durations table to import the name and duration ❷.

All tasks and their durations are imported into Microsoft Project for Windows. Because Name and Duration are the only fields in your table, the other columns—Opt. Dur, Pess. Dur, Most likely, and Std. Dev—in the Microsoft Excel file are ignored. The Gantt Chart now looks like this:

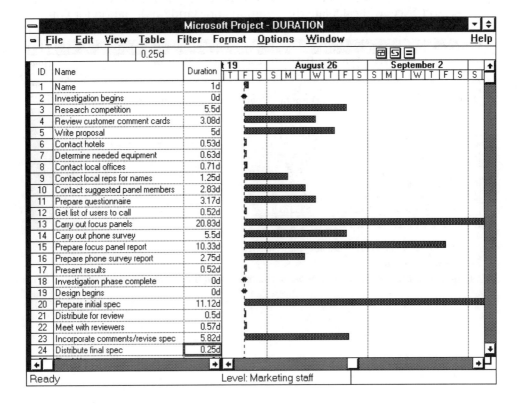

Exchanging Using the Edit Copy and File Paste Commands

To calculate durations for just a few tasks, you can use the Clipboard to export the list of tasks and then import the estimated durations. Remember, to use this method, the application receiving the information must be able to use the Windows Clipboard.

In Microsoft Project: Filter the tasks such that only those tasks for which you need durations calculated are displayed in the view. For example, if the tasks are all those handled by one department, you could filter on "Department," if you have included such a field in your task list. Or you could mark all the tasks for which you need durations calculated using the Marked check box on the Task Form. To mark a group of tasks, select all the tasks you want to mark (these tasks do not have to be adjacent), and then choose Edit Form or click the form icon (▣). Turn on the Marked check box. Now filter the tasks so that only the Marked tasks are displayed.

Apply the table containing only those columns you want to export. For example, apply the Durations table created in the previous example to export the name and duration for the tasks. Choose Edit Copy.

In Microsoft Excel: Choose Edit Paste. Add the columns for the three duration estimates and one for the standard deviation. Add the equations for weighted average and standard deviation as described earlier in this example. Gather the three estimates for each task and enter them on the spreadsheet. When you are finished, select the tasks and durations (columns A and B), and choose Edit Copy.

In Microsoft Project: Select where you want the tasks to be pasted. Choose Edit Paste. The tasks will be pasted starting from the left-most field of the selected row.

Exchanging Information with Lotus 1-2-3 or dBase

Exchanging information with Lotus 1-2-3 or dBase is similar to exchanging information with Microsoft Excel. You create a table containing columns for the information you want to import or export. To import, you open a WKS or WK1 file for Lotus 1-2-3, or a DBF file for dBase. Microsoft Project asks for the table, and places the information either in the open project or a new project, as you specify. To export, you save the file in the WKS or WK1 format for Lotus 1-2-3, or DBF 2 or DBF 3 format for dBase.

USING PROJECT INFORMATION IN MICROSOFT WORD FOR WINDOWS

You can also share information from Microsoft Project with a word processing application, such as Microsoft Word for Windows. Using the Clipboard, you can copy a view from Microsoft Project, and place it in a document you are creating in Microsoft Word for Windows. For example, if you are preparing a report on various alternatives to solve a schedule conflict, you could place a Microsoft Project Gantt Chart in the report to support your conclusions.

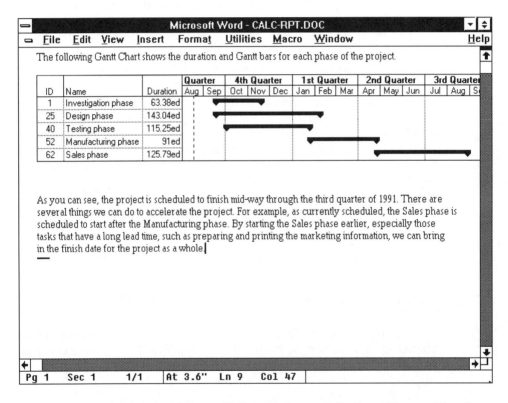

To do this, hold down Shift and choose Edit Copy Picture. The Copy Picture command is available only when you hold down the Shift key as you select the Edit menu.

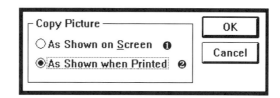

Choose As Shown On Screen ❶ if you want to display the picture on screen.
Choose As Shown When Printed ❷ if you will be printing the file containing the copied picture.

You have two choices when you copy a picture. The option you select depends on how you plan to use the picture. If you plan to display the picture on screen, choose the As Shown On Screen option; if you plan to print the file containing the picture, choose the As Shown When Printed option. Be sure the correct printer is selected in the File Printer Setup dialog box before copying the picture, or you will have to copy it again. If you choose As Shown When Printed, the picture will not look very good in your file on screen, but it will print correctly.

After copying the picture in Microsoft Project, open the other application. Go to where you want to paste the picture and choose Edit Paste.

CHAPTER 16

Using Microsoft Project Tools

The tools in Microsoft Project for Windows are the keys to making the software do just what you want—to see what you want and print what you want. Once you have edited or created one table, filter, view, or report, you'll see that the others are edited or created in a similar manner.

Use this chapter to create the tables, filters, views, and calendars you found useful as you read the chapters. Once you have followed an example or two here, you'll be able to create whatever you need.

This chapter includes the steps for:

- Changing or creating a table
- Changing or creating a filter
- Changing or creating a view
- Customizing the Table, Filter, and View menu to include only those tables, filters, and view you use most often, including those you create
- Changing or creating a calendar
- Sorting—another tool to control the presentation of information in a view
- Changing the Gantt Chart palette to make the Gantt Chart look just as you want
- Additional sample reports

To purchase a companion disk containing all the samples in this chapter and throughout the book, use the order form at the back of the book. This disk also includes many more sample reports and combination views.

TABLES

Tables specify the fields you see in the view. To create a table, merely select the group of fields you want displayed. The names of the fields appear as the column heads across the top of the view.

Choose the Table Define Tables command to begin making any adjustments to a table.

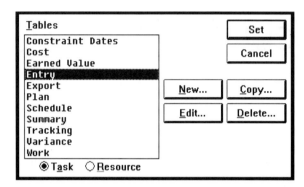

Once in this dialog box, you have three choices: you can copy an existing table, you can edit an existing table, or you can create a new table. The following two procedures show how to copy or edit an existing table (the procedure is the same) and how to create a new table.

Changing an Existing Table

To change an existing table, use one of the following methods:

- If you want to retain the original table, make a copy of the table by choosing the Copy button in the Table Define Tables dialog box.

- If you want to change the original table permanently, choose the Edit button in the Table Define Tables dialog box.

The example in this section shows you how to add the WBS field and the Manager field to the Entry table. You follow the same procedure to add any field to any existing table.

Whenever you want to add a field that doesn't exist in Microsoft Project, use a custom field. Microsoft Project provides six custom text fields for tasks and two custom text fields for resources. Microsoft Project also provides six custom date fields for tasks.

The following example shows you how to make the following changes to a copy of the Entry table:

- Delete a field
- Change the width of a field
- Add the WBS field and the Manager field

Choose Table Define Tables.

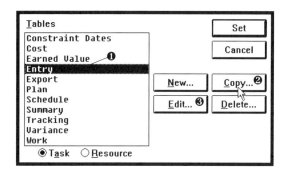

Select Entry ❶, the name of the table you want to change.

If the table is currently displayed in the view, it will already be selected.

Choose the Copy button ❷.

If you want to change the table permanently and don't want to keep the original, choose the Edit button instead ❸.

The table definition dialog box shows all the columns currently in the Entry table, plus the alignment of the information in each column, the width of each column, and a title for the column. If there is nothing in the Title column, the field name is used.

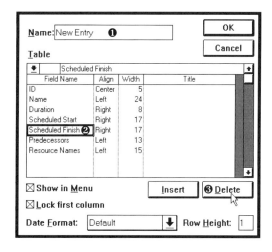

Type "New Entry" as the name for the new table ❶.

To delete the Scheduled Finish column, select Scheduled Finish ❷.

Choose the Delete button ❸.

Now insert the WBS field between the Duration field and the Scheduled Start field.

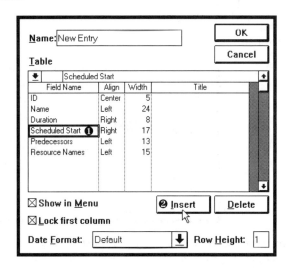

To insert a column, first select Scheduled Start ❶—the row representing the column to the right of where you want to insert the column.
Choose the Insert button ❷.

You'll see a blank space inserted in the table definition.

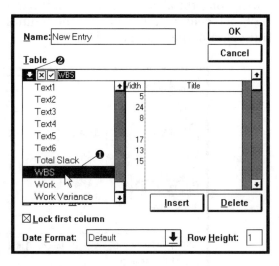

In the Field Name field, select WBS from the entry bar list ❶.
To see the entry bar list, press Alt+Down Arrow or click the entry bar arrow ❷.

Reduce the size of the Predecessors column so you have more room for the new columns.

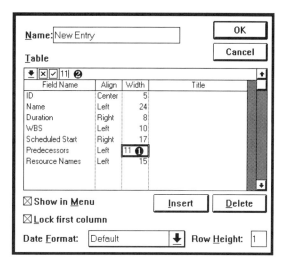

Select the Width field for Predecessors ❶.
Type "11" ❷.

Add the Manager column before Resource Names. Since Microsoft Project doesn't include a manager field, use a custom field.

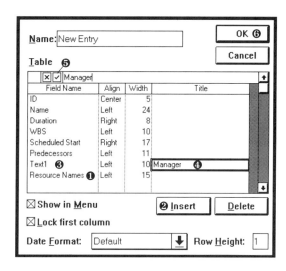

Select Resource Names ❶, *the column to the right of where you want to insert the new column.*
Choose the Insert button ❷.
In the Field Name field ❸, *select Text1 from the entry bar list.*
In the Title field ❹, *type "Manager".*
Press Enter or click the Enter box ❺.
Choose OK ❻.

To apply this table, choose the Set button. When you apply this table to the Task Sheet, it looks like this:

ID	Name	Duration	WBS ❶	Scheduled Start	Predecessors	Manager ❷	Resource Names
1							
2							

Microsoft Project - Project1
File Edit View Table Filter Format Options Window   Help

The WBS field is here ❶.
The custom field is here ❷, with the title of Manager, as you indicated.

Creating a New Table

You can create any table you want, with whatever fields you need for any purpose. Follow the steps in this section for creating the following tables:

- Data collection table in Chapter 11, "Tracking Progress and Updating the Schedule"

- Table for importing resource information (name, standard rate, overtime rate) in Chapter 15, "Sharing Information"

- Table for exporting task name and duration in Chapter 15, "Sharing Information"

The following example shows how to create the data collection table. Choose Table Define Tables.

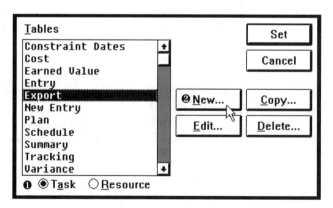

To indicate you want to create a task table, select the Task option ❶.
Choose the New button ❷.

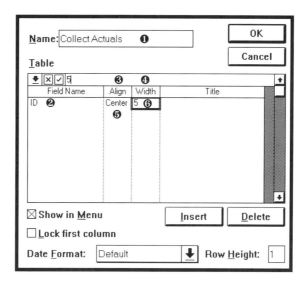

In the Name box ❶, type "Collect Actuals".

In the Field Name field ❷, select ID from the entry bar list.

Microsoft Project enters default values of "Left" in the Align field ❸ and "10" in the Width field ❹.

Change the Align field to Center ❺, and the Width field to 5 ❻.

You can use the entry bar to select alignment and width. If the width you want isn't an increment of five, which are your choices in the entry bar list, you can type any value.

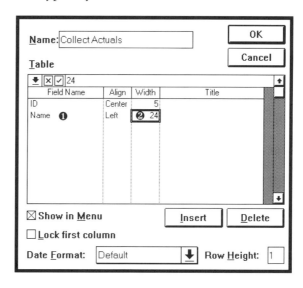

In the next Field Name field, select Name from the entry bar list ❶.

Change the width to 24 ❷.

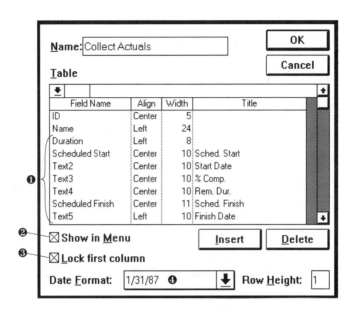

Continue selecting field names until the list looks like this ❶.

Leave the Show In Menu check box ❷ turned on to add this table to the Table menu. You can then apply the table by choosing Table Collect Actuals.

Turn on the Lock First Column check box ❸ so the ID numbers in the first column do not scroll out of the view.

Select 1/31/87 as the date format ❹.

Choose OK.

Choose the Set button to apply the table. When you apply the table to the Task Sheet, the columns look like this:

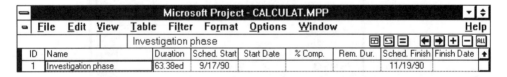

Creating a table may take a bit of trial and error. Once you create a table and apply it to a view, you'll probably discover titles you forgot to change, or columns that are too narrow or wide, or perhaps that the order of fields is not what you want, and so on. Just edit the table by choosing the Edit button in the Table Define Tables dialog box until it is just as you want it.

You can also change the width of the columns with the mouse. Point to the line between the column heads in the table and drag the divider to the left to make it narrower or to the right to make it wider.

FILTERS

Filters control which tasks or resources are displayed—all, or a subset based on the filter you apply. For example, if you apply the Critical filter, only those tasks that are critical are displayed. Microsoft Project checks the Critical field to determine which tasks to display. If the Critical field contains Yes, the task is displayed; if the Critical field contains No, the task is not displayed.

You can create any type of filter you want. When you create a filter, all you are doing is telling Microsoft Project which field to look at and what you want the field to contain. A filter can do one of three things:

- Always look for the same thing, such as the Critical filter does
- Look for a value you specify each time you apply the filter—called an interactive filter—such as finding all tasks that use the resource you enter when you apply the filter
- Compare the values in two fields—called a calculated filter—such as comparing the planned start date and the actual start date for a task

The easiest way to understand how to create and change filters is to look at some of the filters that come with Microsoft Project.

The following illustration shows the Critical filter in the filter definition dialog box.

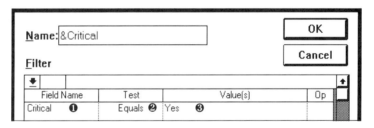

The field you want Microsoft Project to check is listed here ❶.

The test ❷ tells Microsoft Project how to compare what it finds in the Critical field to the value in the Value(s) field ❸.

The value ❸ tells Microsoft Project what to look for in the Critical field.

For the Critical filter, Microsoft project checks the Critical field for each task. If the value in the field is (equals) Yes, the task is displayed. If the field contains No, the task is not displayed.

The next illustration shows the Date Range filter, an interactive filter that prompts you to enter the first date and last date of the date range every time you use the filter.

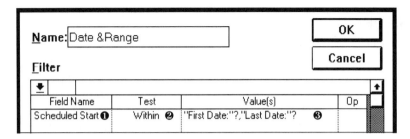

The Scheduled Start field ❶ is checked by Microsoft Project.

The Within test ❷ tells Microsoft Project that information in the Scheduled Start field must be between the two dates you specify when you apply the filter.

By typing a prompt in quotes, followed by a question mark ❸, you tell Microsoft Project to display a dialog box in which you enter the two dates. This dialog box is displayed every time you apply the filter.

When you apply the filter, you see the following dialog box. Note how the text between the quotes in the Value(s) field matches the text in the dialog box.

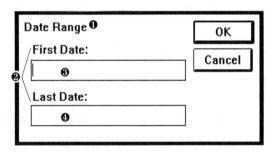

The name of the dialog box ❶ matches the name you gave the filter in the filter definition dialog box.

This text ❷ matches the text in the Value(s) field.

Type the date for the earliest scheduled start date you want Microsoft Project to display ❸.

Type the date for the latest scheduled start date you want Microsoft Project to display ❹.

Choose OK.

You type the first date and last date; Microsoft Project displays all tasks that have a scheduled start date between the two dates.

The next illustration shows two things: It shows a calculated filter that compares the values in two fields and it shows how to use one filter to check more than one field.

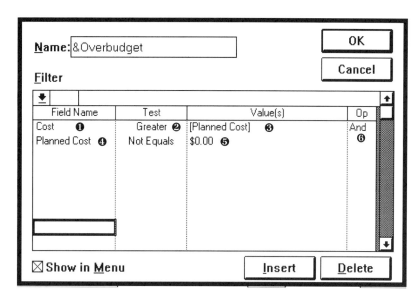

The first row tells Microsoft Project to check the Cost field ❶ and display the task if the cost is greater ❷ than the value in the Planned Cost field ❸. By entering a field name in square brackets in the Value(s) field, you tell Microsoft Project to compare the values in two fields.

The second row tells Microsoft Project to check the Planned Cost field ❹ for $0.00 ❺—the value it contains if you have not chosen Options Set Plan to copy the scheduled costs into the planned cost fields. If the field contains $0.00, you do not want the filter to display the task because it is meaningless information—naturally the cost field will be higher than planned if you did not save the baseline schedule.

The And ❻ tells Microsoft Project that for a task to be displayed, the task must have a cost greater than planned cost (line 1) AND that the planned cost must have been saved (line 2).

Microsoft Project will display only those tasks for which a planned cost exists and scheduled cost is greater than planned cost.

When you create a calculated filter, use the entry bar list to select the field name for the Value(s) field. All the names in the list include the square brackets so you don't have to type them.

Changing an Existing Filter

To change an existing filter, choose Filter Define Filters. Suppose you want to find all tasks scheduled to start before a date you specify. You could change the Date Range filter as follows.

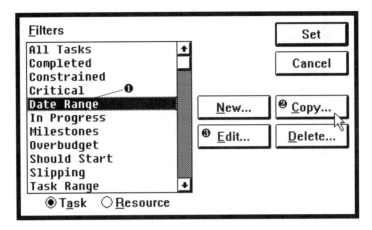

Select the filter you want to change ❶.

Choose the Copy button ❷.

You can also choose the Edit button ❸ if you don't want to keep the original filter.

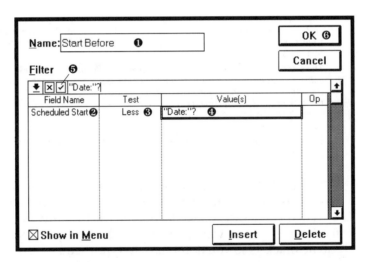

Change the name to "Start Before" ❶.

Since you are still interested in the scheduled start date, don't change the field name ❷.

Change the Test field to Less ❸. The Less test tells Microsoft Project to look for all dates prior to the date in Value(s). You can select the test from the entry bar list.

Change the text in the Value(s) field to just ""Date:"?" ❹ since you no longer are looking for a range. Be sure to put quotes around Date and a question mark at the end. This tells Microsoft Project to display the dialog box for you to enter the date.

Press Enter or click the Enter box ❺.

Choose OK ❻.

To apply the filter, choose the Set button. When you apply this filter, you'll see the following dialog box.

Type the date here ❶.
Choose OK ❷.

All tasks scheduled to start before the date you typed will be displayed.

Creating a New Filter

You can create a filter to look for any information in any field. You can, of course, also filter using custom fields. For example, if you used resource custom field Text1 as the Manager field, you can filter to see all resources reporting to a certain person. Or if you used task custom field Text3 as the Department field, you can filter to see all tasks performed by one department, such as Design.

The following example shows how to create a resource filter using a custom text field.

Choose Filter Define Filters.

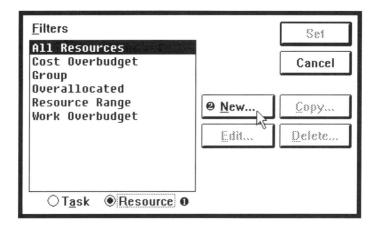

To indicate you want to create a resource filter, select the Resource option ❶.
Choose the New button ❷.

Name the filter "Manager" ❶.

In the Field Name field, select Text1 ❷ from the entry bar list.

In the Test field, select Equals ❸.

In the Value(s) field, type ""Manager:"?" ❹.

Press Enter or click the Enter box ❺.

Choose OK ❻.

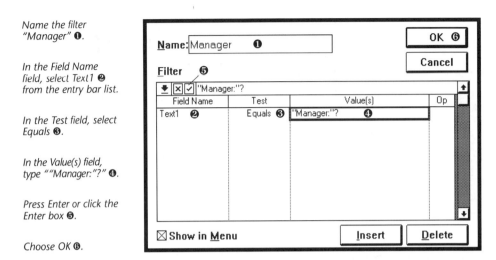

The test looks for a matching value in the Text1 field for each resource. The value "Manager:"? makes this an interactive filter so that each time you use the filter, you can specify the name of the manager you want to find.

When you apply the filter, you see the following:

Type the manager's name here ❶.

Choose OK ❷.

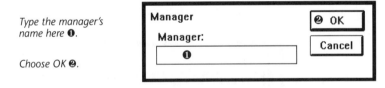

The next example shows how to create a filter to display all marked tasks.

Choose Filter Define Filters.

Select the Task option ❶.

Choose the New button ❷.

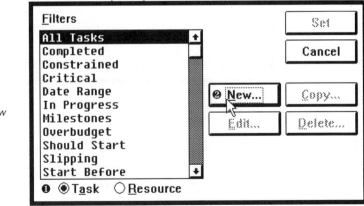

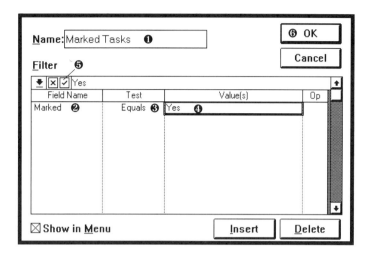

Type "Marked Tasks" as the name ❶.
In the Field Name field, select Marked ❷ from the entry bar list.
In the Test field, select Equals ❸.
In the Value(s) field, type "yes" ❹.
Press Enter or click the Enter box ❺.
Choose OK ❻.

When you apply this filter, Microsoft Project checks the Marked field for the value Yes. Those tasks you have marked—by turning on the Marked check box in the Task Form or Edit Form dialog box for tasks—have Yes in the Marked field and will be displayed when you apply the filter.

VIEWS

When you discover the perfect combination of view, table, and filter to create reports for your company or analyze your schedule, you can save the combination as a new named view that you or anyone can display. This is a simple way to standardize reports in your company, and an easy way for anyone to generate reports.

All views are saved in the view file, as are the tables and filters. For more information about view files, see Chapter 15, "Sharing Information."

Again, you have three choices when you work with views. You can create a new view, or change an existing view by either editing the original or changing a copy of the original.

> **Want Your Original Views, Tables, Filters, and Reports Back?**
>
> Just open the view file called BACKUP.MPV. To open a view file, choose View Define Views, and then choose the Open button. The file should be located in your Microsoft Project directory.

Changing an Existing View

When you change an existing view, the Edit View dialog box shows the table and filter currently used for the view. When you choose the Edit or Copy button, you can change one part and leave the other parts as they are. For example, you can start with the Task Sheet, which has the Entry table applied and the All Tasks filter applied, change the name to Tracking Task Sheet, and change the Entry table to the Tracking table. Then any time you display the Tracking Task Sheet, you'll see the Task Sheet with the Tracking table applied. You can, of course, use any tables and filters you have created in a view. The procedures are different for single-pane views and combination views.

Single-pane View

The following example shows how to start with the Task Sheet and create the Tracking Task Sheet.

Choose View Define Views.

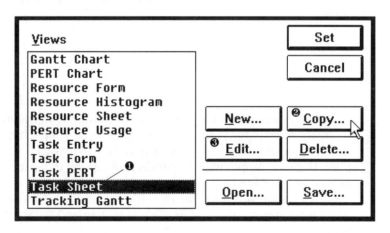

Select Task Sheet ❶.

Choose the Copy button ❷.

You can also choose the Edit button ❸ if you don't want the Task Sheet anymore.

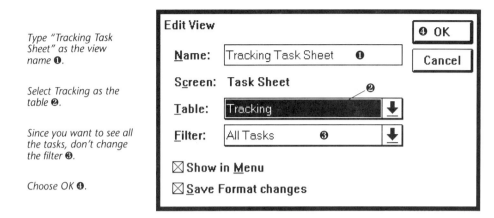

Type "Tracking Task
Sheet" as the view
name **❶**.

Select Tracking as the
table **❷**.

Since you want to see all
the tasks, don't change
the filter **❸**.

Choose OK **❹**.

When you apply the Tracking Task Sheet, you'll automatically have
the Tracking table applied to the Task Sheet.

Combination View

When you change a combination view, you change the top and bottom views, but not the table and filter used in the views. If you want to
change that information, create a new single-pane view with the appropriate task and filter and use that as one of the views in the new combination view.

Suppose you've found that you use the Gantt Chart over the Task
PERT Chart quite often to check relationships as you look at the schedule. Instead of creating the combination view on screen every time you
want to use it, you can create a named view to apply any time you want
to use the combination. You can copy and change the Task Entry view
so that it contains the Gantt Chart over the Task PERT chart.

Choose View Define Views.

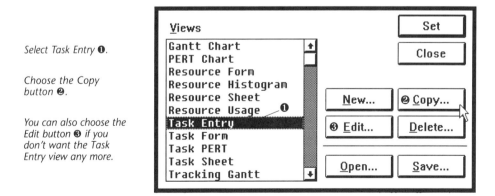

Select Task Entry **❶**.

Choose the Copy
button **❷**.

You can also choose the
Edit button **❸** if you
don't want the Task
Entry view any more.

Type "Gantt/Task PERT" as the new name ❶.

Since you want the Gantt Chart on top, don't change anything here ❷.

Select Task PERT here ❸.

Choose OK ❹.

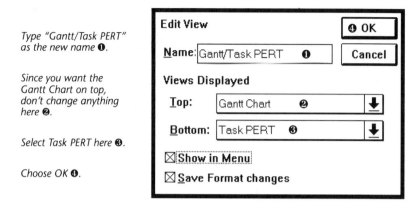

Each time you apply this view, you'll see the Gantt Chart over the Task Pert Chart.

Creating a New View

Creating a new view is just as easy as changing an existing view, except you may have to select more information.

New Single-pane View

Suppose when you collect progress data, you apply to the Task Sheet the Collect Actuals table you created for collecting actual data, and the Date Range filter to limit the tasks displayed. When you display this view, you'll be prompted for the date range to use, and then see only those tasks scheduled to start during the time you specified. By printing this view, you have your form for collecting progress data. The procedures are different for single-pane views and combination views.

Choose View Define Views.

Choose the New button ❶.

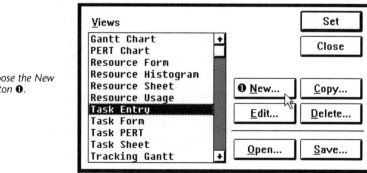

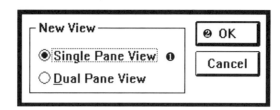

Select Single Pane View ❶.
Choose OK ❷.

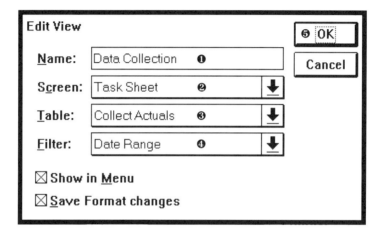

Type "Data Collection" as the name ❶.
Select Task Sheet here ❷.
Select Collect Actuals here ❸.
Select Date Range here ❹.
Choose OK ❺.

When you display this view, the filter will prompt for the two dates, and then only those tasks scheduled to start during the two dates will be displayed.

New Combination View

Suppose you find that you are often combining two views—for example, the Resource Usage view and the Task Sheet. It would be easier and quicker for you to create a named combination view so that in the future you can display this view instead of combining the two on screen.
Choose View Define Views. Choose the New button.

Select Dual Pane View **❶**.

Choose OK **❷**.

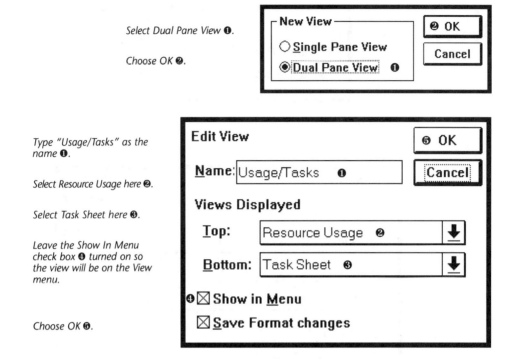

Type "Usage/Tasks" as the name **❶**.

Select Resource Usage here **❷**.

Select Task Sheet here **❸**.

Leave the Show In Menu check box **❹** *turned on so the view will be on the View menu.*

Choose OK **❺**.

Now any time you want to display this view, you can choose it from the View menu.

CUSTOMIZING THE MENUS

In Microsoft Project, you can make the Table, Filter, and View menus contain only those tables, filters, and views you use most often or those you have created for the company to use. You control the tables, filters, and views appearing on the menus using the Show In Menu check box. When the Show In Menu check box is turned on, the name appears on the menu; when the check box is turned off, the name does not appear on the menu.

If you want to be able to choose a table, filter, or view name from the menu using the keys, you can specify the letter in the name you want to be used. This letter will be underlined in the name on the menu, just as in the other names on the menus. Any letter in the table, filter, or view name can be the one. All you have to do is put an ampersand (&) before the letter in the name.

The following illustration shows how to add a table to the Table menu. The procedure is identical for the Filter and View menus, except you use the filter definition dialog box or Edit View dialog box.

Choose Table Define Table, select the table you want on the menu, and choose the Edit button.

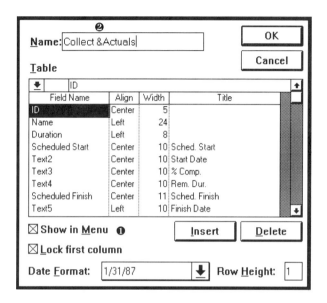
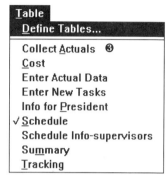

To have the table name appear on the Table menu, be sure the Show In Menu check box is turned on ❶.

To allow users to select the table using the keys, include an ampersand (&) in front of the letter you want to use to select the table ❷.

On the Table menu, the table Collect Actuals is included, with the A in Actuals underlined ❸ to indicate you use A to select the table with the keys—press Alt, T, A.

To create a custom menu, turn off the Show In Menu check box for everything you do not want on the menu. Be sure the check box is on for everything you want on the menu. This information is saved in the view file. When you open the view file, the custom menus will appear.

Customizing the Table Menu

To remove tables currently on the Table menu, choose Table Define Tables, select a table you do not want on the menu, choose the Edit button, turn off the Show In Menu check box, and choose OK. Continue this process until all tables you want off the menu have been removed.

To add tables to the Table menu, choose Table Define Tables, select a table not on the menu that you do want on the menu, choose the Edit button, and turn on the Show in Menu check box. If you want to specify the letter to be used to apply the table with the keys, add an ampersand in front of the appropriate letter in the name. Choose OK. Continue this process until all tables you want on the menu are on it.

Customizing the Filter Menu

To remove filters currently on the Filter menu, choose Filter Define Filters, select a filter you do not want on the menu, choose the Edit button, turn off the Show In Menu check box, and choose OK. Continue this process until all filters you want off the menu have been removed.

To add filters to the Filter menu, choose Filter Define Filters, select a filter not on the menu that you do want on the menu, choose the Edit button, and turn on the Show in Menu check box. If you want to specify the letter to be used to apply the filter with the keys, add an ampersand in front of the appropriate letter in the name. Choose OK. Continue this process until all filters you want on the menu are on it.

Customizing the View Menu

To remove views currently on the View menu, choose View Define Views, select a view you do not want on the menu, choose the Edit button, turn off the Show In Menu check box, and choose OK. Continue this process until all views you want off the menu have been removed.

To add views to the View menu, choose View Define Views, select a view not on the menu that you do want on the menu, choose the Edit button, and turn on the Show in Menu check box. If you want to specify the letter to be used to display the view with the keys, add an ampersand in front of the appropriate letter in the name. Choose OK. Continue this process until all views you want on the menu are on it.

Calendars

If you want to create several base calendars, perhaps because you need three shifts each day, this section will help you do it.

First, create a calendar for one of the shifts, say the day shift, which includes all holidays and the normal working days for the company or project as a whole. Then copy this calendar, rename it, and change it to reflect the work hours for the different shifts.

Creating a New Calendar

Suppose the normal working days for your company are Monday through Friday, and working hours are 7 a.m. to 11 a.m. and 11:30 a.m. to 3:30 p.m. To create a base calendar with these settings, plus one day off for the founder's birthday (April 1), choose Options Base Calendars.

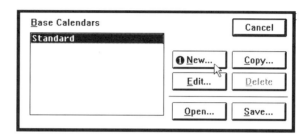

Choose the New button ❶.

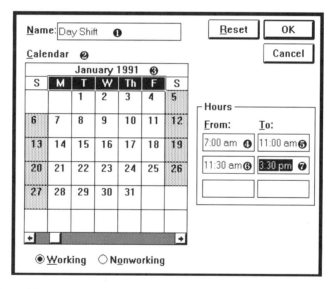

Type "Day Shift" as the calendar name ❶.

The working days already are Monday through Friday, no need to change anything here ❷.

To change the working hours, first select the day titles M, T, W, Th, and F ❸.

Type "7:00 am" here ❹.

Type "11:00 am" here ❺.

Type "11:30 am" here ❻.

Type "3:30 pm" here ❼.

Next, add the founder's birthday as a holiday.

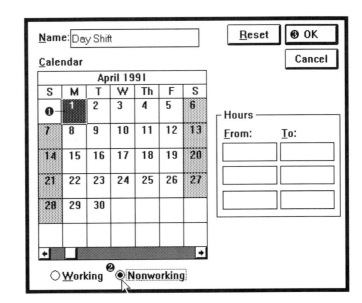

Select April 1 ❶.

Select the Nonworking
option ❷.

Choose OK ❸.

The day shift calendar is created; select this calendar in the Calendar box in the Options Project Info dialog box. All resource calendars will initially be based on this calendar, until you change their base calendar.

Changing an Existing Calendar

Now that you have created one calendar with the basics in it, you can copy this calendar for the other two shifts.

Suppose the swing shift works 3 p.m. to 11:30 p.m., with one-half hour for dinner from 7 to 7:30. Make a copy of the day shift calendar, and then change the hours to match the swing shift.

Choose Options Base Calendar.

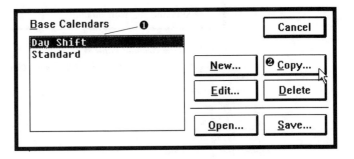

Select Day Shift ❶.

Choose the Copy button ❷.

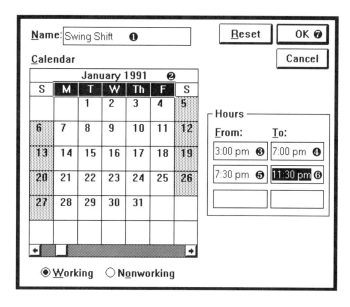

Type "Swing Shift" here ❶.

To change the working hours, first select the day titles M, T, W, Th, and F ❷.

Type "3:00 pm" here ❸.

Type "7:00 pm" here ❹.

Type "7:30 pm" here ❺.

Type "11:30 pm" here ❻.

Choose OK ❼.

The holiday for the founder is already in the calendar because you copied the Day Shift calendar.

Last, create the calendar for the graveyard shift. Their hours are 11 p.m. to 3 a.m., and 3:30 a.m. to 7:30 a.m. Since they start their work week on Sunday nights, you'll change the working days. Because their hours cross midnight, setting up the hours is different.

Choose Options Base Calendar.

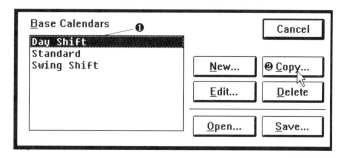

Select Day Shift ❶.

Choose the Copy button ❷.

Type "Graveyard Shift" as the name ❶.

Select the Sunday heading ❷.

Select the Working option ❸.

Type "11:00 pm" here ❹.

Type "12:00 am" here ❺.

Delete the values that were here ❻.

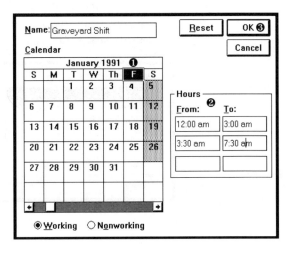

Select the M, T, W, and Th headings ❶.

For hours, type "12:00 am" to "3:00 a.m.", "3:30 am" to "7:30 am", and "11:00 pm" to "12:00 am" ❷.

Select the Friday heading ❶.

Type "12:00 am" to "3:00 am" and "3:30 am" to "7:30 am" ❷.

Choose OK ❸.

As you assign resources, if the resource works a shift other than day, be sure to assign the correct base calendar to each resource group, depending on their working schedule.

SORTING

Sorting is another tool you can use to control the presentation of information in the views. Initially, all tasks are in task ID number order, starting with 1, and all resources are in resource ID number order, starting with 1. You can change the order by sorting on any field, even a custom field. You can sort in ascending order (from low to high) or in descending order (from high to low).

To sort, choose the Format Sort command. In the Key box, select the field you want to be sorted. For example, if you want to sort the list of resources so they are in alphabetical order, select the Resource Name field. Or if you want to sort by duration, with the longest task at the top of the list, and start date, do the following:

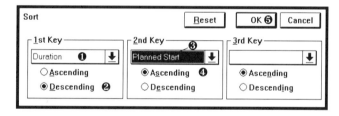

To sort the tasks by duration, select the Duration field here ❶.

To place the longest task at the top of the list, select the Descending option ❷.

To further sort the tasks that have the same durations in order by start date, select the Planned Start field here ❸.

To sort the earliest start date first, select the Ascending option here ❹.

Choose OK ❺.

The tasks in the displayed view will be rearranged such that the longest task is at the top of the list; any time two or more tasks have the same duration, the task with the earlier start date will appear first.

Because it wouldn't be useful to do so, you can't sort the PERT Chart.

Using the Gantt Chart Palette

The Gantt Chart palette allows you to change the appearance of the Gantt Chart. You can create a chart to meet virtually anyone's reporting requirements, from adding special symbols, to defining new bars, to adding text to the bars.

The Format Palette dialog box contains a considerable amount of information, but it is easy to work with, once you understand what it is telling you.

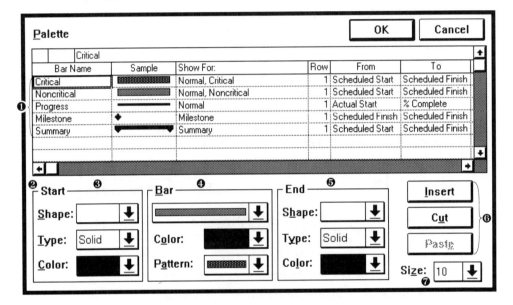

Each row describes one type of bar on the Gantt Chart ❶.

The information across the bottom ❷ describes the bar and symbols for the bar name selected above.

The Start box ❸ describes the shape, type, and color for the symbol at the start of each bar.

The Bar box ❹ describes the bar width, color, and pattern.

The End box ❺ describes the shape, type, and color for the symbol at the finish of each bar.

Use the buttons ❻ to change the order of the bar descriptions.

If you change the size of the text on the Gantt Chart, you may want to change the size of the bars to match. Select a point size for all the bars here ❼.

The information in each row tells you the following:

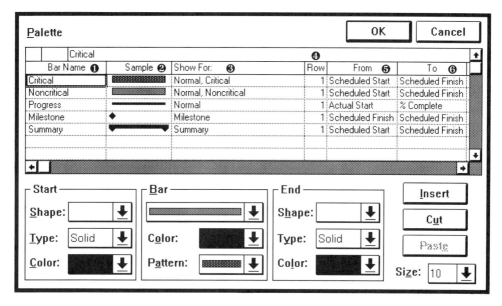

The name ❶ reminds you of the bar's purpose.

The sample ❷ shows what the bar looks like now; you change it by changing the options in the Start box, Bar box, and End box at the bottom.

The Show For column ❸ specifies the kind of tasks the bar is displayed for.

The Row ❹ specifies where the bar is drawn (each task can have four rows of bars).

From ❺ and To ❻ tell Microsoft Project what the bar spans. You select a field for the beginning and end of the bar.

Scroll right to see the Top, Bottom, Left, and Right text fields, in which you add text to the Gantt Chart.

In the Show For field, "Normal" means a task that is neither a summary task nor a milestone.

Bars are drawn in the order they appear in this dialog box, with the top bar being drawn first. If you have two bars drawn in the same row, one narrow, and the other wide, the wide bar should be listed first in the dialog box so the narrow bar will be superimposed on the wide one, instead of being obscured by it.

There is an endless number of ways you can customize the Gantt Chart; the following example shows how to add one bar, the slack bar. The next section on Reports shows another customized Gantt palette.

Choose Format Palette.

Press Down Arrow or use the scroll bars to move to the bottom of the list of bar descriptions ❶.

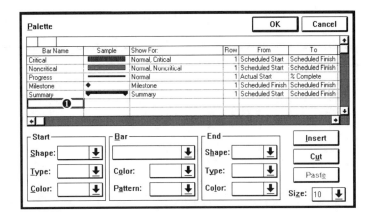

Type "Slack" ❶. The Name you type here is for your convenience— to remind you what the bar shows.

Under Bar, select the narrow bar ❷, the color black ❸, and the solid pattern ❹.

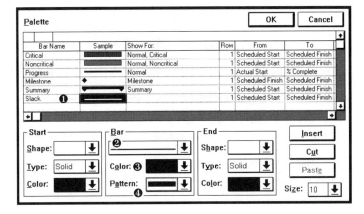

To add a symbol at the end of the bar, select a shape in the Shape box under End ❶.

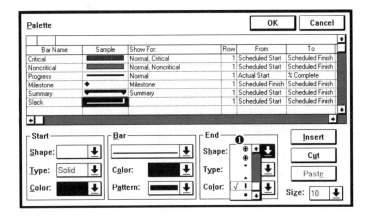

To show total slack, select Scheduled Finish and Total Slack in the From and To fields. You can also show free slack by selecting Scheduled Finish and Free Slack in the From and To fields.

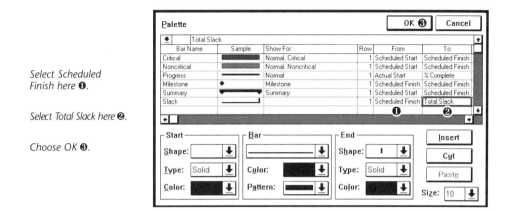

Select Scheduled
Finish here ❶.

Select Total Slack here ❷.

Choose OK ❸.

When you display the Gantt Chart, you'll see the slack bars drawn for the tasks that have slack, from the end of the schedule duration bar.

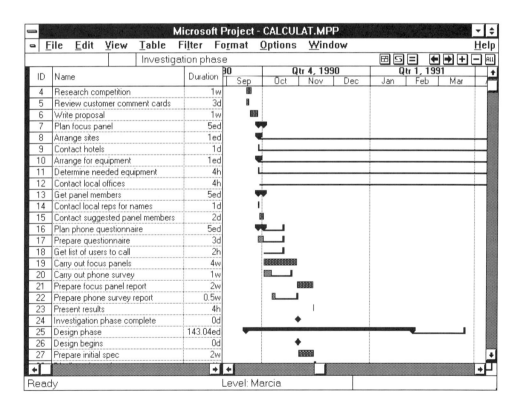

REPORTS

In this section are two more reports, showing what you can do to customize your views and reports to get just the look you want. Creating custom reports combines all the tools you learned about in this chapter.

Comparing Schedules Over Time

The following Gantt Chart shows graphically the differences in the finish dates as your schedule has changed over time. By saving start and finish dates at various points in the project, you can compare where you originally planned to finish tasks when you saved the baseline plan with where you were at some later date, and with where you are today. For each task, three Gantt Bars are drawn: one for the "original" schedule you saved as the baseline schedule, one for the "current" schedule, saved in the Start1 and Finish1 fields, and one for the "last" schedule—an interim schedule you saved in Start2 and Finish2 fields.

To use this view, you must have saved the schedule as the schedule progressed, such as once a month. For example:

- You save the baseline or original schedule before the project gets under way
- After a month, you save the first set of dates by copying the Scheduled Start/Finish fields into the Start1/Finish1 fields
- After another month, you move last month's schedule dates from Start1/Finish1 into Start2/Finish2, and then copy the current schedule into Start1/Finish1
- Each month, you repeat the last step, copying last month's schedule dates into Start2/Finish2 and the latest schedule dates into Start1/Finish 1

All three sets of dates are saved using the Options Set Plan command.

- To save the "original" schedule, you select Scheduled Start/Finish in the Copy box and Planned Start/Finish in the Into box in the Options Set Plan dialog box. You do this, of course, before you start tracking your project.
- The "last" schedule is saved by selecting Start1/Finish1 in the Copy box and Start2/Finish2 in the Into box.
- The "current" schedule is saved by copying the Scheduled Start/Finish into the Start1/Finish1 fields.

Also on the Gantt Chart is text showing the resources assigned to each task and the current finish date for the task. This text is added to the Gantt Chart using the Format Palette command, as are the additional bars.

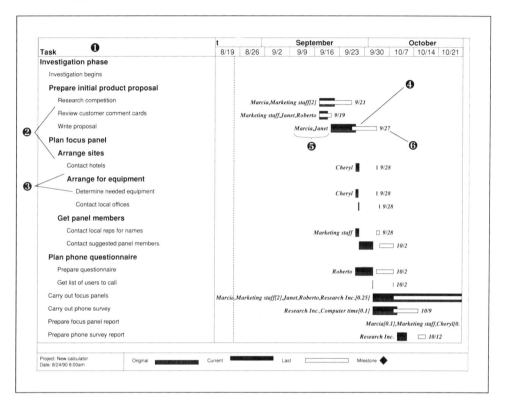

Table ❶.   Gridlines ❷.   Fonts ❸.
Multiple bars ❹.   Left text ❺.   Right text ❻.

To duplicate the report, you do the following:

- Create a table
- Create a view
- Change the gridlines
- Change the Gantt palette
- Change the fonts

Create the Table

Choose Table Define Tables, and then the New button. Enter the following information in the table definition dialog box:

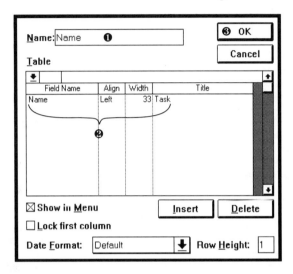

Type the table name ❶.
Enter this information for the table columns ❷.
Choose OK ❸.

Create the View

Choose View Define Views, select Gantt Chart in the Views box, and then choose the Copy button. In the Edit View dialog box, do the following:

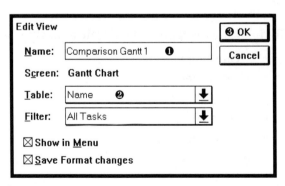

Change the View name ❶.
Select the table you just created ❷.
Choose OK ❸.

Change the Gridlines

Use the Format Gridlines command to change the gridlines. To place gridlines after every fourth task, change the information in the At Interval box.

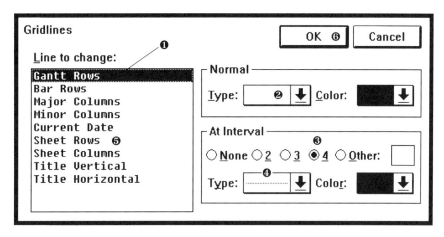

Select Gantt Rows ❶. These are the gridlines drawn on the chart side.

"Normal" gridlines are drawn after every task. This view has no normal row gridlines, so select the blank pattern in the Type box under Normal ❷.

In the At Interval box, you specify the interval at which gridlines are to be drawn. This view has an interval of 4—a gridline after every fourth task. Select the 4 option ❸.

In the Type box ❹, select the dotted lines (the third pattern).

Select Sheet Rows ❺. These are the lines drawn on the table side.

Remove the lines under Normal, and make the lines the same in the At Interval box as they are for the Gantt Rows.

Choose OK ❻.

Changing the Gantt Palette

To change the Gantt bars, and add the text to the left and right ends of the bars, choose the Format Palette command.

To remove the existing rows which, except for Milestone, do not appear in the Comparison Gantt, select each row, except Milestone, and choose the Cut button.

To insert rows for the new Gantt bars, choose the Insert button ❶ *three times.*

Enter the information for the new Gantt bars ❷.

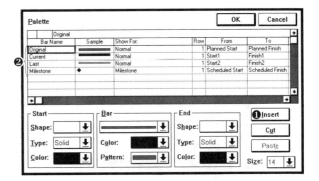

Scroll the dialog box to the left until you can see the Left Text ❶ *and Right Text* ❷ *columns.*

In the Left Text column for the Original bar, select the Resource Names field ❸.

In the Right Text column for the Last bar, select the Finish1 field ❹.

Choose OK ❺.

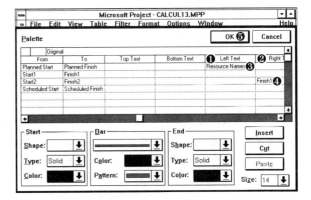

Change the Fonts

In the Format Text dialog box, change the following:

Select	Turn on the
Summary Tasks	Bold check box
Column titles	Bold check box
Bar Text—Left	Bold check box Italic check box
Bar Text—Right	Bold check box Italic check box

Printing the Comparison Gantt

Whenever you want to print the Comparison Gantt, just display the view (choose View Comparison Gantt), and then choose File Print. You will see the usual dialog boxes in which you indicate the period of time you want to print, the number of copies, and the page range.

Printing a Bi-weekly Task List

The next illustration shows a report listing tasks scheduled to occur during two week periods. Within the two week periods, the tasks are sorted by the individual responsible for the task. The individual responsible for each task was entered in the custom field Text3. You'll need to add this field to a table and enter the individual responsible to have this information in the report.

❶

❷ **Compusystems New Calculator**
Bi-Weekly Tasks

Task	Current	Last	Responsible
Week of September 16			
Investigation begins	9/17/90	9/17/90	
Fix old bugs	9/17/90	9/28/90	Bill
Write proposal	9/26/90	10/3/90	Janet
Research competition	9/17/90	9/26/90	Marcia
Review customer comment cards	9/17/90	9/20/90	Roberto
Week of September 30			
Test all bug fixes	10/1/90	10/12/90	
Contact hotels	10/3/90	10/3/90	Cheryl
Determine needed equipment	10/3/90	10/3/90	Cheryl
Contact local offices	10/4/90	10/4/90	Cheryl
Get list of users to call	10/8/90	10/8/90	Cheryl
Write proposal	9/26/90	10/3/90	Janet
Contact local reps for names	10/3/90	10/4/90	Janet
Contact suggested panel membe	10/4/90	10/8/90	Janet
Carry out focus panels	10/8/90	11/5/90	Marcia
Prepare questionnaire	10/3/90	10/8/90	Roberto
Carry out phone survey	10/8/90	10/15/90	Roberto
Week of October 14			
Carry out focus panels	10/8/90	11/5/90	Marcia
Carry out phone survey	10/8/90	10/15/90	Roberto
Prepare phone survey report	10/15/90	10/17/90	Roberto
Week of October 28			
Investigation phase complete	10/31/90	10/31/90	
Design begins	10/31/90	10/31/90	
Prepare initial spec	11/1/90	11/14/90	Dave
Prepare focus panel report	11/5/90	11/19/90	Janet
Carry out focus panels	10/8/90	11/5/90	Marcia
Week of November 11			
Testing begins	11/15/90	11/15/90	
Review spec	11/15/90	11/22/90	
Create testing scripts	11/22/90	12/12/90	
Prepare initial spec	11/1/90	11/14/90	Dave
Prepare focus panel report	11/5/90	11/19/90	Janet
Revise manual	11/15/90	2/6/91	John
Present results	11/19/90	11/19/90	Marcia
Distribute for review	11/15/90	11/15/90	Terri

❸ (sorting bracket)
❹ (Week of October 14)
❺ (Week of October 28)
❻

Page 1   **❼**   12/17/90 8:00am

Table **❶**.   Header **❷**.   Sorting **❸**.   Fonts **❹**.
Shading **❺**.   Border **❻**.   Footer **❼**.

The report was created as follows:

- Create a table
- Create the report, which includes sorting, fonts, and shading
- Change the page setup

Create the Table

Choose Table Define Tables, and then the New button. Enter the following information in the table definition dialog box:

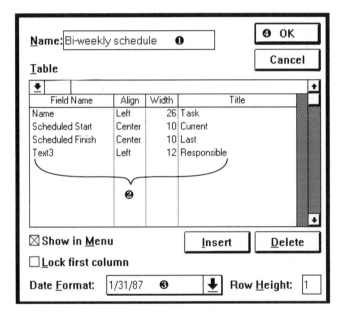

Type the table name ❶.
Enter this information for the table columns ❷.
Change the Date format ❸.
Choose OK ❹.

Create the Report

Choose File Print Report, select Periodic Task in the Print Report box, and then choose the Copy button. In the Edit Periodic Report dialog box, do the following:

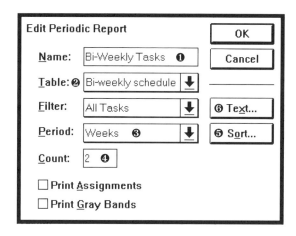

Change the Report name ❶.

Select the table you just created ❷.

Select Weeks as the Period ❸.

Type "2" as the Count ❹. This, along with Weeks in the Period box, is what makes the report bi-weekly.

Choose the Sort button ❺. To sort the tasks occurring in each two week period by the individual responsible for the task, select Text3—the custom field containing the name of the responsible staff member—in the 1st Key box.

Choose the Text button ❻.

In the Text dialog box, change the following:

Select	Turn on the
Noncritical Tasks	Italic check box
Critical Tasks	Italic check box
Column Titles	Bold check box Shade check box
Period	Bold check box Shade check box

Choose OK as necessary to close all the dialog boxes.

Set Up the Page

Choose the File Page Setup command.

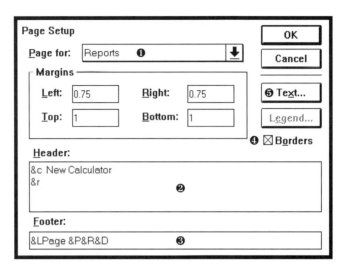

Select Reports in the Page For box ❶.

The information in the Header box ❷ goes at the top of each page. The "&c" tells Microsoft Project to print the company name from the Options Project Info dialog box; the "&r" tells Microsoft Project to print the name you gave the report when you created it, in this case, Bi-Weekly Tasks.

The information in the Footer box ❸ tells Microsoft Project to print the following: at the left side (&L), print the word "Page" followed by the page number (&P); at the right side of the page (&R), print the current date (&D).

To print a border around the report, turn on the Borders box ❹.

Choose the Text button ❺.

In the text dialog box change the following:

Select	Do This
Header (top) Header (middle)	Change Size to 14

Choose OK to close the dialog boxes.

For a list of all the codes used in the Header and Footer box, see Chapter 10, "Communicating the Plan." The codes are also in Microsoft Project Help, which you can display by pressing F1.

Printing the Bi-weekly Task Report

Whenever you want to print the bi-weekly report, choose the File Print Report command. Select Bi-Weekly Tasks in the Print Report box, and choose the Print button.

To purchase a companion disk containing these two reports, as well as others, use the order form at the back of the book.

Index

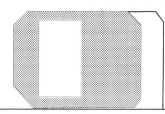

Companion Disk

for

Managing Projects with Microsoft Project for Windows

To receive the companion disk to *Managing Projects with Microsoft Project for Windows*, send this coupon with only $25 (plus postage, handling, and applicable tax), or call the toll-free number. On the disk are alternate view files containing all the tables, filters, views, and reports described in the book, plus a collection of useful combination views and additional sample reports. The disk comes with a booklet showing each report and view included on the disk, along with instructions for using the view files containing the views and reports.

To order the disk, send the coupon below to:

Editorial Services
PO Box 82903
Kenmore, Wa 98028

Or call: 800/878-5704

Yes, please send me _____ copies of the companion disk to
Managing Projects with Microsoft Project for Windows at $25 each. $ _____

_____ 5.25-inch format   _____ 3.5-inch format

Sales tax (8.1% for Washington residents only) $ _____
Postage and handling: $3.50 per disk (U.S. orders) $ _____
                        $6.00 per disk (international orders) $ _____

                        Total $ _____

Payment: _____ Check or money-order enclosed (U.S. funds)
           _____ Bill to: _____ Visa _____ MasterCard

     Acct # _____ Exp. date _____

     Signature _____

Name _____

Address _____

City _____ State _____ Zip _____

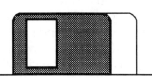

Companion Disk

for

Managing Projects with
Microsoft Project

To receive the companion disk to *Managing Projects with Microsoft Project*, send this coupon with only $25 (plus postage, handling, and applicable tax), or call the toll-free number. On the disk is an alternate view file containing all the table, filters, views, and reports described in the book, plus a collection of useful combination views and additional sample reports. The disk comes with a booklet describing each view, table, filter, and report included in the view file, along with instructions for using the view file.

To order the disk, send the coupon below to:

Editorial Services
PO Box 82903
Kenmore, WA 98028

Or call: 800/878-5704

Yes, please send me _____ copies of the companion disk to
Managing Projects with Microsoft Project at $25 each $_____

      PC: ____5.25-inch format ____3.5-inch format
      Macintosh_____

Sales tax (8.2% for Washington residents only) $_____
Postage and handling: $3.50 per disk (U.S. orders)
                       $6.00 per disk (international orders) $_____

Total $_____

Payment: _____ Check or money order enclosed. Please make check
                   payable to Editorial Services.
               _____ Bill to: ___Visa ____Mastercard

         Account #:_____Exp. date:_____

         Signature_____

Name_____

Company_____

Address_____

City_____State_____Zip_____